THE DIVE S[ITES OF]
THE BAH[AMAS]

LAWSON WOOD

Foreword by the Minister of Tourism, The Bahamas

Series Consultant: Nick Hanna

Lawson Wood has many years' experience as a diver and is one of the world's leading underwater photographers.

First published in 1999 by
New Holland Publishers (UK) Ltd
London • Cape Town • Sydney • Auckland

24 Nutford Place	80 McKenzie Street	Unit 4, 14 Aquatic Drive	Unit 1A, 218 Lake Road
London W1H 6DQ	Cape Town 8001	Frenchs Forest, NSW 2086	Northcote, Auckland
UK	South Africa	Australia	New Zealand

10 9 8 7 6 5 4 3 2 1

ISBN 1 85368 990 4

Project development: Charlotte Parry-Crooke
Series editor: Pete Duncan
Copy editor: Donald Reid
Index and proofread: Paul Barnett
Design concept: Philip Mann, ACE Ltd
Design: Behram Kapadia, Alan Marshall
Cartography: ML Design

Reproduction by Hirt and Carter, South Africa
Printed and bound in Singapore by Tien Wah Press (Pte) Ltd

Photographic Acknowledgements
All photographs taken by Lawson Wood except for the following: Bahamas Ministry of Tourism 78, 88, 130; Bahamas Tourist Office (UK) 6, 17, 29; Pete Bennett–BWP 37, 114, 148; Rob Palmer 27; Photobank/Peter Baker 11, 19, 22, 23, 25, 54.

Front cover: *Diver on Theo's Wreck, Grand Bahama.*
Front cover inset: *Stella Maris dive boat at Conception Island.*
Spine: *Grey angelfish (Pomocanthus arcuatus).*
Back cover: *Rainbow parrotfish (Scarus guacamaia).*
Title page: *Queen angelfish (Holacanthus ciliaris).*
Contents page: *The Bahamas are world-renowned for their caves and caverns.*
Foreword: *The shallow Bahama Banks are perfect for exploration both above and below the waves.*

This book is dedicated to Rob Palmer, whose fame stemmed from his exploration of the blue holes of the Bahamas.

AUTHOR'S ACKNOWLEDGEMENTS

This book would have been impossible without the help, patience and enthusiasm of my wife Lesley, who is not only my dive buddy and partner but also a superb spotter of marine life, the results of which can be seen in the photographs which enhance this publication.

Special thanks go to the Bahamas Tourist Board, both in the Bahamas and in the UK, who have been behind this project 110 per cent. Particular mention must be made of Cleveland Williams – a true friend and superb organizer – Julie Angove, Franz Hepburn, Jeremy Bonnett and, of course, Carmeta Miller on Grand Bahama Island.

In addition: Bahamasair, British Airways, American Airways, American Eagle, Major Air, PanAm Airbridge and Sandpiper Air for all our air travel and inter-island transfers; our regular 'home from home' – Orange Hill Inn, New Providence – thanks to Liz, Rick, Judy and Danny; Rob Palmer and Stephanie Schwabe and the Rob Palmer's Blue Holes Foundation; Stuart Cove and Dive South Ocean; Frazier Nivens and Nassau Scuba Centre; Leroy Lowe and Bahama Divers; Danny Holcomb and Great Abaco Beach Resort Dive Centre; Mary Stevens and Brendals Dive Shop; Paul Christman and Dive Dive Dive; Barry Albury, Gary Adkison and Sea Below; Bob and Rose Vella and Valentine's Dive Centre; Ollie Ferguson, Christina Zenato, Shamie, Pancho and all the guys at UNEXSO; shark veteran Ben Rose who provided invaluable help; Chris Allison and the Dolphin Experience; Kevin Collins, Chris McLaughlin, Luke, Peaches and Raquel and the Riding Rock Inn; Victorin Pelletier, Marcello Guymaraes and Manfred Roon and Club Med Diving; Johnny Ray and the Exuma Dive Centre and Watersports Ltd; Neil Watson's Undersea Adventures; Chris Illing and Randy at the Greenwood Inn Dive Resort; Bill and Knowdla Keefe's Bimini Undersea; Walt DeMartini and his boat *Dry Martini*; Jeff Birch, Peter, Jim, Mike, Paige and Skeebo at Small Hope Bay Lodge; Bimini Big Game Fishing Club, Bimini Bay Hotel, Blue Waters Hotel, Club Med, Club Peace & Plenty, Grand Bahama Beach Hotel, Greenwood Inn, Lucayan Beach Resort, Riding Rock Inn, South Ocean Club, Stella Maris Resort, Valentine's Yacht Club and Walker's Cay Resort.

Diving equipment by The Shark Group, Amble, Northumberland; additional camera and flash equipment from Nikon UK and Sea & Sea Ltd.

PUBLISHER'S ACKNOWLEDGEMENTS

The publishers gratefully acknowledge the generous assistance during the compilation of this book of the following: Nick Hanna for his involvement in developing the series and consulting throughout, Dr Elizabeth M. Wood for acting as Marine Biological Consultant and contributing to The Marine Environment, and Paul Bower for verifying the factual information in the Bahamas.

PHOTOGRAPHY

The author's photographs were taken using Nikonos III, Nikonos V, Nikon F-801 and the Nikon F-90s. Lenses used on the amphibious Nikonos system were 35mm, 15mm and 12mm. The lenses for the housed Nikons were 14mm, 60mm, 105mm, 20–40mm zoom, 28–200mm zoom and 70–300mm zoom. Housing manufacture is by Subal in Austria and Sea & Sea in Japan. Electronic flash was used in virtually all of the underwater photographs; these were the YS30 Duo, YS50, YS120 Duo and YS300 supplied by Sea & Sea Ltd from Paignton in Devon, England and Japan. For the land cameras, the Nikon SB24 and SB26 were used. Film stock used was Fujichrome Velvia and Fujichrome Provia, supplied by KJP in Edinburgh, Scotland and Fuji. Film processing was by Eastern Photo Colour in Edinburgh.

CONTENTS

FEATURES

Foreword

The islands of the Bahamas offer an array of dive experiences like no other destination in the world. There are sunken Spanish galleons, inland blue holes, caves and forest-like coral reefs, all teeming with marine life.

Among the most exciting encounters for divers are at sites off New Providence, Grand Bahama, Walker's Cay and Long Island where enthusiasts can swim with and feed reef sharks.

Visiting divers will find many hundreds of dive sites all across the Bahamas. Moreover, the people of the Bahamas are as committed to the art of hospitality as to preserving the unique ecology of this island home.

The Ministry of Tourism is therefore delighted that *The Dive Sites of the Bahamas* will share the underwater wonders surrounding our islands with a large audience of both new and experienced divers.

THE HONOURABLE C.A. SMITH
Minister of Tourism, The Bahamas

How to Use this Book

THE REGIONS

The dive sites included in this book are divided into twelve island regions: Grand Bahama, the Abacos, the Bimini Islands, the Berry Islands, Andros, New Providence, Eleuthera, the Exumas, Cat Island, Long Island Group, San Salvador and the Undiscovered Bahamas. Regional introductions describe the key characteristics and features of these areas and provide background information on climate, the environment, points of interest, and advantages and disadvantages of diving in the locality.

THE MAPS

A map is included near the front of each regional section to identify the location of the dive sites described and to provide other useful information for divers and snorkellers. Although certain reefs are indicated, the maps do not set out to provide detailed nautical information, such as exact reef contours. In general the maps show: the locations of the dive sites, indicated by white numbers in red boxes corresponding to those placed at the start of each dive site description; the locations of key access points to the sites, such as ports and beach resorts; drop-offs and wrecks. Each site description gives details of how to access the dive site. (Note: the border round the maps is not a scale bar.)

MAP LEGEND

Land	✈ Airport	**1** Dive site	⚓ Lighthouse	▲ Place of interest
Hills	⋯⋯ Path	⌗ Park headquarters	═ Road	⚓ Wreck	⌐ Jetty

THE DIVE SITE DESCRIPTIONS

Within the geographical sections are the descriptions of each region's premier dive sites. Each site description starts with a number enabling the site to be located on the corresponding map, a star-rating and a selection of key symbols, as shown opposite. (Note that the anchor used for live-aboards is merely symbolic: no boat should ever drop anchor over a reef.)

Crucial practical details on location, access, conditions, typical visibility and minimum and maximum depths precede the description of the site, its marine life, and special points of interest. In these entries, 'typical visibility' assumes good conditions.

The Star-Rating System

Each site has been awarded a star-rating, with a maximum of five red stars for diving and five blue stars for snorkelling.

Diving			*Snorkelling*		
★★★★★	**first class**		★★★★★	**first class**
★★★★	**highly recommended**		★★★★	**highly recommended**
★★★	**good**		★★★	**good**
★★	**average**		★★	**average**
★	**poor**		★	**poor**

The Symbols

The symbols placed at the start of each site description provide a quick reference to crucial information pertinent to individual sites.

 Can be done by diving

Shore dive

 Can be reached by local dive boat

 Can be done by snorkelling

Can be reached by live-aboard boat

Suitable for all levels of diver

The Regional Directories

A regional directory, which will help you plan and make the most of your trip, is included at the end of each regional section. Here you will find practical information on how to get to an area, where to stay and eat, and available dive facilities. Local non-diving highlights are also described, with suggestions for excursions.

Other Features

At the start of the book you will find practical details and tips about travelling to and in the area, as well as a general introduction to the region. Also provided is a wealth of information about the general principles and conditions of diving in the area. Throughout the book there are features and small fact panels on topics of interest to divers and snorkellers. At the end of the book are sections on the marine environment (including coverage of marine life, conservation and codes of practice in the Bahamas) and underwater photography and video. Also to be found here is information on health, safety and first aid, and a guide to marine creatures to look out for when diving in the Bahamas.

INTRODUCTION
TO THE BAHAMAS

The Bahamas, sometimes referred to as the 'Tropic of Paradise', straddle the Tropic of Cancer and are the surface expression of a series of huge limestone plateaus stretching from Florida to Hispaniola. Over millennia, enormous amounts of sand arising in the warm tropical waters have built up to form massive banks, of which the Great Bahama Bank and the Little Bahamas Bank are the largest. On these sit 700 islands and a further 2377 cays and rocks grouped, for the most part, in large strings running in a northwest–southeasterly direction with the edges of the cays beside deep water on the lips of the continental shelf.

Nearly all the islands and cays – small islets formed from oolitic or coral sand – are low-lying, covered in dense scrubby jungle and surrounded by shallow reefs and sandbars. Channels wind their way through the sandbars and reefs to perfect little harbours, old colonial-style villages and quiet coves bordered by sand or fringed by coconut palms. Visitors' first impressions of the islands are generally from the air when flying overhead: the most marvellous colours can be seen in the sandbanks, ranging from pure white and pink sandy beaches to the incredible deep indigo blue of the continental shelf. All this sounds impossibly idyllic – and it is. The Bahamas rank among the most beautiful islands in the Caribbean.

Located between the latitudes of 20°56' and 27°25'N and the longitudes of 71°00' and 79°20'W, the entire island archipelago covers 250,000 sq km (160,000 sq miles) of ocean, though the total land area is just 8580 sq km (5382 sq miles) and only around 25 of the islands have any habitation. Although they are usually described as being in the Caribbean, the Bahamas are actually north of the Caribbean Sea and should perhaps be known collectively (with the Turks & Caicos Islands) as the Gulf Stream Islands.

The shallow banks are a prolific nursery to all manner of vertebrate and invertebrate life and make for some of the most varied and spectacular scuba diving in the Caribbean, with excellent visibility, warm waters, wrecks, caverns, blue holes, a vast abundance of fish, stingrays and dolphins. Most famous of all the Bahamas' underwater attractions is shark

Opposite: *The southern shores of Cat Island feature superb empty beaches.*
Above: *Changing the Guard at Government House in Nassau, capital of the Bahamas.*

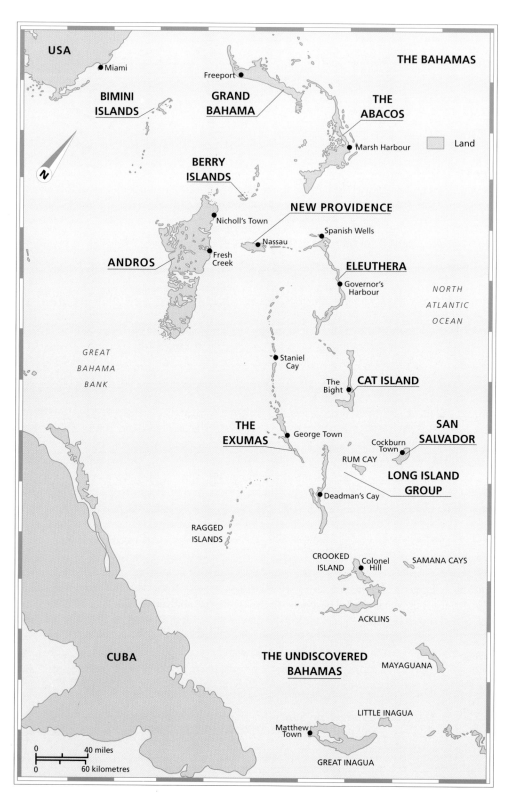

USA

Miami

BIMINI
ISLANDS

Freeport

GRAND
BAHAMA

THE BAHAMAS

THE
ABACOS

Marsh Harbour

Land

BERRY
ISLANDS

N

NEW PROVIDENCE

Nicholl's Town

Spanish Wells

Nassau

ANDROS

Fresh
Creek

ELEUTHERA

Governor's
Harbour

NORTH

ATLANTIC

OCEAN

GREAT

BAHAMA

BANK

Staniel
Cay

The
Bight

CAT ISLAND

THE
EXUMAS

George Town

SAN
SALVADOR

Cockburn
Town

RUM CAY

LONG ISLAND
GROUP

Deadman's Cay

RAGGED
ISLANDS

CROOKED
ISLAND

Colonel
Hill

SAMANA CAYS

ACKLINS

CUBA

THE UNDISCOVERED
BAHAMAS

MAYAGUANA

LITTLE INAGUA

Matthew
Town

0   40 miles

0   60 kilometres

GREAT INAGUA

diving. This is essentially a spectator sport, with divers positioned a safe distance away from a shark wrangler dressed in a chain-mail suit who hand-feeds large Caribbean reef sharks. Initial sensations of pumping adrenalin soon pass to sheer wonder and amazement as the shark handlers stroke the sharks and at times relax them to the point of immobility.

Most divers who come to the Bahamas visit the islands of New Providence and Grand Bahama, where possibly the greatest diversity of diving can be found. However, there is also superlative diving on the less visited Family Islands, where the walls and submarine plateaus of Cat Island, Rum Cay, Conception Island, Eleuthera and San Salvador are outstanding.

THE CAST OF ISLANDS

Nassau, the capital of both **New Providence Island** and the Bahamas, along with Freeport, capital of Grand Bahama Island, offers the widest choice of entertainment in the islands, running the gamut from Las Vegas-style nightlife to the simple pleasures of virtually deserted beaches, snorkelling and scuba diving. Nassau has many preserved colonial-style houses, though its waterfront properties have begun to suffer in comparison with the huge commercial developments taking place on Paradise Island, opposite the main town across the harbour, where several multi-million-dollar resorts and casinos are currently under construction. Southern New Providence is better known for its world-class diving and for attracting the rich and famous, who hang out on Lyford Cay.

Grand Bahama is the second largest tourist destination, with over 30% of its visitors arriving by cruise ship from Florida. Freeport/Port Lucaya is where most of the action is, with casinos, duty-free shopping and the Dolphin Experience. Eco-tourists can scuba dive or kayak into the mangroves on the north of the island and visit the largest known underground cave system in the Bahamas.

The islands and cays formerly known as the Out Islands – though now they take the name of the **Family Islands** – offer a more relaxed pace of life. With many of these accessible only by boat, they are largely unspoiled. Great Abaco's protected waters and dozens of offshore cays help make it the sailing capital of the islands, though it also offers championship golf and the opportunity to dive with upwards of 150 sharks at Walker's Cay. The Biminis are recognized as one of the best fishing locations in the Caribbean and are home to the 'Atlantis Road', a curious formation of rock underwater which has been claimed as evidence of the lost city of Atlantis. Andros, the biggest but the least populated island for its size, has what is claimed to be the world's third largest barrier reef. Andros is best known in the sea-angling world for its bonefishing and in the diving world for its immense blue holes. On Eleuthera there are classic colonial houses and pink sand beaches, and the Exumas have hosted James Bond films several times in fantastic underwater caverns. Cat Island has the highest peak in the Bahamas, and was at one time thought to be Columbus' original landfall. Most historians have it instead that he landed on San Salvador, which has some pristine coral reefs disappearing into the depths, cut by thousands of gullies and canyons. Long Island has some massive blue and green holes while, last but not least, Conception Island is a designated nature park both above and below water and is reputed to have the best (and certainly the least dived) reef walls in the Bahamas.

More islands lie in the extreme southwest. Far removed from the pressures of New Providence and Grand Bahama, these islands have come to be dubbed the **Undiscovered Bahamas**. Crooked Island is known for its sheltered cruising grounds and fishing, while Acklins Island, a short ferry ride away, is rockier and has numerous caves. In the far south, Inagua is the third biggest island in the Bahamas. A good portion is devoted to salt production, but it also has a National Park which includes the world's largest West Indian flamingo colony.

HISTORY OF THE BAHAMAS

It was Christopher Columbus who christened the islands 'Bahamar', meaning 'shallow seas', after landing on an island known as Guanahani by the Lucayan people who lived there. The Lucayans were Arawak Indians who had migrated north from the Greater Antilles around the 8th century AD, fleeing from the cannibalistic Carib Indians of the Lesser Antilles. After his first landfall Columbus spent just 20 days exploring the archipelago, visiting what is now Rum Cay (which he named Santa María de la Concepción), Long Island (which he called Fernandina) and several other islands. But, finding neither gold nor silver, Columbus set off to explore elsewhere. The Bahamas subsequently became a port of call for ships returning to Spain laden with gold, silver and emeralds from newly discovered Cuba and Hispaniola, and the Lucayans were enslaved in their thousands to work in the gold mines of those islands. In 1513 the explorer Ponce de León came to the Bahamas searching for the legendary Fountain of Youth, but for the next century or so the islands (by now largely depopulated) were left in peace.

When the British founded their first colonies in Virginia in the early 17th century they quickly realized the strategic significance of the Bahamas, formally claiming them in 1629. The first new settlers on the islands, who were escaping religious disputes on Bermuda, arrived in the 1640s. Captain William Sayle, who had been Governor of Bermuda, led a group of around 70 settlers and 30 slaves on board three ships, calling themselves 'The Company of Adventurers for the Plantation of the Islands of Elutheria [*sic*]' (the latter is from the Greek word for freedom). Within a decade the settlers on Cigatoo (which they renamed Eleuthera) had been joined by others from Bermuda and the Carolinas, and townships had developed at Spanish Wells and Dunmore Town. The more centrally located New Providence Island was settled in 1656.

OBEAH

Obeah is an ancient tradition of communicating with the spirit world, sometimes referred to as voodoo in other areas of the Caribbean. It is thought to be related to African religious beliefs brought to the New World by African slaves. Little spoken of, Obeah is revered in many islands where it is used to protect property, cast spells or prevent spells being cast on other people. Physical signs include dead lizards, snakes and spiders immersed in bottles of water with dirt from a graveyard. The casting or making of a spell or counter-spell is called 'foxing' by the spiritual leader or shaman. The practice has never been decriminalized by the authorities, resulting in the practice sinking into anonymity in some places.

There is a strong belief in the islands that the spirits of the dead walk the land. Spirits are believed to be of two kinds: those that are good and those that are evil. The nature of a spirit is determined by how that person acted whilst the person was still alive.

PIRATES AND BUCCANEERS

Over the next two centuries the Bahamas became one of the most notorious pirate bases in the Caribbean. The many islands, inlets, shoals and secret harbours provided perfect hiding places from which to launch attacks on Spanish galleons, which were obliged to negotiate the shallow sandbanks and reefs as they sailed to the northeast in order to catch the trade winds which would carry them home.

By the early 18th century it is estimated that there were between one and two thousand pirates active in the Bahamas – many of them shielded by the various governors, who profited enormously. The roll call of pirates who operated from here during this period includes many whose names have passed into legend, incuding Sir Henry Morgan, Edward (Blackbeard) Teach, Charles Vane, Peter Hynd, Jack (Calico) Rackman, Anne Bonney and Mary Read. The inhabitants of the islands also made a good living salvaging cargo, supplies and booty from ships wrecked on the surrounding reefs.

This lawless situation continued until 1717, when complaints by law-abiding merchants finally led to the

establishment of the Bahamas by the British as a Crown Colony. In 1718 the first Governor, Captain Woodes Rogers, arrived.

SLAVES AND SURVIVAL

Some 300 years of disputed ownership over the islands was resolved in 1783, when the Spanish formally ceded the Bahamas to the British under the Treaty of Versailles. During and after the American Revolution thousands of British loyalists fled the mainland and emigrated to the Bahamas, many of them coming with their slaves. Over the next five years the population rose to over 12,000, around three-quarters of whom were slaves.

The abolition of slavery in the British Empire in 1834 dealt the final blow to the plantations, which were already struggling on the islands' poor soil, and many settlers fled back to England. During this period a number of slaving ships also dumped their human cargoes in the Bahamas to avoid the expense of returning them to Africa. Left to their own devices, the freed slaves settled on remote islands, trading crafts with infrequent visitors. During the years of isolation which followed, the islanders developed their own culture of music, dance and crafts. Modest churches were built and Christianity developed in the islands.

The statue of Christopher Columbus, a central figure in the history of the Bahamas, stands at Nassau on New Providence.

JUNKANOO

Held on Boxing Day and New Year's Day, Junkanoo is a celebration of freedom, thanksgiving and friendship which dates from the 19th century. Drawing on the spirit of the islanders' West African ancestry, Junkanoo is a magical, noisy celebration of bannermen, paraders, dancers and musicians dressed in fantastic costumes and keeping time to a rhythmic beat. Coupled with the sounds of brass horns, bellowing conch shells, goatskin drums and outrageous colour, the event is something not to be missed. If you do miss the real thing, a number of larger resort casinos have Junkanoo shows weekly, which are almost as much fun though without the frenzy.

**HAWKSBILL CREEK
AGREEMENT**

The Hawksbill Creek Agreement of
1964 created a 325 sq km (200 sq
mile) free trade zone on Grand
Bahama Island known as Freeport. It
has a harbour capable of handling as
many as five cruise ships at any one
time and, along with duty-free
shopping, the area also attracts
offshore bankers and a huge
number of private investors seeking
to take advantage of the tax
exemptions on profits, capitals and
real estate. The agreement extends
to the year 2054.

EARLY TOURISM

Despite the distance, the equitable winter climate of the
Bahamas began to attract visitors from Britain in the early
1800s. The first US visitors arrived in 1860, when a Cunard
steamship berthed in Nassau, and although the development
of tourism came to a halt with the American Civil War
(1861-65), the Bahamas prospered during this time on trade
with the Confederacy.

Tourism resumed again when Henry Flagler, the
Florida railroad baron, decided that the islands were ripe
for tourist development. He bought the Royal Victoria
Hotel and built the Colonial Hotel in 1900, and also started
a steamship service to Miami. The presence of British
aristocracy helped add to the islands' glamorous image
for Americans.

THE US CONNECTION

The passing of Prohibition laws by the US Congress in 1919 provided the Bahamas with a
major economic boom, allowing fast boats to run illicit supplies of rum to the US
mainland. The US Coast Guard waged a ceaseless war against the rum-runners' fast boats,
but it was not until the repeal of Prohibition in 1933 that this large sector of the Bahamian
economy was put out of action.

During the 1920s the Bahamas became popular with a wealthy American and Canadian
clientele and in 1929 Pan American Airlines made the first flight into the islands from
Miami. During World War II the USA built a large airfield in New Providence, which
became Nassau's first international airport in the 1950s. It is sometimes referred to as the
Windsor Field in honour of the Duke of Windsor, who became Governor of the colony
when he arrived with Wallis Simpson in 1940 after his abdication.

In the post-war years visitors increasingly sought out quieter destinations away from
the hubbub of Nassau. Freeport was also established, but it was slow to get off the ground
and required a last-ditch attempt to save the project. The government issued the first
gaming licences here in 1963 and almost overnight the economy of Grand Bahama
boomed. Encouraged by this success, developers turned their attention to Hog Island,
which was renamed Paradise Island and quickly became one of the most popular resorts
in the Caribbean. During 1966-8 Nassau's deep-water harbour was extended and dredged
to 12m (40ft), leading to a boom in cruise ship arrivals.

Party politics had begun to develop in the Bahamas in the 1950s and by1953 the first
political party, the Progressive Liberal Party (PLP), was formed. A campaign for majority
rule got underway, and, though racial equality was slow to take hold, civil rights legislation
banning segregation was passed in 1956. The mainly white United Bahamian Party retained
power until 1967, when the PLP won a close election and its leader Lynden Pindling (later
Sir Lynden) became Prime Minister. In the 1972 elections the Bahamiam people voted for
full independence from Britain, which was granted on 10 July 1973.

THE REGION TODAY

One ongoing problem for the islands today is the fact that a significant percentage of
cocaine imported into the USA passes through the islands. In a bid to halt this, the
government has instituted several campaigns against drug-running and corruption, and

works closely with the United States Drug Enforcement Agency, which maintains a constant presence throughout the islands.

However, tourism has undoubtedly increased the economic well-being of the islanders. As well as improved harbours, clinics, hospitals and schools, small restaurants have opened at virtually every crossroads and the value of beachfront property has risen exponentially. At beachside resorts, more water-based facilities have appeared, including scuba diving. More specifically, the shark awareness programmes now in operation in the Bahamas are responsible for a huge rise in tourism income. The Bahamians have gone as far as to put a price – a tourism price – on each shark's head, and it is claimed that each live shark in the shark feeding arenas is worth in the region of up to $200,000 in income to the local economy.

On the larger islands of Grand Bahama and New Providence, the local populace are fully aware of the impact tourists have on the economy of the islands and on their livelihood. Whilst visitors may find local residents in the Family Islands more shy and wary, the inhabitants of the larger islands are nearly always extremely gracious and gregarious.

Locally made products can be bought at the many straw markets in the Bahamas.

BAHAMAS TOURISM OFFICES

Canada: 121 Bloor St. East, Suite 1101, Toronto, Ont. M4W 3M5; tel (416) 968 2999, fax (416) 968 6711.

Germany: Leipziger Strasse 67d, 60487 Frankfurt/Main; tel (49) 699 708 340, fax (49) 699 708 3443.

UK: 3 The Billings, Walnut Tree Close, Guildford, Surrey GU1 4UL; tel (44) (1483) 448 900, fax (44) (1483) 571 846.

USA: 2957 Clairmont Rd, Suite 150, **Atlanta**, GA 30345; tel (404) 633 1793, fax (404) 633 1575.
8600 W. Bryn Mawr Ave., Suite 820, **Chicago**, IL 60631; tel (312) 693 1500, fax (312) 693 1114.
World Trade Centre, 2050 Stemmons Freeway, Suite 116, PO Box 581408, **Dallas**, TX 75258-1408; tel (214) 742 1886, fax (214) 741 4118.
3450 Wilshire Blvd., Suite 208, **Los Angeles**, CA 90010; tel (213) 385 0033, fax (213) 383 3966.
1 Turnberry Place, 19495 Biscayne Blvd., Eighth Floor, Aventura, **Miami**, FL 33180-2321; tel (305) 932 0051, fax (305) 682 8758.
150 East 52 St., 28th Floor North, **New York**, NY 10022; tel (212) 758 2777, fax (212) 753 6531.

http://www.gobahamas.com/bahamas

TRAVELLING
TO AND IN
THE BAHAMAS

The Bahamas see an influx of around 3.5 million tourists each year, approximately two-thirds of whom arrive by cruise ship, and these mainly from Miami. Of these cruise ships, most are on the very popular two-day, one-night cruises to Nassau and Freeport which offer gambling and duty-free shopping.

GETTING THERE BY AIR

The international airport on New Providence is southwest of Nassau. Over 85% of all visitors to the Bahamas are from the USA, with many arriving on regular daily flights with a variety of airlines, notably American Airlines/American Eagle, Delta/Comair, USAir and Paradise Island Airlines. The Bahamas national airline, Bahamasair, has scheduled flights linking Miami with Nassau, Freeport and various Family Islands settlements. PanAm AirBridge operates between Miami and Nassau and Bimini. Other airlines link further US and Canadian airports direct to some of the Family Islands. Walker's Cay Airline serves the island of the same name from West Palm Beach, and numerous charter flights operate inter-island throughout the Bahamas. Flights from Miami and Fort Lauderdale to Nassau or Freeport take around one hour.

From Europe, there are direct flights to Nassau from Amsterdam on Martin Air, from Shannon, Ireland, on Aeroflot, from London on British Airways, from Paris on AOM, from Frankfurt with Condor Air and a flight to Eleuthera from Milan with Air Europe.

From the 'hub' of Nassau, you can pick up connecting flights to any of the Family Islands. These are scheduled to keep transfer times to a minimum, but be aware that travel times with major air carriers Bahamasair and American Eagle can be slow. Delays at some Family Island airports may occur as flights connect with ferries from outlying cays, so make sure to allow yourself plenty of time on your return jouney to be able to catch your international connnections.

Opposite: *Snorkelling boat trips are popular around the islands, including Long Island.*
Above: *Tourists can take a ride in a Surrey around downtown Nassau on New Providence.*

BAHAMAS INTER-ISLAND AND CHARTER AIRLINES

American Eagle; tel (800) 433 7300 or (242) 377 5124, fax (242) 377 7998.
Bahamasair; tel (800) 222 4262 or (242) 377 8519, fax (242) 377 7409.
Gulfstream; tel (800) 992 8532 or (242) 377 4314, fax (242) 377 2118.
Island Air; tel (800) 444 9904.
Island Express; tel (954) 359 0380, fax (954) 359 7944.
Major Air; tel (242) 352 5778, fax (242) 352 5788.
PanAm AirBridge; tel (800) 424 2557 or (242) 363 1687, fax (242) 363 3649.
Sky Unlimited; tel (242) 377 8993, fax (242) 377 3107.
Twin Air; tel (954) 359 8266, fax (954) 359 8271.
Cherokee Air; tel (242) 367 2089.
Cleare Air; tel (242) 377 0341, fax (242) 377 0342.
Congo Air; tel (242) 377 8329, fax (242) 377 7413.
Dolphin Atlantic Airlines; tel (800) 353 8010 or (954) 359 8003, fax (954) 359 8009.
Sandpiper Air; tel (242) 377 5602, fax (242) 377 3143.
Taino Air; tel (242) 327 5336.

North Bimini is serviced by PanAm AirBridge seaplane.

There is an international departure tax of US$15 payable in cash. When you pay the departure tax at the ticket check-in counter you will be required to present your flight tickets and hand over the white copy of your immigration form.

HEALTH

There are no vaccinations required when visiting the Bahamas. Make sure that you have good medical insurance. The drinking water is safe, though it is best to enquire in more remote areas as the water will be from either cisterns or desalinated; the food is always prepared to a very high standard. The greatest health risk is the sun, and you must protect yourself with a high-factor sun block and tan gradually. Many a holiday is ruined by sunburn.

VISAS AND IMMIGRATION

Visas are not required when entering the Bahamas, and in the case of Americans and Canadians a tourist card and proof of citizenship (generally either a passport or original birth certificate and photograph ID) are sufficient for entry. All other foreign citizens are required to carry a full passport and a tourist card, which is, in effect, the counterfoil from your immigration form. Do not lose this as it must be returned to Immigration on your departure.

CUSTOMS

Customs officers are well used to thousands of divers arriving with lots of baggage and will generally let you walk straight through after a cursory examination of your documents and questions about your diving destination. If

you are carrying a large amount of photographic equipment, it is advisable to write down a list of everything you are carrying, all serial numbers and the value of each item. This list can then be presented to customs and stamped. The list will also have to be checked and cleared on your departure.

MONEY

US Dollars and Bahamian Dollars are on a par, but unless you request otherwise, you will get change in Bahamian currency even if you hand over US$. Remember to exchange any remaining Bahamian currency at a bank on the islands before your return home, as charges will be made for currency exchange outside the islands.

Banking hours are Monday to Thursday 09:30 to 15:00 and Friday 09:30 to 17:00. All credit cards are accepted.

GETTING AROUND

Taxis are available from the airports, and although most work on a set charge, prices do vary depending on the number of passengers, how much luggage you have and whether the taxi driver thinks it worth the hassle of taking you to your destination. Metered cabs are the best value. Note that taxi fares from your hotel to the airport work on a different scale of charges and will cost more. It is always a good idea to ask what the taxi fare will be before you get in: your hotel will be able to inform you of the going rate. One set of charges applies for journeys around town and another from each hotel into the town.

On the Family Islands, it is worth checking in advance how close your hotel is to your arrival point, as a number of the islands have several airports and you may end up having a taxi ride of over one hour, which can cost as much as $100.

HOLIDAYS	
New Year's Day	1 January
Good Friday	
Easter Monday	
Whit Monday	(seven weeks after Easter)
Labour Day	(first Friday in June)
Independence Day	10 July
Emancipation Day	(first Monday in August)
Discovery Day	12 October
Christmas Day	25 December
Boxing Day	26 December

TIME ZONE

The islands' time zone is Eastern Standard Time (5 hours behind Greenwich Mean Time). During the summer, Eastern Daylight Savings Time is adopted to avoid scheduling confusion between the Bahamas and the USA.

MAILBOAT SCHEDULE (FROM NASSAU)

Travelling by mail boat is an inexpensive and rewarding way to see another side of the Family Islands. It costs around $75 for the round trip from Potter's Cay in Nassau to most of the islands. Tel (242) 393 1064 to confirm separate times.

	Time	Destination	Travel Time
Mondays			
Captain Moxey	23:00	South Andros	8 hours
Abilin	n/a	East Long Island	17 hours
Sherice	16:00	West Long Island	15 hours
Tuesdays			
Mia Dean	18:00	Marsh Harbour, Abaco	12 hours
Champion	19:00	Bullock's Harbour & Abaco	11 hours
Bahamas Day Break III	12:00	Bluff & Harbour Island	6 hours
Lady Francis	18:00	Rum Cay & San Salvador	18 hours
Lady D	12:00	Fresh Creek, Andros	5 hours
Lady Gloria	14:00	South Central Andros	5 hours
Grand Master	n/a	George Town, Exuma	14 hours
Wednesdays			
Marcella III	16:00	Freeport, Grand Bahama	12 hours
Bimini	12:00	Bimini	13 hours
N. Cat Island	14:00	North Cat Island	11 hours
Sea Hauler	12:00	South Cat Island	8 hours
Lady Mathilda	16:00	Crooked Island	n/a
Thursdays			
Lisa J. II	10:00	North Andros	5 hours

Above: *One of the prettiest old colonial towns is Dunmore Town on Harbour Island.*
Opposite: *The Romora Bay Club enjoys an idyllic setting on Harbour Island.*

TIPPING

It is common practice to tip baggage handlers up to $1 per bag depending on the weight and size of the item. Hotel maids would expect to receive around $2 per day, depending on the size of the apartment. (Experienced travellers recommend that you tip the hotel maids on arrival, to ensure extra special attention and prompt daily cleaning.) Tipping may also be expected on the day dive boats at the end of your vacation. Always carry at least $20 in one dollar bills for contingencies, since tipping is customary almost everywhere.

ELECTRICITY

The Bahamas run on 120 volts/60 cycles, as in the USA. Travellers from Europe should take a two pin adapter for recharging flash and batteries.

If you ask around, you may be able to get a taxi and driver for the day and get the driver to give you an unofficial guided tour. Between four or five people, this is a great way to see the area and inexpensive.

There is little public transport available in the Bahamas, except on New Providence Island, where small buses called Jitneys operate. These operate on circular and shuttle routes throughout the day until about 6pm and cost $1 (50c on Paradise Island). Horse-drawn Surreys are another way to get about Nassau and take an informative and inexpensive tour. This costs $5 per person for around 25 minutes.

To hire a car you must have a valid driver's licence from your country of origin. Rental agencies will take a signed credit card imprint as a deposit: without a credit card you will not be able to hire a car. If you plan to rent in the Family Islands rental agencies will cover you for Third Party claims, but you should bring your own proof of car insurance against damage to the car you hire, or you rent at your own risk. Major rental firms such as Hertz, Avis, National and Budget cover you comprehensively in Nassau and Freeport, but do not have depots in the Family Islands. Rental prices are in the region of $55–120 per day. Check the vehicle out prior to rental to avoid any unnecessary problems later on.

Driving is on the left hand side of the road (British style), although as the majority of the hire cars are left hand drive American models and many of the drivers are more used to driving on the right, a certain amount of confusion prevails on the roads. All distance markers are in miles. On the Family Islands, keep your car filled with fuel as there are very few filling stations.

Motor scooter hire costs around $35 per day including fuel. Insurance costs an additional $5 and a deposit is required (usually an imprint of your credit card). Crash helmets must be worn at all times. Bicycles are usually available for rent for $10 per day with a $10 deposit.

ACCOMMODATION

The accommodation available on Grand Bahama, New Providence and the Family Islands covers a wide variety of styles, size and budget. In Nassau, Cable Beach and Paradise Island on New Providence there are 65 hotels, including guesthouses, suites and self-catering apartments, offering over 7000 rooms.

TELEPHONES

You can make international calls from most hotels, but be warned that charges will automatically start after the fifth ring, even if the number is engaged or unanswered. Credit card calls from Bahamas Telecommunications Corp. (BaTelCo) phone boxes (on most streets) are very reasonably priced and phone cards ranging from $5–$20 can be purchased in places such as gift shops and supermarkets. In the Bahamas you can access 1-800 freephone numbers on mainland USA by dialling 1-880, or a BaTelCo operator. The country area code for the Bahamas is 242, which has to be used whenever you telephone inter-island. For further information when you are in the Bahamas call 352 7778.

Virtually all resort hotels in the Bahamas are either located on the coast or a short walk away. The larger facilities have access to golf and most offer a variety of watersports including diving, snorkelling and parasailing. Prices vary tremendously, between around US$80 to $995 per night in Nassau, Cable Beach and on Paradise Island, and around US$85 to $495 per night on Grand Bahama. For $80 you can expect a room for two in a small hotel or guest house, but this may not always include breakfast. Divers can anticipate paying around $100–$150 for good quality accommodation and breakfast, or approximately the same for a self-catering apartment.

There is a room occupancy tax of 8% (Cable Beach and Paradise Island hotels charge an extra 2%). When booking into a hotel you will be asked to sign a blank imprinted credit card slip for incidental charges. This is standard practice in all hotels.

Hotel packages are based on the Modified American Plan (room, breakfast and dinner) or the European Plan (room only). Guest houses tend to be less expensive and, although they offer little choice in dining, there is usually a choice of restaurant nearby, particularly in Nassau and Freeport. In the Family Islands, however, restaurant choice may be limited to the resort you are staying in.

Many diving operations offer all-inclusive packages. These are regularly advertised in the American scuba diving press and usually involve a four night/three day bed-and-breakfast deal with three twin-tank dives plus a night dive. Prices rise during the American holiday season around Easter and Thanksgiving, and locations such as Freeport are often booked up early, so try to book your dives well in advance during holiday periods.

CLIMATE

Rainfall in the Bahamas averages around 130cm (52in) each year, and is most pronounced from May to October. With a tropical maritime climate, the Bahamas experience few extremes of temperature, although on 19 January 1997 a light flurry of snow did occur in the northern Bahamas. During the summer months, coastal areas are cooler with the eastern trade winds felt on the eastern seaboard of virtually all of the islands. For most of the year, the skies are blue with huge columbiform clouds occasionally forming, particularly in June, giving rise to stormy showers and occasional electrical storms in the afternoons. September and October can bring the chance of hurricanes and the skies are often overcast, with rainfall during these periods often more persistent. Winters are generally pleasant.

There is very little change in the air or water temperature through the year, with water temperatures rarely dropping below 17°C (63°F) during the winter months and 28°C (82°F) during the summer. Summer air temperatures rise to between 30 and 40°C (85 to 100°F) and rarely drop below 15°C (60°F) during the winter months.

HURRICANES

A hurricane is a revolving storm of tropical origin accompanied by winds of over 120kph (75mph) which circulate around a central vortex of a lower barometric pressure and travel in an anti-clockwise direction. When the wind speed drops to between 120 and 65kph (40mph) it is called a tropical storm and when the wind speed drops below 65kph the phenomenon is regarded as a tropical depression.

During a hurricane, dangerous and abnormal tides can be experienced, thanks to the shift in atmospheric pressure. This can result in sudden waves causing unknown destruction when accompanied by extremely high winds.

Scientists have discovered that when El Niño is raging in the Pacific Ocean there is increased rainfall in the Bahamas, but less chance of hurricanes forming. The main risk period for hurricanes in the Caribbean is in August, September and October. Hurricane Erin passed through the Bahamas in 1997 causing minimal damage around the Family Islands, although Hurricane Andrew devastated the northern islands on 23–24 August 1992.

SHOPPING

Most luxury goods are exempt from import tax and the islands have no sales tax, so shopping is a major draw for many American visitors. It is possible to save between 20 and 50% on some imported goods, though always be aware of the price you might have paid back home, as the savings aren't always what they seem. Bargains can be found, principally on items such as glassware, fine china, linens, perfume, jewellery and watches. Remember to check your customs allowance (for US citizens, for example, US$600 worth of untaxed goods).

Nassau's Bay Street is one of the main shopping hubs, with most of the smarter shops represented here or in the adjoining side streets. Hotel shopping arcades feature a less varied selection, but there are also numerous outlets in the

Paradise Beach near Nassau on New Providence has all manner of watersports available.

various malls in Freeport/Port Lucaya and Nassau. International chains such as Body Shop, Benetton and Gucci are well represented. Note that bargaining is not normal in shops but is expected in markets.

Most people will head at some point to the local straw markets, the largest of which is in Nassau. Here you will find hats, shopping bags, handbags, place mats and much more besides – many of these items are made in the Far East, as a quick glance at the labels will confirm. Expect to pay more for a genuine Bahamian-made item, such as those found at the Bahamas Straw Market or The Plait Lady, both in Nassau.

SPORTS

Salt water fishing in the Bahamas is superb. Licences are available all the year round and this extended season for particular fish species makes the area a very popular destination. Most tour operators are able to give you advice on combined fishing packages, while the local tourist offices can offer advice on where and when to go. Andros, Long Island, Bimini and the Exumas are regarded very highly for bonefishing; Walker's Cay and Bimini are also known for their marlin, wahoo and tuna fishing off the edge of the continental shelf in the Straits of Florida, through which courses the Gulf Stream.

The Bahamas are also regarded as an excellent destination for windsurfing, with above-average facilities and good conditions over enormous flat, shallow, sandy lagoons. All major international resort hotels have windsurfing boards for hire and many offer instruction, often at little or no additional cost. Because much of the Bahamas is low-lying and relatively exposed, there is nearly always a good sailing wind.

DIVING AND SNORKELLING IN THE BAHAMAS

The Bahamas have long held a reputation as one of the most popular destinations for diving in the Caribbean thanks to their proximity to the USA and the diversity of conditions which they offer. Among the highlights are the eastern seaboard of Andros, claimed to be the second largest barrier reef in the northern hemisphere and the third largest in the world, virgin offshore reefs, superb wrecks, famous underwater movie sets, pristine vertical walls dropping 1800m (6000ft), and some exciting and challenging cave diving in spectacular blue holes. For the adventurous, new territory is being opened up constantly by the live-aboard dive boats which explore the outer reefs, atolls and submerged mountain ranges, particularly west to Cay Sal, the least known of the Bahama Banks, where there is spectacular diving on oceanic walls and shark-filled blue holes.

The Bahamas are regarded as the shark-diving capital of the world, and divers here have an amazing opportunity to get close to sharks in a number of different ways with a minimum of fuss and in as controlled a situation as you can be with these wild creatures. There are also encounters with bottle-nose dolphins run by UNEXSO on Grand Bahama Island and open-ocean experiences with pods of spotted dolphins off Bimini.

The Bahamas are in the hurricane zone and the last ten years have seen three major hurricanes which have caused considerable damage in specific localities above water, although very little damage was caused underwater. Fish life around the islands is exceptionally varied and marine species from both the Caribbean and the Atlantic Ocean are found. To the west of the majority of the islands are massive shallow sandy areas, bordered by rich mangrove forests which are breeding grounds for most species found in the eastern Caribbean.

The best time to visit the Bahamas for diving is April to October when the weather is more settled, barring the occasional tropical storms. Easter and Thanksgiving (late November) are busy with Americans, and high season is from Christmas to Easter, when prices are highest.

Opposite: *Divers on a decompression line, after an open ocean dive in Bimini.*
Above: *Rob Palmer was one of the pioneers who first explored the blue holes of the Bahamas.*

DIVING CONDITIONS

Diving conditions vary around the islands and the visiting diver will experience the full range of reef conditions found elsewhere in the eastern Caribbean. Lying in the path of the Gulf Stream, the four large plateaus that make up the Bahamas are fed by regular currents which are responsible for the higher than average diversity of marine life to be found on these shallow banks. Water temperatures in the Bahamas rarely drop below 17°C (63°F) during the winter months and 28°C (82°F) during the summer.

The strongest currents are located off the west coast of Bimini along the edge of the continental shelf where the Gulf Stream pours up the Florida Straits and onwards past Bermuda, and on northern Eleuthera where the Current Cut can reach incredible speeds as it passes through a narrow gap between two islands. If you are unsure of your ability in strong current, always check with the dive master on the boat you are diving from.

Surge conditions are a problem during the winter months and the sheltered southern and western shores of New Providence, Grand Bahama, Cat Island, Rum Cay, Eleuthera and San Salvador are where the majority of diving takes place. Exposed areas such as Andros are saved from the worst of the surge conditions by massive barrier reefs of elkhorn coral which take the force out of the worst of the oceanic swells.

The northern shores of New Providence, the Abacos and Eleuthera suffer from periodic winter storms which move across from the USA and out into the far Atlantic, resulting in a long low swell which can make boat trips and times between dives uncomfortable. This is where diving in the blue holes really comes into its own. These pools and underground rivers are crystal clear with a visibility of over 60m (200ft) even during the winter months, when perhaps the seaward diving is too rough and visibility consequently impaired.

Nevertheless, the islands of the Bahamas cover such a vast expanse of ocean that many of their shores form a barrier against whichever weather conditions prevail. With sheltered conditions usually to be found even in remote locations, you can dive virtually all year round.

TIDAL STREAMS

Waters circulating twice each day around the Caribbean Sea and the Gulf of Mexico help push the Gulf Stream up through the Straits of Florida and through the Bahamas chain before it makes its way across the Atlantic. The Gulf Stream accounts for the higher than average concentration of marine life to be found in the Bahamas, as well as a constant supply of fresh, clear water.

During the full moon the gravitational forces of the moon exert more pull on the world's oceans and so tidal movements play a greater part: these are called spring tides. When the tidal streams and currents are slower, these are called neap tides. During the spring and autumn equinoxes, when the sun is also closer to us, the pull is strongest and tidal currents will be faster and higher than at any other time of the year.

WATER VISIBILITY

The water visibility in the Bahamas is generally very good, improving as you travel further to the south away from the major shallow sandbanks. Several important factors help ensure the clarity of the water – most significantly the complete absence of rivers and the massive deep-water trench known as the Tongue of the Ocean which separates Andros from New Providence Island and the Exumas, dropping to 1800m (6000ft). Although the Bahamas do experience seasonal planktonic fluctuations, the associated particulate matter quickly falls away into this trench, keeping the inshore, shallow reefs clear of sedimentation. Any bad visibility is usually localized, caused by adverse weather patterns.

Visibility does vary according to your location and the time of year, averaging 18m (60ft) in the winter, and 45m (150ft) during the summer off the edge of the wall though only 25m (80ft) amongst the inner reefs. In the southeast and San Salvador in particular, visibility averages 30m (100ft) in the winter and well over 60m (200ft) in summer.

The Bahamas are susceptible to rain storms from July through to September, particularly in years when the

Hundreds of kilometres of reefs and cays stretch south through the central Bahamas.

El Niño phenomenon has been noted. This heavy rainfall causes localized flooding, resulting in fresh muddy water being expelled from the islands onto the shallow reefs. Fortunately the period of poor visibility and rough topside conditions soon passes.

DIVE FACILITIES

Very little shore diving is done in the Bahamas as the edge of the continental shelf or wall is deemed to be too far from the shore to swim; the majority of diving is done by boat. All dive operations have boats leaving at regular times from the dock.

The diving operations are usually extremely professional, though some more so than others. The larger companies located on New Providence and Grand Bahama islands, where the majority of the diving takes place, offer excellent instruction and sales of diving equipment. The further you travel south, the smaller and less up-to-date the facilities generally become, with the exception of San Salvador, where both diving operations are superbly outfitted with retail stores, new boats and rental equipment.

On the Family Islands, diving tends to be relatively informal. This may not suit everyone, as dive times can be erratic, but overall the service is much more personal, and you can sometimes be the only divers staying in a particular resort. It is a good idea to contact smaller dive resorts well in advance of your holiday to ensure they are open and that there are qualified staff on hand to assist you.

SURGE

During the winter months, the oceanic swell from the Atlantic and prevailing easterly wind create surge conditions along the eastern shores of the islands from the Abacos to San Salvador, as well as Andros. These conditions make diving tricky when in proximity to reefs, and you may be inadvertently pushed against the corals. To avoid damaging the reef (and yourself), swim in the direction of the surge. When the pull is against you, do not fin against it, as swimming against the surge can be very tiring; when the pull reverses, this is the time to fin so that you can cover ground safely.

As in all Caribbean dive locations, a typical day's diving consists of a twin tank dive in the morning, a single tank dive (often a training dive) in the afternoon and a night dive on request. The morning dives will be to approximately 33m (110ft) (the maximum depth allowed by the dive operations), followed shortly by a much shallower dive on a nearby reef or wreck.

Night diving is a bonus and there are a number of popular locations close to the dive centres, although again it is sensible to check in advance that a night dive is taking place and reserve your space. Night dives are generally on a shallow reef surrounded by wide sandy areas, or on a popular wreck such as the *WiLLaurie*, southwest of New Providence Island, the Vulcan Bomber also off the south shore of New Providence or, best of all, Theo's Wreck off Grand Bahama Island.

The majority of dive sites are marked by a permanent mooring buoy. In addition there are often anchor drops available in confined sandy areas, away from places where corals might be damaged.

DIVERS DOWN LIGHTS

These are used when divers are diving at night. A series of three lights, red over white over red, they are visible for a distance of 180m (600ft), and 360 degrees. It is an offence to show such lights if diving is not in progress.

DIVE BOATS

Dive boats come in two categories – day boats and live-aboards. On day boats, the usual programme is a twin-tank dive in the morning and a single tank dive (or training dive) in the afternoon. Night dive trips may mean losing one of your day dives. However, some operators such as Stuart Cove and Nassau Scuba Centre on New Providence Island and UNEXSO on Grand Bahama Island offer a greater number of trips, with the chance to

UNEXSO is the largest and oldest of the numerous diving operations on Grand Bahama.

dive up to five times per day. Times to the sites by boat are relatively short, as boats will only generally venture on a 30-minute radius from their base, except when offshore expeditions are planned from Nassau to the Andros Ocean Blue Hole or the United States Naval Buoy in the Tongue of the Ocean.

Live-aboard dive boats are one of the best ways to get the most from the massive diversity that the Bahamas offer, with opportunities to visit largely unexplored reefs, wrecks, walls and blue holes. Much of the diving from live-aboards is done on remote reefs which are only visited a couple of times each year, and therefore offer an above average likelihood of finding dolphins, sharks, turtles and, in the south in the early part of the year, humpback whales.

LEARNING TO DIVE IN THE BAHAMAS

Many thousands of experienced SCUBA (Self Contained Underwater Breathing Apparatus) divers visit the Bahamas each year and most are well versed in the area's dive sites and the particular location that they want to revisit. Nevertheless, many scuba divers wish to upgrade their diving skills, and the inter-island dive shop network has an enviable reputation for instruction to the highest level. For people wanting to learn to dive, the diversity of experience and warm water also make the Bahamas a great place to do it.

All Bahamian dive operations are affiliated to one of the major schools of instruction (PADI, NAUI and BSAC), with PADI (Professional Association of Diving Instructors) the

---

DIVING RULES

Divers often inadvertently cause serious damage to coral reefs. Listed below are a few reminders when diving in Bahamian waters.

- Avoid touching coral with hands, fins, tanks etc.
- Do not wear gloves
- Never stand on coral
- Do not collect any marine life
- Avoid overweighting, and work on buoyancy control
- Do not feed the fish alien foods harmful to them
- Do not use spear guns
- Do not molest marine life, in particular turtles, pufferfish and sea urchins
- Do not climb inside barrel sponges

LIVE-ABOARD BOATS IN THE BAHAMAS

Most live-aboard boats offer itineraries leaving from Freeport, Nassau, Miami or Fort Lauderdale. A few have on-board marine scientists and photographic experts, and most have full E6 processing facilities. The operations listed here all have vast experience of the Bahamas, the diving conditions, and special needs of their guests. All provide a relaxed, friendly atmosphere and the opportunity of unlimited diving in one of the top diving destinations in the world.

Bottom Time Adventure
PO Box 11919,
Fort Lauderdale,
Florida 33339-1919.
tel (800) 234 8464 or (954) 921 7798
fax (954) 920 5578
Main dive areas: Exuma Cays,
Cat Cay, Eleuthera.
E6 processing on board. 28 passengers.

Blackbeard's Cruises,
PO Box 66-1091,
Miami,
Florida 33266.
tel (800) 327 9600 or (305) 888 1226
fax (305) 884 4214
Main dive areas: Bimini, Victories, Cat Cay, Grand Bahama, Nassau, Exumas, Berry Islands.
Three boats carrying 23 passengers, one carrying 12 passengers.

Nekton Diving Cruises,
520 S.E. Street,
Fort Lauderdale,
Florida 33316.
tel (800) 899 6753 or (954) 463 9324
fax (954) 463 8938
Main dive areas: Cay Sal, Bimini, Grand Bahama, Rum Cay, Conception Island, San Salvador, Exumas.
E6 processing on board. 30 passengers.

Out Island Voyages,
PO Box N-7775,
Nassau,
New Providence, Bahamas.
tel (800) 241 4591 or (242) 394 0951
fax (242) 394 0948
Main dive areas: Exumas, Andros, Cat Island, San Salvador, Conception Island, Long Island, Crooked Island.
E6 processing on board. 20 passengers.

Sea Dragon,
717 S.W. Coconut Drive,
Fort Lauderdale,
Florida 33315.
tel (954) 522 0161
Main dive areas: Exuma Cays, Conception Island, San Salvador.
8 passengers.

Sea Fever Diving Cruises,
PO Box 443-3837,
Miami Beach,
Florida 33239.
tel (800) 443 3837
or (305) 531 3483
Main dive areas: Cay Sal, Shark Blue Hole, Exuma Cays, Berry Islands, Little Bahama Bank, Dolphin grounds north of Bimini.
E6 processing on board.
16 passengers.

dominant association in use throughout the Bahamas, and responsible for the certification of 85% of all visiting scuba divers. A number of the larger dive operators have instructors who are also qualified with NAUI (National Association of Underwater Instructors) and the BSAC (British Sub Aqua Club).

You must gain certification before you are allowed to rent equipment and head off to dive independently with a buddy. The most popular way to start is to enrol in a resort course, known around the world as the Discover Scuba Programme. This 2–4 hour basic instruction course is a combination of lectures, swimming pool techniques and open water work designed to give you a taste of diving, fire your enthusiasm and teach basic water safety and conservation. Those with a medical problem such as asthma or epilepsy which they are unsure of should always consult their doctor first. A resort course is available to everyone over the age of 12 (teenagers up to age 18 must have full parental consent), and will cost around $100 including rental equipment. Note that it does not, however, lead to a qualification.

If you decide to take your training further and invest several hundred dollars and rather more time, you can take a five-day Open Water certification course under the PADI scheme. This gives you the chance to dive with a fully qualified dive instructor to a depth of 18m (60ft). The Open Water qualification course is taken by 25% of all first-time resort course participants and will cost around $200.

The PADI system is designed in modular form to allow you to advance your skills depending on the time and money that you have available. For a further $250, divers qualified in the Open Water course are able to go on to an Advanced Open Water course. Subsequently, divers are able to enrol in many other speciality courses including wreck diving, cave and cavern diving, underwater photography and dive instruction. All of these courses are offered at the major diving operations in the Bahamas. UNEXSO, Stuart Cove and Nassau Scuba Centre also offer further speciality courses on rebreather systems, wall diving with underwater scooters, shark feeding and dolphin handling.

Once fully qualified, your certification or 'C' card serves as your diving passport and is recognized worldwide. It is valid for life, but, if you are unable to dive from one year to the next, it is recommended that you enrol in a refresher course at any PADI-affiliated dive centre around the world.

Opposite: *Shark feeding sessions by UNEXSO bring divers and sharks into close proximity together.*

DISABLED DIVERS

A number of diving operations are specifically geared to cater for disabled divers. Certain boats are specially adapted for wheelchairs, and dive centres are able to certify people of all disabilities, including paraplegics, quadriplegics and those with impaired hearing or sight, providing that the individual is medically able to dive. Any prospective student must consult a doctor prior to taking a certification course. As a general rule, any dive operator with its own jetty will be accessible for disabled divers, whereas smaller operators whose access to their dive boat is by beach cannot offer the service.

DISABLED DIVING

For further information on disabled organizations and training, contact:

BSAC: Telfords Quay, Ellesmere Port, South Wirral, Cheshire L65 4FY, UK; tel (+44) (151) 350 6200, fax (+44) (151) 350 6215

Handicapped Scuba Association (HSA): 116 West El Portal, Suite 104, San Clemente, CAL 92672, USA; tel (+1) (714) 498 6128

SNORKELLING

Entering the water for the first time wearing a mask, snorkel and fins can be quite daunting, but with the correct techniques you will quickly discover that snorkelling requires little physical effort. Only the ability to swim is essential.

With correct instruction you will quickly be able to enjoy the splendours of coral reefs suitable for snorkelling, such as those found very close to the south shore of New Providence, or to swim with wild dolphins near Bimini. It is wise to check with the local dive shop whether the area you are planning to snorkel in is safe enough for you and your family. If in any doubt, do not enter the water, and seek advice first.

Instruction is offered at nearly all top hotels and dive resorts and may take place in a dive centre's swimming pool. Equipment can normally be rented from a dive centre, though snorkelling is not an expensive sport and it is possible to purchase your own.

JEAN-MICHEL COUSTEAU'S FAMILY ISLANDS SNORKELLING ADVENTURES

Jean-Michel Cousteau has devised a snorkelling programme with the Family Islands Promotional Board on some of the best snorkelling reefs in the world. Developed in conjunction with the various diving centres on the main islands, the course offers all participants trained instruction, a snorkelling guide book, rental equipment, waterproof marine identification cards and a personalized certificate from Jean-Michel Cousteau. The cost varies and local dive operators should be contacted for full details.

The Family Islands are the perfect setting for this programme as there are literally thousands of kilometres of charted and uncharted coral reefs just waiting for exploration. The elkhorn reefs around the Abacos, Andros, Eleuthera, Cat Island, Bimini, San Salvador, Long Island and the Exumas are some of the best in the Caribbean and, with depths of less than 1m (3ft) in many areas, are ideal for snorkelling and gaining an understanding of the diverse marine ecosystems of the Bahamas.

SNORKELLING AND DIVING EQUIPMENT

Snorkelling equipment consists of a mask with an adjustable strap and toughened glass. The mask must be of a kind that enables you to adjust the air pressure inside through your nose. Several types of mask also have the provision for optical lenses to be installed. For those people who wear contact lenses, a close fitting, low volume mask should normally be adequate.

The snorkel should not be too long or have too wide a bore, as you need to be able to clear the water out of it in a single breath if you submerge yourself too far. Some modern snorkels make use of a self-draining device which will remove any excess water. The snorkel must fit snugly in the mouth and be free of any type of restriction which might impair breathing.

In addition to the basic equipment of mask, snorkel and fins, it is sensible to wear either a Lycra swim-skin or a thin full wetsuit. This will not only shield you from the sun's rays, but also afford protection against any stinging microscopic plankton which may be found in the water. If you have no other protection, at least wear a T-shirt to keep off the sun's rays.

Supplementing the basic snorkelling equipment, diving equipment consists of an air tank and air; a regulator or demand valve through which you breathe; a contents gauge to indicate how much air you have left in your tank; an easy-to-read depth gauge to indicate your current depth and maximum depth reached; a watch with an adjustable bezel or timer device to let you know how long you have been at a specific depth and the duration of your dive; a weight belt and weights, which help counteract the body's natural positive buoyancy; and a buoyancy compensator or life jacket of some description that allows you to adjust buoyancy at depth in order to remain at that depth or keep off the corals. During the winter months the water temperature can drop as low as 17°C (63°F) and it's advisable to wear a full wetsuit instead of the much thinner Lycra suit. There is no real need for equipment such as dry suits or hoods in the Bahamas, although some people like to wear a hood whilst diving at night. A small knife may be worn, in case you need to use it to cut yourself free from impediments such as fishing line loose in the water. A computer is recommended for more experienced divers who are on an unlimited dive package, to assist them with repetitive dive profiles.

A dive boat from Small Hope Bay, the oldest family-owned dive resort in the Bahamas.

GRAND BAHAMA

Grand Bahama, the fourth largest island of the Bahamas, lies near the top of the Bahamas chain and is separated from Florida by only 90km (55 miles) of the Gulf Stream. To the north of the island lie shallow banks dotted with coral heads, while to the south is a deep trench called the North West Providence Channel. The island, 150km (95 miles) long, is the southwestern part of the Little Bahama Bank, which also comprises the Abacos and some 300 islands and cays, and boasts some of the best diving in the entire region.

The main town of Freeport/Port Lucaya is relatively new, still ranking second to Nassau in terms of visitor numbers. Whereas parts of the centuries-old Nassau waterfront show their age, Freeport/Port Lucaya is consistently modern, up-market and extremely popular with tourists who enjoy tax-free shopping and some great entertainment. Freeport is the commercial centre, while Port Lucaya is the tourist/yacht/shopping centre.

A large amount of development has taken place around Freeport, where a massive canal system was constructed in the 1960s to allow investors to have their homes by the sea. By contrast, the eastern approaches to Grand Bahama are mainly shallow marshland with hardly any development. The west end of the island was once a notorious home for rum-runners during the days of Prohibition, and is now destined for new hotel resorts.

As you fly over the island, you will be struck by the colour of the water, which ranges from light turquoise blue to the near black of the circular sink holes inland, and from the green of shallow grass beds dropping off to an indigo blue beyond the wall. The dive centres on Grand Bahama all operate along the same stretch of coastline. Operators include the Underwater Explorers' Society (UNEXSO) at the market place in Freeport, one of the oldest established dive businesses in the Bahamas. Within UNEXSO, but run as a separate business, is the Dolphin Experience, where divers and non-divers are allowed the chance to interact with these fascinating, intelligent creatures in their natural habitat.

Opposite: *Hobie cats lie on a Grand Bahama beach at sunset.*
Above: *Diamond-backed blennies (Malacoctenus boehlkei) are frequently found near large anemones.*

Because of the parallel formation of the reefs and the close proximity of the many dives, the dive sites in this section are arranged into three different depth ranges to suit different standards of diver. Sites 1 to 8 are dives on shallow reefs down to 12m (40ft) deep, Sites 9 to 23 are medium-depth reefs between 12m and 20m (66ft) deep, and Sites 24 to 35 are deep dives. Site 36 is a Blue Hole. All of the dive sites are protected by mooring buoys to prevent anchor damage.

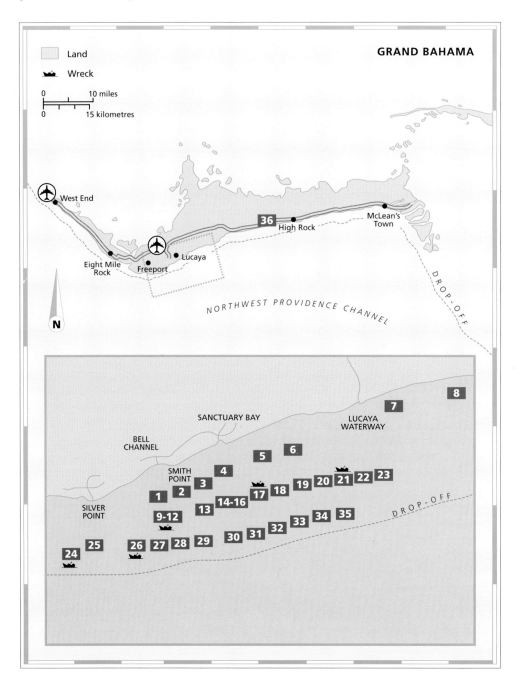

1 FISH FARM (Treasure Channel)
★★★☆

Location: At the eastern end of Bell Channel.
Access: By boat, but can be reached from the shore.
Conditions: Generally choppy with some light surge.
Average depth: 3m (10ft)
Maximum depth: 6m (20ft)
Average visibility: Reduced to 10m (33ft) due to sandy location.

The site is known for its overly friendly fish, which have been hand-fed for years. Residents include a large mixed school of yellowtail snapper (*Ocyurus chrysurus*), Bermuda chub (*Kyphosus sectatrix*) and sergeant majors (*Abudefduf saxatilis*) around the mooring line as well as numbers of snapper and grunt which appear to seek shelter under the elkhorn corals. The shallow-water corals make this a popular snorkelling site.

2 TREASURE REEF SOUTH
★★★★★

Location: Opposite Smith Point, midway between the shore and Octopussy Garden (Site 13).
Access: By boat only.
Conditions: Being so close to shore, this site is subject to surge and surface chop.
Average depth: 7m (25ft)
Maximum depth: 11m (36ft)
Average visibility: 12m (40ft)

During 1960–3 a group of four snorkellers was taken to this reef by a local dive shop and ended up discovering a horde of Spanish treasure. For many years previously coins had washed up on the shoreline and it was thought that there could be an ancient wreck in the area. The discovery was estimated at US$3 million (the book *Finders Losers* tells the tale of the find and how the millions were lost to unscrupulous investors). Elkhorn and brain corals predominate on this low-lying, ancient spur and groove reef which is topped with sea plumes. Fish life comprises snapper and grunt.

3 PILLAR CASTLE
★★★☆

Location: East of Treasure Reef (Site 2).
Access: By boat usually, but can be reached from shore.
Conditions: Can be choppy, but little or no current.
Average depth: 4m (15ft)
Maximum depth: 6m (20ft)
Average visibility: 12m (40ft)

The site is named after two large stands of pillar coral (*Dendrogyra cylindrus*): one to the north of the mooring on a narrow finger of reef, the other directly across from the mooring. Near the latter the reef has been sculpted out by wave action, forming a small cavern which becomes filled with silversides from July to September. A large green moray eel (*Gymnothorax funebris*) is often seen in this area. Common snapper and grunt are found in abundance on this reef.

4 RAINBOW REEF
★★★☆

Location: The next mooring east from Site 3 along the inner reef system.
Access: By boat only.
Conditions: Choppy and liable to oceanic surge.
Average depth: 4m (15ft)
Maximum depth: 7m (24ft)
Average visibility: 12m (40ft)

Midway between the Bell Channel and Sanctuary Bay, this is a continuation of the inner strip reef which runs parallel to the south shore of Grand Bahama Island. On the broken coral-rubble bottom to the north one can find yellowhead jawfish (*Opistognathus aurifrons*) and banded jawfish (*Opistognathus macrognathus*) – the latter are much more timid than the yellowhead jawfish, which stand vertically in the water column above their holes. Schools of yellowtail goatfish, grunt and sergeant majors can be found all over. Silversides and glassy sweepers (*Pempheris schomburgki*) can be found under a huge stand of elkhorn and boulder star coral (*Monastrea annularis*).

5 SEA HUNT REEF
★★★★☆

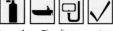

Location: The first mooring east of the Sanctuary Bay channel.
Access: By boat only.
Conditions: Can be choppy on the surface with oceanic surge during stormy weather.
Average depth: 3m (10ft)
Maximum depth: 6m (20ft)
Average visibility: 12m (40ft)

Much of the reef filming for *Sea Hunt*, the first television drama to popularize scuba diving, was done here. A shallow section of strip reef and single isolated coral heads, this site is made up of star corals and brain corals topped with sea fans and sea plumes. French grunt (*Haemulaon flavolineatum*) are common, as are sergeant majors and yellowtail snapper. Damselfish are everywhere, protecting their 'gardens' of algae.

Above: *Great shoals of silverside minnows swarm around the Papa Doc wreck (Site 12).*

6 BLACKBEARDS
★★☆☆☆

Location: A continuation of the strip reef running east from Sanctuary Bay, with three separate moorings.
Access: By boat only.
Conditions: Can experience surge and surface chop.
Average depth: 9m (30ft)
Maximum depth: 12m (40ft)
Average visibility: 12m (40ft)
This is a long, widely spread section of reef, with a varied terrain of long strips of reef and hundreds of individual coral heads, many of which are mushroom-shaped. They are primarily constructed of star corals and all are topped by sea fans, feathers and sea plumes. Virtually all the coral heads are sculpted out around their base, providing shelter for small grouper, bigeye (*Priacanthus arenatus*) and squirrelfish (*Holocentrus adscensionis*). This is a popular training site and although not in great shape, due to hurricane damage and excessive algal growth, it is still a delight. It is split into three separate mooring sites; the second mooring

(known as Blackbeard's Castle) has an enormous pillar coral and the eastern site (known as Blackbeard's Springs) has a blue hole 30cm (12in) in diameter.

7 BUDDHA HEADS
★★★☆☆

Location: East of the Lucayan waterway which bisects the island and opposite the National Park.
Access: By boat, but can be reached from the shore.
Conditions: This site can be choppy on the surface, with surge during stormy weather.
Average depth: 9m (30ft)
Maximum depth: 13m (43ft)
Average visibility: 15m (50ft)
A series of large squat coral heads, this site has a profusion of fish and invertebrate life. Normally the dive boats rarely venture this far, but from a photographic point of view the site is well worth the journey time, as it normally yields reef sharks, southern stingrays and the occasional turtle. All of the coral heads are topped by huge stands of sea plumes (*Pseudopterogorgia* spp.)

and giant split-pore sea rods (*Plexaurella nutans*). Fish life includes barred hamlets (*Hypoplectrus puella*), schools of brown chromis (*Chromis multilineata*) and creole wrasse (*Clepticus parrae*).

8 GOLD ROCK
★★★☆

Location: Last mooring buoy travelling east along the inner strip reef opposite the eastern end of the National Park.
Access: By boat only.
Conditions: Surge and surface chop to be expected.
Average depth: 11m (36ft)
Maximum depth: 14m (46ft)
Average visibility: 15m (50ft)
Gold Rock is a large patch reef system with lots of individual coral heads packed close together, creating some interesting swim-throughs and gullies. Although the sides and reef crest are largely overgrown by a light tan-coloured algae, there are also excellent examples of the smaller single corals such as the ridged cactus coral (*Mycetophyllia lamarckiana*) and lettuce coral (*Agaricia humilis*). Sea fans, rods and sea plumes all top the coral heads, which are fringed with an ever-moving curtain of blue chromis (*Chromis cyanea*).

9 HYDRO LAB (Shark Junction)
★★★★

Location: One of the closest sites to the Bell Channel entrance to Freeport/Port Lucaya.
Access: By boat, ten minutes from the UNEXSO dock.
Conditions: Reduced visibility can be expected with some surge and surface chop.
Average depth: 14.5m (47ft)
Maximum depth: 14.5m (47ft)
Average visibility: 6m (20ft) in the arena and 15m (50ft) everywhere else.
This is an incredible first introduction to diving with sharks. It can be a nerve-racking experience for beginners, who often feel that they are in a giant inter-active aquarium with a number of Caribbean reef sharks (*Carcharhinus perezi*). The shark handlers undertake thorough training to build up a safe relationship with the sharks, but even so they wear chain-mail suits (the first question most people ask when they see them is 'Why isn't everyone else wearing one?'). Before the dive, there is a comprehensive lecture on what to expect on the dive and a brief introduction to the biology of sharks. You must sign a waiver declaring that you will not sue if you get bitten.

WRASSE

Some wrasse are born either male or female, others as hermaphrodites. Most then develop first into a female, then a male. The male escorts and protects his 'harem'. If he dies or is killed, the next dominant female in the hierarchy will change sex and continue the dynasty.

The dive itself takes place on a wide sandy floor with UNEXSO's old recompression chamber behind you to offer an extra level of protection. Divers are arranged in a semi-circle with a 'point' diver at each side wearing chain-mail gauntlets and carrying a billy stick to ward off any sharks which get too close to the audience. Once everyone is in place, the shark feeder arrives; over the years, the feeders have developed such a close and tactile relationship with many of the sharks that they can actually be held and even picked up. This is a spectacular dive for first timers to shark feeding, an activity which also takes place in several other locations in the Bahamas.

To the west of Shark Junction is the upturned wreckage of a former work barge, the *Pretender*. Now upside down, the wreck is often visited as a second dive of the day, but it has few outstanding features and you will find more of interest in the surrounding corals.

10 SPID CITY
★★☆

Location: Next to Shark Junction (Site 9), travelling east.
Access: By boat only.
Conditions: Can be choppy on the surface, but little surge due to the protection of the outer reef system.
Average depth: 12m (40ft)
Maximum depth: 20m (66ft)
Average visibility: 15m (50ft)
SPID is an acronym for the Self-contained, Portable, Inflatable Dwelling that was once used for short-term habitation experiments in the mid- to late 1970s, although there is now no trace left of these. The remains of a twin engine Aztec aircraft, once used in the *Sea Hunt* television series, sits on the sandy bottom surrounded by garden eels (*Heteroconger halis*) and is now regarded as the centre of SPID City.

There are large schools of blue parrotfish, snapper, grunt and grouper all over the reef, but by far the biggest feature of the site are the sharks, which hang around here because it is close to Site 9 where the shark-feeding takes place. They can include large Caribbean reef sharks and nurse sharks, as well as barracuda, Atlantic spadefish and amberjack. This is a popular dive with the chance of seeing sharks on a shallow reef, but it can be rather disconcerting how close they come towards divers. A pretty dive, though the aeroplane wreckage is of interest only because of its television history.

11 ANGELS CAMP
★★☆

Location: Next mooring buoy from Site 10 travelling east from the Bell Channel.
Access: By boat only.
Conditions: Can be choppy on the surface with surge in rougher weather.
Average depth: 12m (40ft)
Maximum depth: 15m (50ft)
Average visibility: 18m (60ft)
As you descend to the mooring pin on the reeftop, you will find fairly high profile corals, sea fans, rods and sea plumes aligned in rows running east to west, interspersed with big coral heads. Running parallel to the first line of strip reef there is a slightly deeper reef with very pretty coral heads which are home to all of the angelfish fish species recorded from the Bahamas. The friendliest are the grey angelfish (*Pomacanthus arcuatus*) and the most timid are the rock beauties (*Holacanthus tricolor*); this is the only species which does not appear to stay in close proximity to its life-long mate.

12 PAPA DOC WRECK (and the Badger)
★★☆

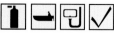

Location: 200m (220yd) east of SPID City (Site 10) on same patch reef system.
Access: By boat only.
Conditions: Can be choppy on the surface.
Average depth: 12m (40ft)
Maximum depth: 14m (47ft)
Average visibility: 15m (50ft)
A group of mercenaries heading for Haiti during the revolution there in 1968 to overthrow 'Papa Doc' Duvalier were en route from Miami when their small gun-running shrimp boat foundered and quickly sank in a storm. Now totally wrecked, there are only a couple of engine blocks and assorted bits and pieces of wreckage scattered around the coral heads. UNEXSO decided to make a better attraction for the area and deliberately sank a small harbour work boat called the *Badger* on the same site in 1996. Sitting upright and resting on a coral head at its bow, the *Badger* has now become known as Papa Doc.

During the summer months the wreck is smothered in silverside minnows which fill the holds and obscure the forward section. The surrounding reef has some curious mushroom-shaped formations, topped with small sea fans and sea plumes.

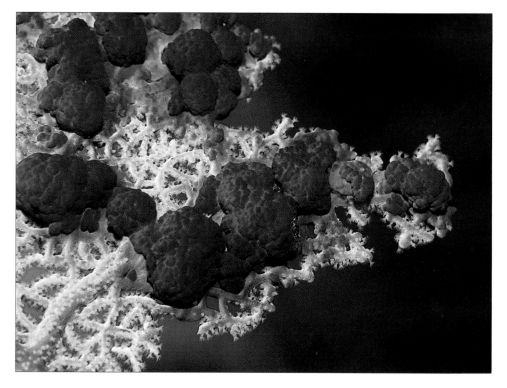

Above: *The flamingo tongue (Cyphoma gibbosum) is the most distinctive of the Caribbean snails.*
Opposite: *The common sea fan (Gorgonia ventalina) often has 'monstrous' growths on its growing fringe.*

13 OCTOPUSSY GARDEN
★★☆

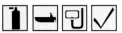

Location: East to the next mooring pin from Papa Doc (Site 12).
Access: By boat only.
Conditions: Surge and surface chop to be expected.
Average depth: 12m (40ft)
Maximum depth: 15m (50ft)
Average visibility: 15m (50ft)

To the east of the mooring pin there are a number of large and very pretty isolated coral heads topped with sea fans and plumes. Surrounding the coral heads is a wide sandy plain, dotted with the nests (built under coral rubble which has been collected into small mounds) of sand tile fish (*Malacanthus plumieri*). Near these mounds you will also find large numbers of bridled sand gobies (*Coryphopterus glaucofraenum*) which dart away in front of you. On the east side of the main reef there is a small blue hole under a dome of brain coral; you can easily find the fresh cold water coming from the hole as it creates a shimmering effect when it mixes with salt water – it is also several degrees colder.

14 ARROW POINT
★★★☆

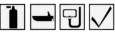

Location: The first deeper mooring pin east of the entrance to Sanctuary Bay.
Access: By boat only.
Conditions: Surface chop and oceanic swell to be expected.
Average depth: 14m (47ft)
Maximum depth: 16m (54ft)
Average visibility: 21m (70ft)

The coral heads at this site form the shape of a rough triangle, arguably part of the reason for its name, though it is also known for numbers of arrow crabs (*Stenorhynchus seticornis*) which can be found under the overhangs. The arrow crabs live near corkscrew anemones (*Bartholomea annulata*), which they use for additional protection and for poaching food which becomes paralysed when straying too close to the anemone's stinging tentacles. There is a tiny blue hole on the sand patch near the mooring pin; you can detect its presence by the temperature change in the water. Stingrays are common on the sand flats, which are home to large numbers of garden eels.

15 PICASSO'S GALLERY
★★★★

Location: The second mooring pin as you travel east from Sanctuary Bay.
Access: By boat only.
Conditions: Surface swell to be expected; no current.
Average depth: 12m (40ft)
Maximum depth: 15m (50ft)
Average visibility: 21m (70ft)

This site is named after its large coral heads, which whoever christened it evidently considered works of art due to their varied and vibrant colours. Arrow crabs, coral banded shrimps (*Stenopus hispidus*) and lots of anemones are common, as are Christmas tree worms (*Spirobranchus giganteus*) and large featherduster worms (*Sabellastartia magnifica*). Algae are present on all of the coral heads, however, making them look a bit untidy. As you swim south into deeper water, the coral heads merge into a continuous strip reef, gradually forming a classic spur and groove shape.

16 DOLPHIN DIVE (Dolphin Flats)
★★★★★

Location: East of Sanctuary Bay on the sand flat before you get to the Ugly Duckling (Site 17).
Access: By boat only.
Conditions: Choppy on the surface, but calm on the seabed.
Average depth: 15m (50ft)
Maximum depth: 15m (50ft)
Average visibility: 24m (80ft)

Any qualms about captive dolphins being exploited to entertain divers can be laid aside at this dive site. It is an open ocean site where two Atlantic bottlenose dolphins (*Tursiops truncatus*) regularly interact with divers – and quite evidently have great fun at the expense of our ungainly underwater antics. Divers are escorted to the seabed and form a rough circle where the dolphins will spin you around and allow you to stroke them. When they see you take your regulator out of your mouth, they will scoot across and expect to be kissed!

This is all great fun, but cannot be entirely guaranteed as the dolphins have been known to leave the area and interact with a group of wild dolphins which live nearby. Although the dolphins are used to human presence, they are still essentially wild animals and should be treated as such, which means you must not hold onto them. A privilege as well as sheer delight, this dive should not be missed.

17 UGLY DUCKLING (Josephine Wreck)
★★★★

Location: 100m (330ft) east of Dolphin Dive (Site 16).
Access: By boat only.
Conditions: Can be choppy on the surface with slight surge underwater.
Average depth: 14m (47ft)
Maximum depth: 14m (47ft)
Average visibility: 15m (50ft), but can be reduced due to the large sandy areas around the site.

Although the wreck is fairly deep, this site is popular with glass-bottomed boats and snorkellers, as it can be seen quite clearly. The wreck is a small 11m (36ft) sailboat called the *Josephine*, which was demasted and ran aground during a severe storm in 1994. It was decided to sink the boat and add it to UNEXSO's artificial reef programme. Although still intact, the boat is not particularly interesting, but the surrounding patch reefs, or bommies, are pretty with a good cover of assorted corals and sponges. Schools of creole wrasse (*Clepticus parrai*) can be found in the water column and clouds of blue chromis fringe every coral head. Yellowtail snapper and Bermuda chub also come quite close to divers.

18 REEF CARIBE
★★★

Location: 90m (300ft) east of the Ugly Duckling (Site 17).
Access: By boat only.
Conditions: Expect surface swell and slight surge.
Average depth: 14m (40ft)
Maximum depth: 18m (60ft)
Average visibility: 21m (70ft)

This site has three lines of isolated coral heads running parallel to each other. The tops of the coral heads are fringed in sea fans, gorgonians and sea plumes, while large hogfish (*Lachnolaimus maximus*) patrol the reefs and Nassau grouper (*Epinephelus striatus*) appear to be everywhere. Damselfish, butterflyfish, snapper, grunt and small jacks are forever lining up for the large number of cleaning gobies which live here. The reef is so large that a second mooring buoy has been placed further to the east, near a large pinnacle-shaped star coral (*Monastrea cavernosa*) with a small blue hole at its base. The blue hole blows and sucks depending on the incoming or outgoing tide, indicating that much of Grand Bahama's interior is linked to the sea. Lobsters and spider crabs are always found in the vicinity of the hole. The site is good for macro-photography.

Originally called the MS *Logna* and then the MV *Island Cement*, the ship now known as Theo's Wreck was built in Norway in 1954. Her current name derives from Theodopolis Galanoupoulos, an engineer working for the Bahama Cement Company when she was ready to be scrapped. It was his idea to deliberately sink the ship as an artificial reef. With the help of UNEXSO, she was sunk on 16 October 1982 off the Silver Beach Inlet off Grand Bahama Island.

Now resting on her port side, the 70m (228ft) ship lies in 29–33m (95–110ft) of water facing away from the drop-off along the Grand Bahama Ledge. Looking upwards through the propeller and rudder, the shaded underside is a carpet of golden cup corals (*Tubastrea coccinea*), as is the underside of the bow, which is also festooned with low-lying red sponges. There are safe entry points in the bridge and accommodation section, in front of which lives a large green moray eel (*Gymnothorax funebris*) which has a habit of coming out of its hole to greet divers.

The superstructure of Theo's Wreck is now covered in soft and hard corals, deep-water sea fans stretch out into the current and large schools of snapper and grunt congregate around the bows and the foredeck. The superstructure is also home to several species of angelfish, while up on the upper railings small shoals of snapper and grunt mill around waiting for lunch to swim by. Divers must not hold onto the rails as they are covered in marine life including stinging hydroids, small tunicates and sponges.

Now earmarked as a special area of conservation by the Bahamas National Trust, Theo's Wreck comes alive at night when the colours of the corals and sponges are illuminated by divers' torches. Gigantic rainbow parrotfish (*Scarus guacamaia*) over a metre long lie sleeping on every large ledge and iridescent blue parrotfish (*Scarus coeruleus*) nestle amidst colourful sponges. A couple of huge tarpon often 'buzz' divers at night. Divers are recommended to take a torch underwater with them even during the day, as it is only with the aid of an artificial light that you will be able to see the true colours.

The underside of Theo's Wreck is a mass of golden cup corals and colourful sponges.

19 BEN'S BLUE HOLE
★★★

Location: The next mooring buoy after the second Reef Caribe (Site 18) mooring buoy travelling east.
Access: By boat only.
Conditions: Surge and surface chop to be expected, but no current.
Average depth: 12m (40ft)
Maximum depth: 15m (50ft)
Average visibility: 21m (70ft)
This blue hole is situated under a ledge which forms part of a much larger fracture line running east from the mooring buoy. Discovered by Ben Rose, who pioneered the tactile relationship which shark feeders in the Bahamas now follow with Caribbean reef sharks, this horseshoe-shaped ledge has several small coral heads growing near its lip. If you follow the fracture line of the blue hole over the next two coral heads, you will find a second blue hole under the further coral head. Snapper, grunt, wrasse, parrotfish and Bermuda chub are common in the area, with the chub often circling lazily around divers.

20 ANCHORS AWEIGH
★★★

Location: The mooring buoy before the Etheridge Wreck (Site 21).
Access: By boat only.
Conditions: Surge and surface swell to be expected, but no current.
Average depth: 14m (50ft)
Maximum depth: 18m (60ft)
Average visibility: 21m (70ft)
This site is a string of scattered coral heads lying next to a line of solid coral made up of boulder star coral (*Monastrea annularis*), ten-ray star coral (*Madracis decactis*), brain coral (*Diploria strigosa*) and finger coral (*Madracis formosa*). Colourful sea fans are found on the top, but there is also considerable algal growth indicating a certain amount of damage caused by periodic hurricanes. Cleaning stations are found on each of the coral heads here, as are small patches of anemones, French angelfish (*Pomacanthus paru*) and the occasional southern stingray (*Dasyatis americana*).

Kissing a dolphin is one of many exhilarating possibilities with the Dolphin Experience (Site 16).

21 ETHERIDGE WRECK
★★★

Location: Ten minutes boat ride east of Bell Channel.
Access: By dive boat only.
Conditions: Can be choppy on the surface with underwater surge, reducing visibility.
Average depth: 15m (50ft)
Maximum depth: 20m (66ft)
Average visibility: 15m (50ft)
This 30m (100ft) car ferry formerly operated in the Carolinas, but is more famous for its appearance in the film *Halloween*. Sunk in early 1992 in an area of scattered coral heads, it sits on top of a low section of reef which has crumpled its starboard hull. The flatbed of the hulk has the remains of a lorry resting up against the intact wheelhouse, which has the name UNEXSO cut out of the metalwork. A large green moray eel is at present residing in the head (ship's toilet) and schools of silversides crowd around from June through to August.

22 ROSE GARDEN
★★★

Location: The buoy after Etheridge Wreck (Site 21).
Access: By boat only.
Conditions: Swell and surface chop to be expected.
Average depth: 18m (60ft)
Maximum depth: 21m (70ft)
Average visibility: 21m (70ft)
This site features long lines of solid coral dissected by surge channels in a spur and groove formation. On the top of one of the coral spurs is a circular blue hole which points upwards. Algal growths and discoloured water stream out of this hole on an outgoing tide. Schools of Bermuda chub (*Kyphosus sectatrix*) and black durgon triggerfish (*Melichthys niger*) inhabit the area. Various snapper and grunt, wrasse and parrotfish abound in the channels and Atlantic spadefish (*Chaetodipterus faber*) appear occasionally.

23 ANN'S REEF (West Ann's, Ann's Paradise, East Ann's)
★★★

Location: The last three mooring buoys to the east of Site 22, before the entrance to the Lucayan Waterway.
Access: By boat only, 30 minutes from the dock.
Conditions: Can be choppy on the surface.
Average depth: 12m (40ft)
Maximum depth: 18m (60ft)
Average visibility: 21m (70ft)

Ann's Reef was named in memory of Ann Leadman, a schoolteacher who loved this reef, tragically killed in a motorcycle accident on Grand Bahama. This massive area is an overgrown spur and groove structure, similar to Rose Garden (Site 22), but with a much higher reef profile and deep sandy surge channels. As the reef extends to the east the reef starts to break up with large coral pinnacles on the crests, gradually forming large scattered coral heads surrounded by sand and garden eel colonies. Pairs of white-spotted filefish (*Cantherhines macrocerus*) can be seen along most sections of the reef, but the much rarer and much harder to find, slender filefish (*Monacanthus tuckeri*) can also be found amid the sea fans and sea plumes on the reef crest.

To the far east, near the last mooring buoy, lies the wreck of a fibreglass yacht which sank on its way to Great Abaco and was pulled back and repositioned in deep water. It sits in the solid coral to the south of the mooring.

24 THEO'S WRECK
★★★★★

Location: Directly opposite Silver Beach Inlet at the drop-off.
Access: By boat only.
Conditions: Can be choppy on the surface with current running across the wreck, but generally sheltered within the confines of the wreck.
Average depth: 25m (80ft)
Maximum depth: 33m (110ft)
Average visibility: 50m (165ft)
Originally an inter-island cement cargo ship, Theo's Wreck was deliberately scuttled at the end of her useful life by UNEXSO. She now rests on her port side in 29–33m (95–110ft) of water. Divers are expected to descend and ascend on either of the two permanent mooring buoys attached to the bow and stern of the ship. There are safe entry points in the bridge and accommodation section, and the hold is completely open, allowing free access. The superstructure is now covered in soft and hard corals,

golden cup corals, tunicates and sponges. Although a deep dive, this wreck is a superb site and should not be missed. For further details see page 45.

25 LATTIMOR'S MOUND
★★★★

Location: The first buoy west of Silver Point Channel.
Access: By boat only.
Conditions: Surface swell and current can be expected.
Average depth: 18m (60ft)
Maximum depth: 21m (70ft)
Average visibility: 30m (100ft)
Appearing almost as one large coral head, this site is in fact made up of a cluster of large coral blocks. They once had swim-throughs and gullies, but these are now overgrown with sheet corals and gorgonian sea fans, with all of the underhanging ledges smothered in hanging vine algae (*Halimeda copiosa*). The top of the reef has a cloud of blue chromis (*Chromis cyanea*) and creole wrasse (*Clepticus parrai*) in the water column picking off passing planktonic titbits. The reef section which extends either side of the mound is of a fairly extensive spur and groove formation, sloping down into an angled, coral gravel and sand plain which eventually reaches the edge of the drop-off. Garden eels are very common, as are yellowhead jawfish (*Opistognathus aurifrons*).

26 JOSE'S WRECK
★★★

Location: Opposite the entrance to the Bell Channel.
Access: By boat only.
Conditions: Surface swell to be expected, and a slight current is common.
Average depth: 18m (60ft)
Maximum depth: 25m (80ft)
Average visibility: 30m (100ft)
A 12m (40ft) former tugboat was sunk here as an artificial reef in 1986. It is balanced between two coral heads, and divers can swim under the hull where there are always various snapper, grunt and porkfish (*Anisotremus virginicus*). Gradually overgrown with sponges and low encrusting corals, the wreck is home to parrotfish and wrasse browsing around it. Silversides are known to congregate here from August to September and large tiger grouper (*Mycteroperca tigris*) can be seen queuing up at cleaning stations on the sand, where corkscrew anemones are host to large numbers of Pederson's cleaning shrimps (*Periclimenes pedersoni*).

27 MORAY MANOR
★★★

Location: Directly out from the Bell Channel to the two furthest mooring buoys.
Access: By boat only.
Conditions: Surface swell and surge to be expected, with slight current common.
Average depth: 18m (60ft)
Maximum depth: 25m (80ft)
Average visibility: 30m (100ft)
This extensive spur and groove reef was once used as a dumping ground for old truck tyres. You can still see the oversized circles embedded in the sand of the surge channels. Schools of snapper and grunt can be found, as well as goatfish, peacock flounders and coronetfish. Large green moray eels are occasionally sighted, but the reef is better known for spotted morays (*Gymnothorax moringa*) which grow up to about 1m (3ft).

28 CAVES
★★★★

Location: East from the Bell Channel entrance to the next deep mooring buoy after Site 27.
Access: By boat only.
Conditions: Expect surface swell and surge during rough weather.
Average depth: 15m (50ft)
Maximum depth: 21m (70ft)
Average visibility: 30m (100ft)
This is a large spur and groove reef with wide surge gullies creating a labyrinth of coral passages. The site is covered by two separate mooring buoys directly out from Shark Junction (Site 9), and sharks are a normal part of the dive here. The first mooring is near a coral cavern which extends for about 30m (33yd), and is inhabited by blackbar squirrelfish (*Myripristis jacobus*) and barred cardinalfish (*Apogon binotatus*). The second is a smaller circular cavern which you are able to swim through, though take care not to touch the sides.

29 GAIL'S GROTTO
★★★

Location: Around 100m (330ft) east of the Caves (Site 28).
Access: By boat only.
Conditions: Surface swell and surge to be expected.
Average depth: 15m (50ft)
Maximum depth: 27m (90ft)
Average visibility: 30m (100ft)

Above: *Foureye butterflyfish (Chaetodon capistratus) are relatively common on the shallow reefs.*
Below: *Golden zoanthids (Parazoanthus swiftii) overgrow many different types of sponge.*

Gail's Grotto is part of the same huge spur and groove reef as Site 28, which forms the primary barrier for all the oceanic storm fronts before the waves hit Grand Bahama. It features wide and deep sandy bottomed surge channels, which stretch down from the reeftop to a sandy plain that gradually slopes to the edge of the drop-off. The group of Caribbean reef sharks (*Carcharhinus perezi*) which regularly visit the nearby shark-feeding area use these channels to navigate from deeper water to the shelter of the inner strip reefs. Spotted eagle rays (*Aetobatus narinari*) are also seen in the area, as are stingrays, barracuda and several species of large jacks, which are attracted to the scent of bait in the water.

30 EDGE OF THE LEDGE
★★★

Location: East of Gail's Grotto (Site 29) to the edge of the drop-off.
Access: By boat only.
Conditions: Surface swell is generally encountered as well as current at the edge of the wall.
Average depth: 30m (100ft)
Maximum depth: Beyond 70m (230ft)
Average visibility: 50m (165ft)
As its name implies, the Edge of the Ledge is just that. The mooring buoy is anchored on a sandy bottom in 30m (100ft) of water: outwards and to the south you can see the edge of the drop-off where there are scattered coral heads. Despite their small size, they are oases of life, attracting many species of fish and invertebrates. Garden eels (*Heteroconger halis*) are all over, as are yellowhead jawfish, sand tilefish, peacock flounders, stingrays and barjacks. It's worth keeping a look-out into the open water, as there is a fair chance of seeing manta rays, eagle rays, hammerhead sharks and the occasional marlin.

31 LITTLEHALE'S LAIR
★★★

Location: The mooring furthest out opposite the Sanctuary Bay entrance channel.
Access: By boat only.
Conditions: Surge and rough surface water to be expected with a slight current underneath.
Average depth: 21m (70ft)
Maximum depth: 27m (90ft)
Average visibility: 30m (100ft)
Named after the *National Geographic* photographer Bates Littlehale, this location has two separate lairs (small caves) created by corals growing over the tightly packed surge channels of an extensive spur and groove reef. It is possible to swim through the westerly of these two caverns. The area is loaded with grunt, snapper, Bermuda chub, porkfish, yellowtail snapper, black durgon triggerfish and

creole wrasse. The reeftop is rather untidy with stands of sea rods and sea plumes. Many of the sea fans look as if they have sustained storm damage and are quickly becoming overgrown by fire coral (*Millepora alcicornis*).

32 PLATE REEF
★★★

Location: Directly opposite the spur and groove reef from Ben's Blue Hole (Site 19).
Access: By boat only, 20 minutes from Bell Channel.
Conditions: Can be choppy from June to October.
Average depth: 16m (53ft)
Maximum depth: 22m (73ft)
Average visibility: 20m (66ft)
This is a well formed spur and groove reef with surge channels overgrown with corals, forming narrow swim-throughs and tunnels. Divers are not encouraged to enter these as their air bubbles can damage the fragile organisms which grow on the ceilings. A large blue hole comes out of the side of a high profile coral wall here: the sides of the hole disappearing into the depths of the reef are circular and smooth, and cool fresh water can be seen flowing out of the hole, creating a shimmering halocline.

33 PYGMY CAVES
★★★

Location: Near Blair House (Site 35).
Access: By boat only.
Conditions: Can be choppy with surge to be expected.
Average depth: 16m (53ft)
Maximum depth: 22m (73ft)
Average visibility: 18m (60ft)
Here the spurs of the coral have overgrown the grooves to such an extent that they have formed enclosed tunnels which are too small for divers to negotiate. The tops of the reef are made up of large sheet corals (*Agaricia grahamae*), star boulder corals, sea plumes

---

UNEXSO

UNEXSO (The Underwater Explorers Society), situated at Freeport on Grand Bahama Island, is one of the oldest scuba diving centres in the Bahamas. They have a daily shark feeding programme at Shark Junction, just 10 minutes' boat ride from the dock, and oversee the Dolphin Experience, located in Sanctuary Bay, where divers can swim with a pair of friendly bottle-nose dolphins. There are also reef dives, deep wall dives and a number of derelict ships sunk by UNEXSO as part of a massive artificial reef programme, such as Theo's Wreck. UNEXSO have highly qualified staff, and with two swimming pools on site are able to offer diving instruction to all standards of qualification. Their diving retail store is the largest in the Bahamas. The recompression chamber on Grand Bahama Island is also located at UNEXSO.

and rods. The channels feature small gorgonian sea fans and wire or whip corals. Creole and bluehead wrasse are common, as are parrotfish, snapper and grunt.

34 LADY OF LUCAYA
★★★

Location: A 20-minute boat ride from Lucaya on the outer ridge of the reef which becomes Blair House (Site 35).
Access: By dive boat only.
Conditions: Choppy on surface, silty in swim-throughs.
Average depth: 16m (53ft)
Maximum depth: 21m (70ft)
Average visibility: 20m (66ft)
Just to the east of the permanent mooring on the reef is a small statue of a winged angel, The Lady of Lucaya, positioned just in front of a large wide tunnel through a coral head. The tunnel has been carved by the cold fresh water coming out of the blue holes at either side of the tunnel, and is easily negotiated, making this a popular dive. The larger of the holes is often filled with silversides. The statue is gradually becoming overgrown with coral growth, but she is still pretty.

35 BLAIR HOUSE
★★★

Location: A 20-minute boat ride towards the East End on the outer ridge of the reef.
Access: By dive boat only.
Conditions: Choppy on surface, silty in swim-throughs.
Average depth: 16m (53ft)
Maximum depth: 24m (83ft)
Average visibility: 20m (66ft)
The depth to the reeftop is a fairly uniform 16m (53ft) under the boat's mooring, but what makes this ancient spur and groove reef interesting are the many instances where the ridges have grown over the grooves. There are numerous swim-throughs and tunnels which wind through the reef; many of them are interconnecting. Although the reef has few fish, there are some very interesting coral formations and bright colourful sponges.

36 LUCAYAN CAVERNS
★★★★

Location: About 32km (21 miles) east from Freeport.
Access: By foot and along a well travelled path past Bat Cave, from the signposted Lucayan Caverns car park.
Conditions: This dive is only for experienced cave divers with a scientific permit and special authorization.
Average depth: 7m (24ft)
Maximum depth: 12m (40ft)
Average visibility: 25m (80ft)

The grey angelfish (Pomacanthus arcuatus) is the largest member of the angelfish family.

The Lucayan Caverns are situated in a National Park managed by the Bahamas National Trust and are one of the most extensive cave systems known in the Bahamas, with over 10km (6 miles) of passageways. The National Park authorities will allow only permitted divers into the cave system, under the direct guidelines set out by Stephanie Schwabe. The main dry entrance is quite easy and involves going down a wooden walkway under a cavernous mouth, where a collapsed cavern ceiling has created a cantilevered arch or dome that drops several metres into the rocky hillside. This cavern is one of the breeding locations for the buffy flower bat (*Erophylla sezekorni*). The same species of bat is found in similar circumstances in Lighthouse Cave on San Salvador Island.

A sloping rock ledge leads you into the cave and light faintly filters through from the cavern entrance. The bottom of the cave slopes off steeply, then makes a sudden rise and turns around to the right where a small opening above allows light to filter through amid a tangle of tree roots. Good quality flow stone, stalactites and stalagmites can be found in the passageways which extend well beyond the light of day. This is an extensive cave system where ongoing research work is being carried out.

HOW TO GET THERE

By air
The main point of entry on Grand Bahama is Freeport International Airport, a modern airport with limited facilities. Direct flights arrive daily from Miami, Fort Lauderdale and the Family Islands, with Bahamasair being the main carrier.

American Airlines fly to Miami and links to American Eagle, who fly direct from Miami and Fort Lauderdale to Grand Bahama and a few of the Family Islands. Continental Connection also flies in from Florida. Martinair flies from Amsterdam via Fort Lauderdale to Freeport, while all other international carriers route through either Miami or Nassau and you will have to make a connection. Princess and LB charters operate (with seasonal changes) weekly from a number of US cities including Chicago, Baltimore, Cleveland, Cincinatti, Richmond, Knoxville, Greenville, Raleigh/Durham and Fort Lauderdale. From the Family Islands, Major Air Services and Taino Air also fly into Grand Bahama.

By boat
Yachtsmen find Grand Bahama a great lure as the deep-water shelf comes close to the south shore and a large number of marinas can be found here. The largest number of visitors arrive on cruise ships and Freeport is the major stop in the Bahamas for duty-free shopping. The cruise ships hang offshore and passengers are collected in their droves on the 'Little Red Boats' which deposit them at Port Lucaya.

VEHICLE HIRE

Avis, Freeport International Airport, tel (242) 352 7666.
Courtesy Rental, Freeport International Airport, tel (242) 352 5212.
Hertz, Freeport International Airport, tel (242) 352 9277.
Sears Rent-A-Car, Atlantik Beach Hotel, tel (242) 373 4938, and at Freeport International Airport, tel (242) 352 8841.

ONE DAY CRUISE LINERS

One of the most popular way for visitors to visit the Bahamas, and in particular Freeport, is on a day cruise offered from Miami. Costs are from around $100.
Seascape Cruises, tel (305) 476 4300, fax (305) 476 9920.
Discovery Cruises, tel (305) 525 7800, fax: (305) 763 7074.

National Car Rental, Freeport International Airport, tel (242) 352 9308.

WHERE TO STAY

During 1998, a massive redevelopment was planned for the Port Lucaya area, with a number of the hotels being pulled down and others undergoing complete refurbishment. All the hotels listed here are easy to find along the south coast, only 15 minutes by taxi from the airport. For an up-to-date list of the hotel resorts available, contact the **Grand Bahama Island Tourism Board** (see Box).

Grand Bahama Beach Hotel, PO Box F42496, Royal Palm Way, Freeport; tel (242) 373 1333, fax (242) 373 2396. This 500-room hotel can seem large and impersonal as it handles hundreds of stop-over cruise ship guests, but is handy for the Port Lucaya marketplace and is close enough to walk to UNEXSO. All rooms have recently been upgraded, although some reports claim that the $20 million face-lift has had little visible effect.

Bahamas Princess Resort & Casino, PO Box F40207, Mall at Sunrise, Grand Bahama; tel (242) 352 6721, fax (242) 352 6842. This massive resort complex is set in over 810ha (2000 acres) of grounds but has no beach. Said to be the most sophisticated resort on Grand Bahama, it also has the largest casino. Its 942 rooms and 23 suites are divided between the Princess Country Club and the Princess Tower; the complex includes numerous restaurants, 12 floodlit tennis courts, two swimming pools, and access to two 18-hole golf courses. There is a shuttle to the beach, where there are full watersports facilities.

Port Lucaya Resort & Yacht Club, PO Box F42452, Bell Channel Bay Road, Freeport; tel (242) 373 6618, fax (242) 373 6652. The resort is characterized by a series of low-rise buildings surrounding a pool area and Jacuzzi. The 160 rooms are attractive and comfortable, if somewhat on the functional side. Next to the Port Lucaya marketplace, it also has a good restaurant.

Pelican Bay at Lucaya, PO Box F42654, Freeport; tel (242) 373 9550, fax (242) 373 9551. This moderately priced hotel has clean, modern rooms with balconies giving sea views. It has a small pool with an excellent pool-side snack bar, and one main restaurant. The beach is across the road but the hotel is very popular with divers due to its location next door to UNEXSO.

Xanadu Beach & Marina Resort, PO Box F42438, Sunken Treasure Drive, Grand Bahama; tel (242) 352 6783, fax (242) 352 5799. Directly attached to Xanadu Undersea Adventures.

Club Fortuna, PO Box F42398, Freeport; tel (242) 373 4000 or (800) 221 6582, fax (242) 373 5555. All inclusive with good facilities, through rather impersonal. Italian in style.

Self-catering
Freeport Resort and Club, PO Box F42514, Rum Cay Drive, Freeport; tel (242) 352 5371, fax (242) 52 8425. Fifty-two efficiency apartments, swimming pool, with dining at nearby resorts.

Taino Beach Resort and Hotel, PO Box F43819, Freeport; tel (242) 373 4677, fax (242) 373 4421. East of Freeport, with a pool, a great restaurant and 104 rooms.

WHERE TO EAT

All the international hotels have a choice of restaurants. Around town you will find various fast food joints typical of large tourist centres. In restaurants, dress sense is very casual except in the casino restaurants in the hotel resorts.

Brass Helmet Restaurant, upstairs at UNEXSO on the waterfront, Port Lucaya, Freeport; tel (242) 373 2032. Popular with divers thanks to good-value international food and handy location. Good atmosphere and ongoing shark-feeding video.

Pub At Port Lucaya, Port Lucaya Market Place, Freeport; tel (242) 373 8450. Serves Bahamian specialities such as peas'n'rice and jerk chicken, but also more traditional steak and ale pie, steaks and fish. Watch out for the Pusser's Rum concoctions – easy to drink and very strong!

Cowboy's Barbecue, Port Lucaya Market Place, Freeport; tel (242) 373 8631. If you can put up with the Country and Western music and very slow service, it is worth the wait for great ribs and steak. With take-out service.

Zorba's Greek Cuisine, Port Lucaya Market Place, Freeport; tel (242) 373 6137. Traditional Greek cuisine, good value, but service is a bit erratic.

Pier One, Freeport Harbour, Freeport; tel (242) 352 6674. A popular seafood restaurant set on stilts in the harbour which has regular shark-feeding every hour virtually below your feet. Serves great steak and lobster, although it is a bit pricey. You will have to book in advance to get a table in the 'shark pit'.

The Stoned Crab, Taino Beach, Lucaya; tel (242) 373 1442. Relaxed atmosphere on the beach, where you can watch the sunset with a beer and massive helpings of freshly caught snapper, grouper, lobster and swordfish.

DIVE FACILITIES

Caribbean Divers, PO Box F43817, Bell Channel Inn, Port Lucaya, Freeport; tel (242) 373 9111, fax (242) 373 9112. A small dive shop offering more personalized diving.

Sun Odyssey Divers, PO Box F44166, 77 Silver Palm Court, Freeport; tel (242) 373 4014, fax (242) 373 1039. A small operation taking only a few divers, but very experienced on all Grand Bahama reefs.

Underwater Explorers Society (UNEXSO), PO Box F42433, Port Lucaya, Freeport; tel (242) 373 1244, fax (242) 373 8956, e-mail info@unexso.com. In USA tel (954) 351 9889 or freephone (800) 992 DIVE (3483), fax (954) 351 9740. Over 30 years' experience, with a large retail store, five boats, multilingual staff and two swimming pools for training.

Dolphin Experience (UNEXSO), PO Box F42433, Port Lucaya, Freeport; tel (242) 373 1250, fax (242) 373 8956. Guests travel to the dolphin sanctuary by flatbed ferry from UNEXSO.

Xanadu Undersea Adventures, PO Box F40118, Sunken Treasure Drive, Freeport; tel (242) 352 3811, fax (242) 352 4731. In USA: tel (954) 462 3400 or freephone (800) 327 8150. A large operation which also offers shark feeding.

Grand Bahama Watersports, Freeport; tel (242) 373 6775. A small dive operation which tends to be open irregular hours.

Ocean Safari, PO Box F42695, Ocean Reef Resort & Yacht Club, 54 Bahama Reef Blvd., Freeport; tel (242) 373 3217 ext. 168. A small dive shop.

FILM PROCESSING

Photo Magic Ltd, 2B Town Centre Mall, Woodstock Street, tel (242) 352 6040. For Instant print as well as E6.

UNEXSO, Port Lucaya, Freeport, tel (242) 373 1244, fax (242) 373 8956. Full E6 service plus video editing.

EMERGENCY INFORMATION

Recompression Chamber: at UNEXSO, tel (242) 373 1244, or on direct ship to shore radio link on channel 19.

Rand Memorial Hospital, East Atlantic Drive, Grand Bahama, tel (242) 352 6735.

Sunrise Medical Centre, East Sunrise Highway, Grand Bahama, tel (242) 373 3333.

Bain Dental Clinic, Pioneers Way, Grand Bahama, tel (242) 352 8492.

Julie Ryan Licensed Massage Therapist, Grand Bahama Beach Hotel, Freeport, Grand Bahama, tel (242) 373 1333 or 373 3848.

LOCAL HIGHLIGHTS

Boat cruises
'Booze cruises' are popular with locals and cruise ship tourists, although they can be a bit much and too noisy after a hard day's diving. If you're still keen to take a cruise in the Bahamian sunset, tickets are sold from the dockside at Freeport Marketplace and cost $25 (including alcohol).

Deepstar Submarine, Waterfront, Port Lucaya, tel (242) 373 8665/6 or 373 8940, fax (242) 373 8667. Operated by Comex, the submarine carries 45 passengers within a completely acrylic hull and offers fantastic views of Grand Bahama's reefs. The total journey time (including the ferry trip from the shore) is two hours.

Nature parks
Garden of the Groves, situated on Midshipman Road and Magellan Drive, tel (242) 352 4045, is a unique 5ha (12 acre) botanical park named in honour of Georgette and Wallace Groves, the founders of Freeport. Admission is around $5, while an organized coach trip with hotel pick-up costs $20. Perhaps a better alternative are the non-profit, non-governmental National Parks under the auspices of the Bahamas National Trust. **Rand Nature Centre** on East Settler's Way, tel (242) 352 5438, has guided walks explaining the medicinal properties of the native plant life. **Lucayan National Park**, 32km (21 miles) east of Freeport, has a variety of ecosystems including two large caves open to the public. **Peterson Cay National Park**, tel (242) 352 5438, is the only cay on Grand Bahama's leeward shore, located 2km (1 mile) off the south

coast. It is one of the smallest national parks in the Bahamas and is a great place for snorkelling, but the island has little shade and visitors by ferry (which leaves from Port Lucaya) are advised to cover up and take plenty of drinking water and sun screen.

Sport
There are several golf courses on Grand Bahama: **the Bahamas Princess Resort & Casino**, tel (242) 352 6721 ext. 4600, with two challenging PGA courses; **Fortune Hills Golf & Country Club**, tel (242) 373 4500; and the **Lucayan Golf & Country Club**, tel (242) 373 1066, an 18-hole par 72 championship course which costs around $60 for non-members.

For fishing, contact Ben Rose, North Riding Point Bone Fishing Club, tel (242) 353 4250, fax (242) 353 4950. The shallow waters around northern Grand Bahama are a bonefisherman's idea of paradise.

The Dolphin Experience (UNEXSO), Port Lucaya, PO Box F42433, Freeport, Grand Bahama, tel (242) 373-1250 or (800) 992-3483, fax (242) 373-8956. A short ferry ride from the UNEXSO base at Port Lucaya takes you to Sanctuary Bay, where, depending on your time, interest and involvement, you can enjoy the thrill of the encounter, watch the show, or take part in a dolphin assistant trainer programme. It is also possible to take a highly recommended dolphin dive in the open ocean.

Shopping
At the **International Bazaar** and **Port Lucaya**. The best purchases are to be found at Columbian Emeralds and the duty-free outlets, where alcohol is especially cheap.

A local free publication called *What To Do* is available everywhere on the island and gives excellent information on all local attractions.

TOURIST INFORMATION

Grand Bahama Island Tourism Board, PO Box F40251, International Bazaar, Grand Bahama; tel (242) 352 8044, fax (242) 352 2714.
Freeport International Airport, Grand Bahama; tel (242) 352 2052.
Port Lucaya Marketplace, Lucaya, Grand Bahama; tel (242) 373 8988. Internet address: http://www.gobahamas.com/bahamas

THE ABACOS

Occasionally referred to as the 'Isles of the old-time Loyalists', the Abacos are an elbow-shaped cluster of islands and cays stretching 208km (130 miles) in a southeasterly direction from Walker's Cay in the north to the tip of Great Abaco in the south. Located 325km (200 miles) east of Miami and 120km (75 miles) north of Nassau, the Abacos consist of two main islands, Great and Little Abaco, and dozens of cays which are bordered by the shallow waters of the Little Bahama Bank to the west and the Atlantic to the east.

The islands, with hundreds of sheltered bays and protected waters, are extremely popular with both yachtsmen and divers. Superb modern facilities exist in the Abacos alongside a distinctive old-world charm. Among the smaller islands of the group are Man-of-War Cay, with its traditional shipbuilding industry, and Treasure Cay, which has a championship golf course and an upmarket hotel and marina complex.

The largest island in the Abacos chain, Great Abaco, is fringed by approximately 25 cays which form part of the inner barrier reef system protecting the island from the worst of the Atlantic storms. There are two further secondary barrier reefs further east from the cays which provide additional protection for the much more exposed cays themselves. The Abacos' only underwater park is the 486ha (1200 acre) Pelican Cay National Park located around the Pelican Cays, southeast of Marsh Harbour, the commercial centre. The park protects an extensive area of shallow reefs and mangroves harbouring a large array of marine life, and is an understandably popular spot with divers and snorkellers.

In Abaco National Park in the south of Great Abaco, 1000 hectares (2500 acres) have been set aside to protect the Bahama Parrot, which is unique as it nests only in holes in the limestone rock. All of the northern parts of the island are covered in dense pine forest while the entire western seaboard is a massive wetland area of small creeks, mangrove

Opposite: *The lighthouse at Hope Town, Elbow Cay, has distinctive 'candy' stripes.*
Above: *Banded coral shrimps (Stenopus hispidus) are the largest of the 'cleaner' shrimps.*

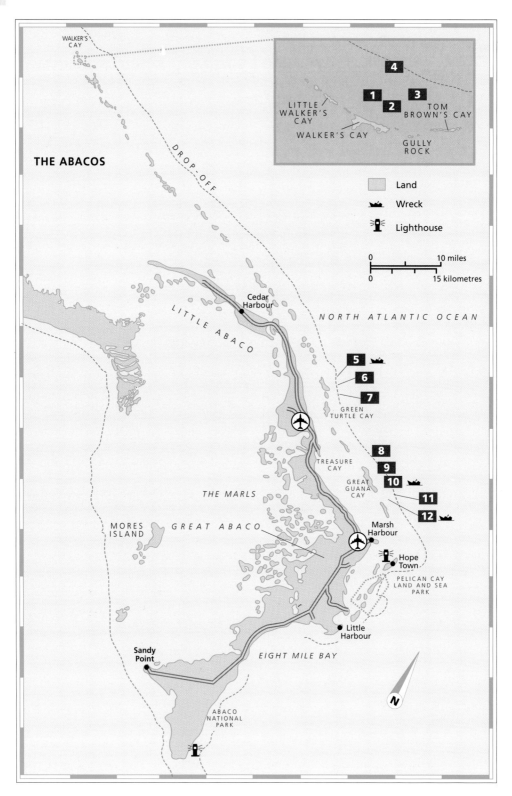

THE ABACOS

WALKER'S CAY

LITTLE WALKER'S CAY

WALKER'S CAY

TOM BROWN'S CAY

GULLY ROCK

4
1 **2** **3**

D R O P - O F F

Land

Wreck

Lighthouse

0   10 miles
0   15 kilometres

Cedar Harbour

LITTLE ABACO

N O R T H   A T L A N T I C   O C E A N

5
6
7

GREEN TURTLE CAY

8
9
10
11
12

TREASURE CAY

GREAT GUANA CAY

THE MARLS

MORES ISLAND

GREAT ABACO

Marsh Harbour

Hope Town

PELICAN CAY LAND AND SEA PARK

Little Harbour

Sandy Point

EIGHT MILE BAY

ABACO NATIONAL PARK

N

forest and small islands known as The Marls which provides an important nursery for many of the reefs' fish and invertebrate populations. The area is a natural habitat for ducks, egrets and herons, and can be explored by kayak.

The main town on nearby Green Turtle Cay is New Plymouth, located at the southern end of this island and occupying most of the headland. Founded in the 18th century, the town retains a great deal of colonial charm with its brightly coloured houses with peaked roofs, old verandas and quiet lanes. A narrow finger of scrubby land juts out between Settlement Creek and Black Sound, offering safe, sheltered anchorage in bad weather. Once a busy port, New Plymouth now has just 400 residents and it takes no more than ten minutes to walk down its main street, Parliament Street. Access to the island is by water taxi from the Treasure Cay airport, a few minutes' ride across a 5km (3 mile) stretch of water.

As the most northerly resort island in the Bahamas, Walker's Cay is known as the 'Top of the Bahamas'. It has been privately owned by Robert Abplanalp (the inventor of the aerosol valve) since 1968. The island covers 40ha (100 acres) and has its own tarmac runway, customs post, marina and resort hotel. As a famous deep-sea fishing resort, the island hosts numerous international competitions. The fish scraps from these are frozen into big drums, or 'chumsickles', which are used on an infrequent basis to attract large numbers of sharks into a feeding arena.

The dive sites around the island are for the most part protected by an outer barrier reef, with all the sites close together and only around ten minutes from the dive centre. Widely known for its interlocking caverns, caves and swim-throughs, much of the diving is very similar to the offshore reefs of Bermuda.

1 SPIRAL CAVERN (Snoopy's Reef) (Shark Rodeo)

★★★★★☆☆☆

Location: 15 minutes northwest of Walker's Cay Marina.
Access: By boat only.
Conditions: Can be choppy on surface.
Average depth: 12m (40ft)
Maximum depth: 12m (40ft)
Average visibility: 15m (50ft), but does reduce considerably during the shark feed.

This is one of the best of all the shark dives on offer in the Bahamas. A frozen bait ball or 'chumsickle' is dropped into mid-water near the dive group, who wait in front of a natural amphitheatre in 12m (40ft) of water. Lots of sharks are already in position as you descend and as many as 200 sharks will make their appearance when the feeding on the bait ball begins. Among the sharks you will see are blacktip, nurse, Caribbean reef and bull sharks, and occasionally hammerhead, lemon and tiger sharks. The dive feels much safer than those on other islands, as the human element has been removed from the shark feed. The sharks completely ignore the divers and seem to regard them as other animals also interested in the bait, along with the grouper and snapper which will try to feed from it.

This is high-voltage action and should not be missed. As the sharks start to feed, a pecking order seems to develop with sharks taking turns at attacking the chumsickle, removing some fish scraps and then leaving the arena for the next shark to move in. Speed this scenario up by about 50 times and you have an idea of the amount of action which is happening just a short space away from your (very wide) eyes!

When the food is finished, divers are given the opportunity to swim into the centre of the arena to look for any sharks' teeth which may have fallen out during the feeding. These make great souvenirs. The shark feeding takes place on an infrequent basis and the same dive is also done more regularly without the bait, allowing divers to take a clear-water reef dive accompanied by sharks, making for some great photographic opportunities.

2 BARRACUDA ALLEY

★★★☆

Location: 15 minutes north of Walker's Cay Marina.
Access: By boat only.
Conditions: Choppy surface conditions and slight current usually present.
Average depth: 7m (24ft)
Maximum depth: 12m (40ft)
Average visibility: 12m (40ft)
Aptly named, Barracuda Alley is home to a few very large barracuda (*Sphyraena barracuda*) which appear at the mooring point above the edge of the reef. They are well used to the presence of divers, and you can approach the larger ones quite closely and take some very dramatic portrait photographs. Like most of the surrounding reefs, there are lots of gullies and canyons to explore, but much of the reef has dense algal growth.

3 PIRATE'S CATHEDRAL

★★★☆☆

Location: 15 minutes northeast of Walker's Cay Marina.
Access: By boat only.
Conditions: Surface chop and slight current to be expected.
Average depth: 7m (24ft)
Maximum depth: 11m (36ft)
Average visibility: 15m (50ft)
At this site, the dive boat drops a sand anchor into a large sandy area surrounded by coral canyons. The sand has a fringe of algal turf grazed by large numbers of mature conch, some of which have large lumps of coral attached to their shell, indicating that they must be many years old. A large barracuda always turns up to follow the divers around, and the reef is of good quality with large Nassau grouper (*Epinephelus*

STINGING CELLS

Anemones, corals and jellyfish are armed with a battery of stinging cells called 'nematocysts'. These cells are actually a tiny barbed harpoon tipped with a paralysing poison which the creature will fire into its prey should they happen to brush against them. These microscopic cells are particularly effective in the case of the Portuguese man-of-war, whose tentacles can trail over 10m (33ft). During late spring and early summer large aggregations of thimble jellyfish (*Linuche unguiculata*) can be found in the waters, which can cause irritation to the softer parts of the skin. Local remedies are known for these conditions.

---

striatus), French angelfish (*Pomacanthus paru*) and blue chromis (*Chromis cyanea*) in residence. The reef features a maze of gullies, canyons, caves and caverns (similar to those found in Bermuda), all of which are easily negotiated.

4 SHARK CANYON

★★★

Location: 20 minutes due north of Walker's Cay Marina.
Access: By boat only.
Conditions: Rather exposed, so expect surface chop and slight surge and current.
Average depth: 20m (66ft)
Maximum depth: 28m (93ft)
Average visibility: 25m (80ft)
This deep dive is known for its sleeping sharks, which can be found at the bottom of several of the gulleys formed from the ancient spur and groove reef. In a number of areas, tunnels have been formed in the coral ridge by fresh water emanating from small blue holes: these tunnels are large enough to swim through, though the water is around ten degrees cooler. A huge school of porkfish (*Anistotremus virginicus*) has been observed at this site hovering over the reeftop amidst sparse stands of gorgonian sea fans, as well as a very large southern stingray (*Dasyatis americana*).

5 THE SAN JACINTO

★★★★☆☆☆

Location: 35 minutes north of Green Turtle Cay.
Access: By boat only.
Conditions: Very exposed site where surge and surface chop can be expected.
Average depth: 12m (40ft)
Maximum depth: 14m (47ft)
Average visibility: 25m (80ft)
The USS *San Jacinto* was the first ever American steam ship, built as an experiment to test propulsion concepts by the New York Navy Yard in August 1847. Launched on 16 April 1850, she was 71m (234ft) long with an 11.5m (38ft) beam, but was plagued by unreliable machinery and finally met her end by running aground on 1 January 1865 while engaged in blockade duty.

Now totally destroyed by the savage pounding of the sea, there is nothing to give a clue of her former stature. Covered in fire coral (*Millepora alcicornis*), small sea fans and sea plumes, brain and boulder corals, the wreck is interesting due to its history and

Great barracuda (Sphyraena barracuda)
become solitary hunters as they reach maturity.

the large numbers of small schooling fish which inhabit the area, including a particularly friendly green moray eel (*Gymnothorax funebris*) which is used to being hand-fed and therefore comes out very close to any divers passing by.

6 CORAL CAVERN
★★★★★☆☆☆☆☆

Location: 20 minutes north of Green Turtle Cay.
Access: By boat only.
Conditions: Can be choppy as site is open and exposed.
Average depth: 10m (33ft)
Maximum depth: 15m (50ft)
Average visibility: 25m (80ft)
This is a lovely dive around a reef profile which is very similar to Pirate's Cathedral (Site 3) at Walker's Cay, with numerous caves, caverns and swim-throughs

absolutely filled with silversides in early summer. The experience can be breathtaking as the fish swarm around you keeping just out of arm's reach. There are always barracuda, jacks and lizard fish waiting around to pick off such morsels, as well as abundant butterflyfish and angelfish.

7 TARPON REEF
★★★★☆☆☆☆

Location: 20 minutes north of Green Turtle Cay.
Access: By boat only.
Conditions: Choppy; best dived between March and September.
Average depth: 1.5–15m (5–50ft)
Maximum depth: 15m (50ft)
Average visibility: 30m (100ft)
This is a reef with high profile corals such as boulder star coral (*Monastrea cavernosa*) and numerous other large stony corals, sea fans, sea plumes and sheet corals. Known for its large tarpon (*Megalops atlanticus*), there is also a hand-fed green moray eel.

8 THE CATHEDRAL
★★★★★☆☆☆☆☆

Location: The first barrier reef west of Guana Cay.
Access: By boat only.
Conditions: This is a shallow surge site and is best dived from March to November.
Average depth: 8m (25ft)
Maximum depth: 8m (25ft)
Average visibility: 18m (60ft)

This dive site is a superb introduction to cavern diving thanks to its shallow depth, large roomy entrance and three large chambers which are cut by sunlight streaming in from above. The reeftop is teeming with fish life, namely threespot damselfish (*Stegastes planifrons*), red-lipped blennies (*Ophioblennius atlanticus*), bluehead wrasse (*Thalassoma bifasciatum*) and striped parrotfish (*Scarus croisensis*). The cavern walls are covered in very fragile, spiky coral forms; shade-loving white and cream sponges adorn the walls, and during the summer months you can find glassy sweepers (*Pempheris schomburgki*).

9 GROUPER ALLEY
★★★★☆☆☆

Location: The outer reef of Scotland Cay.
Access: By boat only.
Conditions: Can be choppy with surge, but no current.
Average depth: 13m (43ft)
Maximum depth: 15m (50ft)
Average visibility: 18m (60ft)

A massive coral formation made up of many different species and layers of hard coral rises from 15m (50ft) to within 3m (10ft) of the surface. This formation is dissected by a winding channel where there are lots of large and overly friendly Nassau grouper (*Epinephelus striatus*) and red grouper (*Epinephelus morio*). Caribbean reef sharks and nurse sharks are commonly found cruising through this patch reef system, as is a large friendly barracuda known locally as Fang.

10 DEBORAH K II
★★★

Location: 20 minutes by dive boat to the outer reef between Fowl Cay and Man-of-War Cay.
Access: By boat only.
Conditions: Choppy but no surge or current.
Average depth: 30m (100ft)
Maximum depth: 34m (115ft)
Average visibility: 25m (80ft)

The *Deborah K II* is a recently scuttled coastal freighter which used to carry supplies around the Abacos. At 50m (165ft) long, she sits perfectly upright and intact on a sandy bottom with some nice coral swim-throughs at her stern. The first colonists on the boat are algae, which create a sort of fuzz that attracts different wrasse and damselfish.

11 THE TOWERS
★★★★☆☆☆

Location: Northeast of Marsh Harbour to the first line of cays and located on the outer reefs between Fowl Cay and Man-of-War Cay.
Access: By boat only.
Conditions: Can experience surge conditions from November through to March.
Average depth: 15m (50ft)
Maximum depth: 18m (60ft)
Average visibility: 25m (80ft)

Popular as a night dive, this reef is marked by towering coral formations which come close to the surface in many areas. There are numerous swim-throughs and caverns providing shade for fish such as squirrelfish (*Holocentrus adscensionis*) and glasseye snapper (*Priacanthus cruenatus*). Nurse sharks are commonly found sleeping under overhangs during the day and eagle rays are often seen swimming through the surge channels.

12 ADIRONDACK WRECK
★★★☆☆☆

Location: On the inner reef off Man-of-War Cay.
Access: By boat only.
Conditions: There can be surge on this shallow dive, so take care of fire coral.
Average depth: 8m (25ft)
Maximum depth: 8m (25ft)
Average visibility: 18m (60ft)

The *Adirondack* was a former Ossipee class wooden screw sloop launched in June 1862, 62m (207ft) long and weighing 1240 tons. A gun ship, she ran aground while en route from Port Royal to Nassau. Unable to be salvaged, the ship quickly broke up in the surf and her well-scattered remains now lie in 3–8m (10–25ft) of water. Two of her 3.5m (11ft) cannon can be clearly seen, as well as a further 12 smaller cannon scattered amid the barely discernible wreckage. The hard, ancient coralline limestone seabed has a few scattered coral heads and sea fans. Sergeant majors abound at this site and territorial damselfish are also commonly seen.

HOW TO GET THERE

Walker's Cay has its own airline which flies out of Fort Lauderdale, along with a daily (except Tuesday) PanAm AirBridge seaplane. American Eagle and Continental Connection serve Marsh Harbour and Treasure Cay from various US cities via Fort Lauderdale and Miami. Bahamasair is the major carrier from Nassau to Marsh Harbour and Treasure Cay. Abaco Air flies charters from Miami, Fort Lauderdale, West Palm Beach, Fort Pierce, Freeport and the Family Islands.
Abaco Air tel (242) 367 2266.
PanAm Air Bridge US tel (954) 359 0329.
Continental Connection tel (800) 231 0856.

VEHICLE HIRE

Car and scooter rentals at Shell Marsh Harbour Service Station; tel (242) 367 2840. Car and boat rental at Banyan Beach Club, Treasure Cay; tel (242) 365 8111.

WHERE TO STAY

Walker's Cay Hotel & Marina, Walker's Cay; US tel (800) 327 8150 or (954) 462 3400, local tel (242) 352 5252. A delightful private resort in need of refurbishment in some parts, but with good food, lots of space, two pools and tennis courts.

Treasure Cay Hotel Resort & Marina, Treasure Cay; US tel (800) 327 1584 or (954) 525 1699, local tel (242) 365 8847. Beside a spectacular 5km (3 mile) white sandy beach, with an 18-hole golf course and sea view restaurant.

Banyan Beach Club, Treasure Cay; US tel (888) 625 3060, local tel (242) 365 8111. Condominiums with two or three bedrooms, on same superb beach as Treasure Cay, with 18-hole golf course, car and boat rental, and several restaurants.

Green Turtle Club & Marina, Green Turtle Cay; tel (242) 365 4271, fax (242) 365 4272. Family atmosphere with large rooms, three secluded beaches, pool and good food.

HOPE TOWN LIGHTHOUSE

In the 17th and 18 centuries wrecking thrived as an occupation on the Abacos, with wreckers using bogus lights to mislead ships as they navigated the nearby reefs. The lighthouse at Hope Town on Elbow Cay was delayed in its construction by the sabotage of wreckers. Finally completed in 1838, the red-and-white striped lighthouse is now a distinctive feature of the Abacos, safely guiding ships.

Longsnout seahorses (Hippocampus reidi) are a rare find in the Bahamas.

Pelican Beach Villas, Marsh Harbour, PO Box AB20304, Great Abaco Island; US tel (800) 642 7268, local tel (242) 367 3600, fax (242) 367 3603. Beachfront villas.

Abaco Towns by the Sea, PO Box AB20486, Marsh Harbour, Great Abaco Island; US tel (800) 322 7757, local tel (242) 367 2221, fax 9242) 367 2227. Typical condominiums with two bedrooms and two bathrooms with either pool or ocean views, as well as car, bicycle and scooter rentals.

WHERE TO EAT

All resort hotels have restaurants and bars. However, there are also local restaurants:

Golden Grouper Restaurant, Don Mackay Blvd., Marsh Harbour; tel (242) 367 2301. Excellent, reasonably priced fish restaurant.

Mother Merle Fishnet, Dundas Town, Marsh Harbour; tel (242) 367 2770. Serves local and American dishes including peas'n'rice, jerk chicken and burgers.

Lee's Diner, Treasure Cay; tel (242) 365 8575. Local and international fare, specializing in fish, lobster and steak.

DIVE FACILITIES

Sea Below, Walker's Cay; US tel (800) 327 8150 or (954) 462 3400, local tel (242) 352 5252; NealWatson@aol.com. An excellent operation offering shark feeding and a small shop. At Walker's Cay Hotel & Marina.

Dive Abaco, PO Box AB20555, Conch Inn Marina, Marsh Harbour, Great Abaco Island; US tel (800) 247 5338 or (305) 895 2825, local tel (242) 367 2787, fax (242) 367 4779; stm@mail.bahamas.net.bs. A well-established operation with good rental equipment and a small shop. Associated with Lofty Fig Villas, Abaco Towns by the Sea and the Conch Inn.

Divers Down at Treasure Cay, Treasure Cay Hotel; US tel (800) 327 1584 or (954) 525 7711, local tel (242) 365 8465, fax (242) 365 8508; e-mail JIC@oii.net. A small operation and shop specializing in island exploration. Associated with Harbour House at Treasure Cay.

Brendal's Dive Shop, Green Turtle Club Marina, Green Turtle Cay; US tel (800) 780 9941 or (954) 467 1133, local tel/fax (242) 365 4411. A large shop offering personalized dive packages. Associated with Green Turtle Club, Bluff House and Coco Bay Cottages.

Abaco Beach Resort Dive Centre, Marsh Harbour, Great Abaco Island; US tel (800) 327 8150 or (954) 462 3400, local tel/fax (242) 367 4646; danny@greatabaco.com. Caters to small groups of divers. Linked to Great Abaco Beach Resort (on property).

EMERGENCY INFORMATION

Abaco Medical Clinic, Don Mackay Blvd., Marsh Harbour; tel (242) 367 4240.

The Chemist Shoppe, Don Mackay Blvd., Marsh Harbour; tel (242) 367 3106.

The nearest **recompression chamber** is at UNEXSO on Grand Bahama, tel (242) 373 1244, or by direct ship to shore radio link on channel 19.

LOCAL HIGHLIGHTS

Equipment for kayaking in The Marls, a massive wetland full of creeks, mangrove islands and waterfowl, is available from hotels.
    Alternatively, stroll around the old settlements, with their colourful colonial-style buildings. Most towns have a museum.

TOURIST INFORMATION

Bahamas Tourist Office – Abaco
PO Box AB-20663, Dove Plaza, Marsh Harbour, Abaco; tel (242) 367 3067.

The Bahamas are widely recognized as the world's number one shark-diving destination following lengthy familiarisation with humans of Caribbean reef sharks (*Carcharhinus perezi*). These largely feared creatures appear as the star attraction in a number of different locations all over the Bahamas. Although the sharks are now well used to human presence, they still present a daunting prospect to divers. The 'what if?' factor can creep into your thoughts when you see shark handlers and feeders wearing chain mail suits while the diver audience has no protection. There are also a few misgivings on both the moral issue of feeding sharks – with little known about effects on any natural ecological processes – and on the possible consequence for other divers of hungry sharks coming to frequent specific areas. However, the feeding and handling is for the most part well controlled, though some operations are much more professional than others.

Stella Maris Resort on Long Island was the first dive resort to start regular shark feeding, over 20 years ago, and the method has remained largely unchanged in the rest of the Bahamas since those days. Stella Maris

organize their dive on Shark Reef as a fairly haphazard feeding frenzy with sharks already circling beneath you even before you enter the water from the dive boat. The bucket of fish which is thrown over the side of the boat in front of the waiting divers is quickly devoured in what can only be described as absolute mayhem. The ferocity of the attack quite close by can be unsettling, especially when all the bait has gone and the sharks are still milling around looking for more.

CHUMSICKLES AND CHAIN-MAIL SUITS

With Sea Below on Walker's Cay in the Abacos, a similar ritualized feed has been developed, but here literally hundreds of sharks attack a large frozen bait ball or 'chumsickle' which is lowered into a wide, sandy-bottomed arena. The experience is not for the faint-hearted or people with a nervous disposition. However, on balance this is the best shark-feeding programme in the Bahamas.

Possibly the greatest variety of shark encounters are on offer south of Nassau – from Stuart Cove's Dive South Ocean, Dive Dive Dive and Nassau Scuba Centre. With all these operations, the first of two dives is

Above: *The shark feeder is in control at Shark Junction (Site 9, Grand Bahama).*
Opposite: *Larger female sharks enjoy being handled by the shark feeders.*

always an open water experience in deep water, swimming with the sharks along the lip of the oceanic trench. There are at least a dozen resident Caribbean reef sharks and several large grouper which accompany you on your dive. On the second dive, the shark feeder leads you a short way in from the lip of the wall into a wide, sandy natural amphitheatre. Here, dressed in either a full chain mail suit or a minimum of chain mail sleeves and gauntlets, the feeder serves the sharks by means of a blunt polespear, extracting commercially caught fish scraps from a large container. Nassau Scuba Centre has a shark-handling programme where for $300 you are given some training in how to feed the sharks wearing a chain mail suit.

The Nassau dive operators, as well as Small Hope Bay Lodge on Andros, also have a much freer encounter with silky sharks (*Carcharhinus falciformis*). This smaller pelagic shark is encountered in the offshore waters between New Providence Island and Andros Island. The dive here is more of a meeting of man and shark adrift in the blue of the ocean.

SHARK STUDIES

UNEXSO (Underwater Explorers Society) on Grand Bahama Island offers a daily shark-feeding programme out at the Shark Junction, a short boat ride from the dock. A detailed lecture is given before each trip. When the shark feeder arrives with a load of fish bait held in an enclosed PVC tube, he or she is soon surrounded by snapper, grouper, horse-eyed jacks, amberjacks, stingrays, nurse sharks (*Ginglymostoma cirratum*) and Caribbean reef sharks. Due to the regular nature of this activity, the sharks are now able to recognize particular handlers.

Inevitably, there are differing levels of safety attached to each experience, and more steps could be taken to study the long-term effects this can have on a reef population. However, some operators have begun to address these issues. UNEXSO routinely monitor the sharks' feeding behaviour and apply it with a number of marine-orientated universities to gain a further understanding of these much-maligned apex predators.

THE BIMINI ISLANDS

Bimini is often referred to as the 'Gateway to the Bahamas'; it is the closest point of the Bahamas to the US mainland, just 79km (49 miles) due east of Miami. It has two main islands, North and South Bimini, a few rocky cays and a massive area of sand flats used by sports fishermen hunting bonefish. Anglers coming to Bimini are able to take part in several fishing competitions during the year with deep-water catches of barracuda, tuna, wahoo, sailfish and marlin a speciality.

Bimini is rich in legends, notably that it is the supposed location of the mythical Fountain of Youth, which Ponce de León sought here. More fantastically it is also claimed to be the location of the lost city of Atlantis – a theory supported by the discovery in 1968 of the 'Bimini Road', a huge formation of column-like limestone blocks at a constant depth of 6m (20ft) which are clearly visible from the air. Certain similarities to ancient Greek constructions, as in the perfectly cut parallel square grooves in one of the underwater piers, have given rise to speculation that the 'road' was built by an ancient civilization.

The Biminis had their heyday during US Prohibition, when the islands became legendary for running rum to the Florida mainland; the wreck of the *Sapona* on the Turtle Rocks is testimony to this trade. The writer Ernest Hemingway also popularized the islands, where he found inspiration for his book *Islands in the Stream* and won notoriety for his hard drinking at The Compleat Angler in the capital, Alice Town. Martin Luther King sought inspiration in the islands to write his Nobel Prize acceptance speech and fished regularly with the famous local bonefisherman Ansil Saunders. He told him, 'I feel I could reach up and touch the face of God in this peaceful place.'

Much of the diving here is done around the shallow inshore reefs and cays, which are home to some of the largest schools of fish to be found in the Bahamas, with sightings on every dive of reef sharks, nurse sharks and barracuda. Bimini Undersea also offer two other exhilarating underwater experiences: the first is to dive in the strong north-running Gulf

Opposite: *A boat races into the shallows off South Bimini.*
Above: *The rock beauty (Holacanthus tricolor) is very shy, hiding under corals when approached.*

Stream off the edge of the continental shelf by hanging onto a vertical, buoyed shot line which drops 45m (150ft) into the blue; the other is to snorkel with a pod of wild spotted dolphins (*Stenella plagiodon*) at a location several kilometres to the northeast of Bimini.

All of the Bimini dive sites have permanent mooring buoys attached which have been paid for and placed by Bill and Knowdla Keefe's Bimini Undersea. Donations towards the upkeep of these buoys and lines are welcomed.

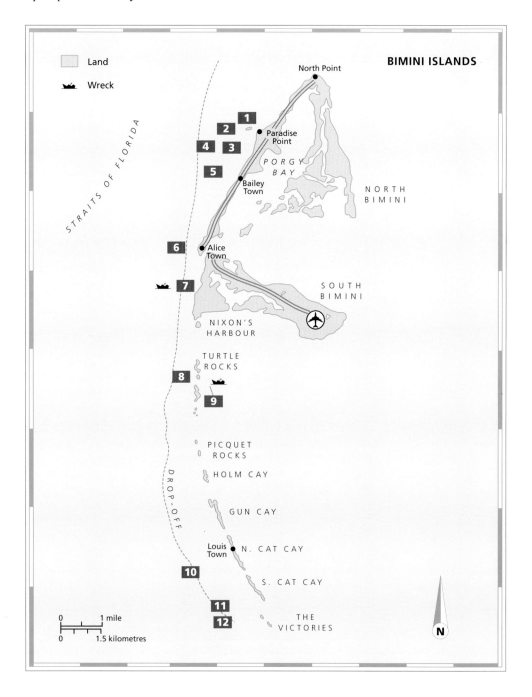

1 ATLANTIS ROAD (Bimini Road)
★★★★

Location: West of North Point on North Bimini, opposite the Bimini Bay Hotel, 60m (200ft) beyond the visible spur of rocks.
Access: By boat only.
Conditions: Visibility variable due to the proximity of the sand flats and shallow water which creates surge and surface chop.
Average depth: 6m (20ft)
Maximum depth: 8m (27ft)
Average visibility: 6–18m (20–60ft)
But for the presence of mysterious stone blocks found underwater, this dive would be rather dull, and there is little sea life to be seen. However, the folklore which has built up around the discovery of what appears to be an ancient road has fuelled many theories. Often thought to be the remains of Atlantis, they also lie at the southern tip of what is widely known as the Bermuda Triangle. The stone blocks are of locally hewn limestone known as 'caprock' or 'micrite', an incredibly hard carbonate substance formed as a result of recrystallization from rainwater, and can only have been excavated from dry land. The site is undoubtedly intriguing, and it is easy to imagine that it could indeed be part of a lost civilization.

2 HAWKSBILL REEF
★★★★

Location: Northwest of Porgy Bay, about 25 minutes from the Bimini Undersea dock at Alice Town, North Bimini.
Access: By boat only.
Conditions: Surge and surface chop can be expected.
Average depth: 10m (33ft)
Maximum depth: 12m (40ft)
Average visibility: 15m (50ft)
This dive is on a series of scattered coral heads which rise around 3m (10ft) off the sandy seabed. Marked by three separate permanent moorings, the reef heads, or bommies, are widely spaced and are home to some of the largest schools of snapper and grunt I have found in the Bahamas. Stingrays (*Dasyatis americana* and *Urolophus jamaicensis*) are common and quite approachable. Nurse sharks (*Ginglymostoma cirratum*) are also common on every dive, and often hide under ledges in groups of two or three. The seabed is home to large numbers of sand tilefish (*Malacanthus plumieri*) and yellowhead jawfish (*Opistognathus aurifrons*), a species which lives in holes in the ground.

Cleaning gobies (Gobiosoma genie) are a common sight on all corals.

3 RAINBOW REEF
★★★★★

Location: Due east of Little Caverns (Site 4) off Porgy Bay, North Bimini.
Access: By boat only.
Conditions: Can be choppy with surface surge from the northwest only.
Average depth: 6m (20ft)
Maximum depth: 8m (27ft)
Average visibility: 15m (50ft)
This reef is one of the oldest dedicated marine sanctuaries in the Bahamas. Established over 20 years ago by a Canadian environmental group, it is now registered with the Bahamas Ministry of the Environment. The reef is for the most part sheltered by Sister Rocks to the north and the island to the east. Popular as a night diving location, the area is known for its nurse sharks, clouds of juvenile fish and lots of overhanging ledges with resident lobsters.

4 LITTLE CAVERNS
★★★

Location: West of Rainbow Reef (Site 3), off Porgy Bay, North Bimini.
Access: By boat only.
Conditions: Can be choppy on the surface, as the site is fairly exposed.
Average depth: 21m (70ft)
Maximum depth: 26m (84ft)
Average visibility: 18m (60ft)
These large, widely spaced coral heads dot the sandy seabed and have a vertical profile of around 6m (20ft). Marked by two mooring buoys, the coral heads are topped with sea plumes (*Pseudopterogorgia* spp.), venus sea fans (*Gorgonia flabellum*) and a moving mass of blue chromis (*Chromis cyanea*) and creole wrasse (*Clepticus parrai*). The underhanging ledges always hide sleeping nurse sharks and, in addition, blacktip as well as Caribbean reef sharks are spotted on most dives.

5 THE STRIP
★★★

Location: Northwest of Bailey Town, North Bimini.
Access: By boat only.
Conditions: Due to tidal movements, current is to be expected on this dive, but only about half a knot.
Average depth: 11m (36ft)
Maximum depth: 11m (36ft)
Average visibility: 12–25m (40–80ft)
Consisting of a very low-lying narrow strip of corals running parallel to the shore, this site has two permanent mooring buoys attached (at the northern and southern ends). There is little else in the surrounding sandy plain, so the dive is concentrated on the reef. Large, hollowed-out narrow caverns have nurse sharks resting during the day and massive grey angelfish (*Pomacanthus arcuatus*) keeping tabs on you during the

The queen angelfish (Holacanthus ciliaris) is a beautiful resident of the reef.

BLACK CORAL

Products made from black coral are popular with tourists, but environmental groups are discouraging this trade by pointing out that all corals are endangered species and that corals are not always harvested carefully. It is illegal to collect coral from Bahamian waters, so this coral will have been imported from countries with less strict conservation laws. We recommend not buying any shell or coral products.

---

entire dive. Huge rainbow parrotfish (*Scarus guacamaia*) are always found on this strip reef, as are Bermuda chub (*Kyphosus sectatrix*).

6 THE BIG BLUE (Drift Wall Dive)
★★★

Location: Running north from the southern tip of North Bimini at the edge of the continental shelf.
Access: By boat only.
Conditions: Strong Gulf Stream current running north at 3–4 knots.
Average depth: 40m (132ft)
Maximum depth: Beyond 70m (230ft)
Average visibility: 45m (150ft)
When tidal current conditions make some of the deeper dives hazardous, Bimini Undersea have developed a fairly safe way to ride the current off the edge of the continental shelf which forms the eastern wall of the Florida Straits. Through this 79km (49 mile) wide channel the bulk of the Gulf Stream is funnelled, creating strong tidal movements and now some exhilarating diving.

A large buoy is deployed into the water with 45m (150ft) of heavy rope and chain attached, which drops into the abyss. Divers then all congregate on the surface and swim down the line to their preferred depth to ride the Gulf Stream, to a maximum of 45m (150ft) depth, depending on the experience of the diver. With a bottom time of only eight minutes, you spend your time looking into the blue to catch rare sightings of marlin, hammerhead sharks and even the occasional whale shark. Divers literally climb up the rope to the surface buoy at the end of the dive and are picked up by the following dive boat.

7 BIMINI BARGE
★★★

Location: Due west of the range markers at the edge of the drop-off off South Bimini.
Access: By boat only.
Conditions: Current is to be expected, running north with the Gulf Stream.
Average depth: 25m (80ft)
Maximum depth: 30m (100ft)
Average visibility: 30m (100ft)
This 81m (270ft) long flatbed barge was formerly used as a supply vessel between Miami and South Bimini. It sank in 1988, landing inside the edge of the drop-off in only 30m (100ft) of water. With a vertical relief of only 4m (13ft), the easily penetrated hulk is now home to large black coral bushes (*Antipathes* spp.), soft corals, gorgonian sea fans, big grouper and thousands of juvenile jacks.

8 MIDDLE TURTLE ROCK
★★

Location: West of the middle set of low rocks south of the Biminis, 25 minutes from the Alice Town dock.
Access: By boat only.
Conditions: Sheltered, easy dive.
Average depth: 12m (40ft)
Maximum depth: 12m (40ft)
Average visibility: 25m (80ft)
At this site the middle mooring is placed between two huge stands of star coral (*Monastrea cavernosa*) which suffered coral bleaching in recent summer temperature changes, but otherwise the coral blocks are in good shape. A long ridge of limestone reef runs north and south from the coral heads, indicating that this was once dry land. Large barracuda are common, as are chub and snapper.

9 SAPONA WRECK
★★★★★★

Location: East of Turtle Rocks; southeast of South Bimini.
Access: By boat only.
Conditions: Shallow and exposed.
Average depth: 5m (17ft)
Maximum depth: 5m (17ft)
Average visibility: 18m (60ft)
The *Sapona* was a rum-runner working between the Bahamas and Florida during Prohibition. Built in 1904, she ran aground during the 1926 hurricane. Over half of the ship is visible above water, and the wreck is popular with snorkellers, who can swim amongst the open ribs of the ship and see a vast amount just a short distance underwater. She was later used for target practice by the Bahamas Militia, and spent cartridges and shells can still be seen. When swimming or diving here, one should beware the fire coral which covers all of the jagged metal surfaces close to the surface.

10 TUNA ALLEY
★★★★

Location: Northwest of South Cat Cay at the southern end of the Bimini chain of islands.
Access: By boat only.
Conditions: Exposed and tidal, with current.
Average depth: 25m (80ft)
Maximum depth: Beyond 70m (230ft)
Average visibility: 30m (100ft)

There are six permanent boat moorings on this 11km (7 mile) stretch of reef, which forms a barrier between the cays and the continental shelf. The first barrier drops in a mini-wall from 12m (40ft) to 36m (120ft) then rises back up to 21m (70ft) before dropping once more into the abyss. Tuna Alley is a cut in this barrier reef where large pelagics such as tuna, amberjacks, eagle rays and sharks are generally seen. The corals include large sheet corals, black corals, gorgonian sea fans and sea plumes. There are huge barrel sponges (*Xestospongia muta*) everywhere and a mass of colourful fish.

11 BLUE HOLE, CAT CAY
★★★

Location: 0.5km (¼ mile) due west from the southern tip of South Cat Cay.
Access: By boat only to the site, then very restricted into the entrance of the cavern.
Conditions: Silty, which can quickly reduce visibility.
Minimum depth: 14m (45ft)
Maximum depth: Reputed to be beyond 70m (230ft).
Average visibility: 12m (40ft) but can silt up.
This is a dive for experienced divers only. The entrance to the blue hole is very narrow and located under an overhanging limestone ledge. Some divers prefer either removing the tank from their back and pushing it ahead of them or wearing side-mounted air tanks. Once past the restriction, the cavern bells out and drops to the first level at 14m (45ft). You can taste and smell the sulphurous water which comes up through the blue hole. It is advisable not to drop further than the first restriction without proper equipment and training. There are lines attached inside, which should not be tampered with.

12 THE VICTORIES
★★★★

Location: 3km (2 miles) south of Tuna Alley (Site 10), and west of Victory Cay.
Access: By boat only.
Conditions: Expect surface surge and tidal current.
Average depth: 18m (60ft)
Maximum depth: 26m (85ft)
Average visibility: 30m (100ft)
This is a mini-wall which drops from 12m (40ft) to 26m (84ft). It is cut by hundreds of holes, caverns, swim-throughs and channels, and is covered in pretty corals, including large orange elephant ear sponges (*Agelas clathrodes*), barrel sponges (*Xestospongia muta*) and azure vase sponges (*Callyspongia plicifera*). Indigo hamlets (*Hypoplectrus indigo*) are dotted about the reef as are lots of fairy basslets (*Gramma loreto*).

HOW TO GET THERE

Most people arrive in the Biminis by boat, due to the short distance between the islands and the US mainland. The mail boat MV *Bimini Mack* serves both Bimini and Cat Cay out of Potter's Cay Dock in Nassau. PanAm AirBridge offer a seaplane service from Miami, Fort Lauderdale and Paradise Island in Nassau to Alice Town on North Bimini. The trip takes around 40 minutes, but be warned that there is a very limited baggage allowance. The dry airstrip on South Bimini is used by private charter flights from Fort Lauderdale and Miami.

WHERE TO STAY

Bimini Big Game Fishing Club & Hotel, Alice Town, North Bimini; US tel (800) 737 1007, local tel (242) 347 3391, fax (242) 347 3392, VHF Channel 68. This self-contained resort with a good reputation is the largest on the island, and has a large pool and two excellent restaurants.

Bimini Blue Water Resort, Alice Town, North Bimini; tel (242) 347 3166, fax (242)

BIMINI ROAD

The Rebikoff Institute of Marine Technology has carried out surveys of the so-called Bimini Road site using transit lines, sextant, photomapping systems and low-altitude aerial photography. This has revealed that the 'road' formation lies at a constant 6m (20ft) depth, constructed in a huge 'U' shape, consisting of multiple rows of large square blocks standing on short square pillars allowing a flow of tidal water under the blocks. There are three parallel piers and on further aerial surveys it was noticed that an area a few hundred metres to the southwest had also been levelled to the same depth of 6m.

On the side of one pier two long parallel grooves were discovered, both cut perfectly square, giving the impression of having been made by a machine, like the causeway itself. These would appear to indicate an early railway such as that found in the area of the present day Corinth Canal in Greece. The 'road' may have been the foundation of a substantial shipbuilding drydock, where ships were hauled up and repaired. Links have also been made to the quarrying and cutting techniques used by the Inca and Mayan empires of South and Central America.

347 3293, VHF Channel 68. Good sea views, although the rooms are small and dark and in need of renovation. Swimming pool.

Bimini Bay Hotel, North Creek, North Bimini; tel/fax (242) 347 2171. Beautiful Art Deco style hotel with spectacular views. 5km (3 miles) out of town.

Seacrest Hotel and Marina, Alice Town, North Bimini; tel (242) 347 3071. Centrally located in Alice Town. Comfortable and functional.

WHERE TO EAT

The main hotels all have good restaurants for evening meals and some will organize a packed lunch for you if you are off diving or fishing for the day. Other restaurants are all located along Alice Town's main street. Most are open for breakfast to cater for the fishermen and divers staying in hotels that do not serve early breakfast.

The Compleat Angler, Alice Town, North Bimini; tel (242) 347 3122, fax (242) 347 3293. In front of the Seacrest Hotel. Hemingway's old haunt with live music several nights each week, typical Bahamian peas'n'rice, local fish and steaks.

The New Red Lion Pub, Alice Town, North Bimini; tel (242) 347 3259. Run by Dolores 'LaLa' Saunders, a place with great atmosphere, great steaks, lobster and local food.

Captain Bob's, Alice Town, North Bimini; tel (242) 347 3260. Open early for big breakfasts as well as ribs, burgers and fish.

The New Fishermen's Paradise, Alice Town, North Bimini; tel (242) 347 3082. Next to the dive dock and PanAm AirBridge terminal. Plain and simple, this is the place for great local soups and sandwiches.

DIVE FACILITIES

Bill & Knowdla Keefe's Bimini Undersea, Alice Town, North Bimini; US tel (800) 348 4644 or (305) 653 5572; local tel (242) 347 3089, fax (242) 347 3079; e-mail biminiua@web2000.net. Bimini Undersea also offer wild dolphin snorkelling excursions two to three times weekly, depending on demand. The dolphin site is located approximately 13km (8 miles) northeast. Trips here are generally done in the afternoon and can take from three to five hours. These are wild spotted dolphins and there is no guarantee that you will find a friendly group or be able to interact.

MYSTERY OF THE MOSELLE SHOAL

To the north of Bimini, the Moselle Shoal was according to legend the site of a ruined city made of granite. Granite is not native to the Bahamas, so the blocks must have been brought from afar.

Richard Wingate, author of *The Lost Outpost of Atlantis*, has spent many years exploring the area, discovering granite boulders which contain evidence of human engineering such as star-like drill holes, bore holes and even an ancient type of glue, similar to that used in bronze age Mediterranean cultures. Granite blocks still litter the seabed near a massive sunken barge which was used to salvage the area. Theorists now debate whether the ruined granite temples of the Moselle Shoal were abandoned by Atlanteans, an ancient Mediterranean culture such as the Phoenicians or even by an advanced group of Lucayan Indians.

Bahama Island Adventures, Inc. (Bimini); Bailey Town, South Bimini; US tel (800) 329 1337; e-mail islifs@sprintlife.com. A small, seasonal dive operation with limited facilities catering to condo owners and fishermen.

EMERGENCY INFORMATION

Government Clinic, Alice Town, North Bimini; tel (242) 347 3210.

The only **recompression chambers** are on New Providence and Grand Bahama.

LOCAL HIGHLIGHTS

Visit the Healing Hole in the middle of the mangroves. This sulphurous spring is reputed to be a cure for most ills. Any of the local bonefishermen will guide you. Another attraction is bonefishing, which costs around $175 for a half day. The hooked fish are weighed and then released back into the wild.

Visit the Hemingway Museum along the main street in Alice Town which is filled with memorabilia and try the Gateway Gallery next door to Bimini Undersea for Bimini arts and crafts.

TOURIST INFORMATION

Bahamas Tourist Office – Bimini
Alice Town, Bimini; tel (242) 347 3529, fax (242) 347 3530.

THE BERRY ISLANDS

The Berry Islands, located east of Bimini and 55km (35 miles) northeast of Nassau, stretch northwards for 53km (32 miles) and comprise some 50 or so small islands and cays which offer quiet beaches, snug harbours and moorings for the many sailors who come to this popular yachting region.

The largest island is Great Harbour Cay to the north, part of which has been developed into a luxurious resort complex with a nine-hole golf course, waterfront townhouses and condominiums. The resort has long powder sand beaches, offers most watersports and caters for yachtsmen and fishermen. There is also a small but very quiet settlement called Bullock's Harbour. North of Great Harbour Cay are the Stirrup Cays, which border the southern wall or drop-off of the Northwest Providence Channel. This steeply sloping, classic spur and groove reef system is open to some rather adverse weather conditions, so little or no diving takes place on it.

As you travel south through the cays, the light turquoise shading indicates very shallow water, much of it to the east covering a massive sandbank only a couple of metres deep. To the south of the sandbank, the tidal streams have created a number of low scrubby and swampy islands, including Bond's Cay, Whale Cay, Bird Cay and the twin islands of Frazer's Hog Cay and Thompson's Cay, known collectively as Chub Cay. Following the massive destruction inflicted by Hurricane Andrew on 23–4 August 1992, much of the local population left for the larger islands. It is only now with the resorts re-opening that locals are once more returning for work. However, the Berry Islands remain sparsely populated and the last official census in 1990 put the overall population of these islands at around 800. The reefs here are usually only visited by passing yachtsmen and the occasional live-aboard dive boat making its route south towards Nassau and Andros. For divers wishing to stay on the islands, the only resort capable of handling divers is the Chub Cay Club.

Opposite: *Chub Cay is occasionally dived by visiting live-aboards.*
Above: *Rainbow parrotfish (Scarus guacamaia) are the largest of the Caribbean parrotfish.*

These southwestern reefs are fairly sheltered, with the wall starting at 18m (60ft). The shallower sites have a lot of algal growth, but the deeper sections of the walls all have excellent coral growth and fish life. Mama Rhoda Reef (Site 2) is one of the best snorkelling reefs around, due to its size, close proximity to the dock and sheltered conditions, and has been designated a marine park. The islands are also fished extensively for lobster.

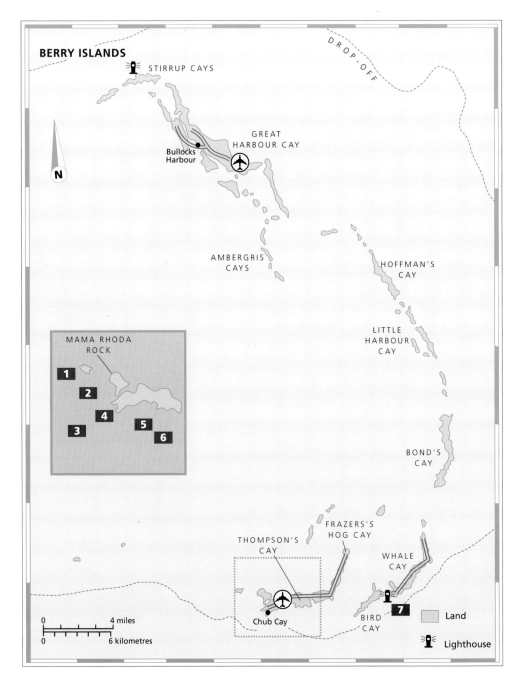

1 CHUB CAY WALL
★★★★

Location: Due west of Mama Rhoda Rock, about 20 minutes from Chub Cay Marina.
Access: By boat only.
Conditions: Can have a slight to moderate current, but almost always diveable.
Average depth: 18m (60ft)
Maximum depth: Beyond 70m (230ft)
Average visibility: 30m (100ft)
This is a vertical drop with overhangs created by growths of sheet coral (*Agaricia grahamae*). Wire coral (*Cirrhipathes leutkeni*) is common, as are black corals and deep-water gorgonian sea fans. There is a particularly large underhang at 33m (110ft) where you will find various squirrelfish and basslets. The wall is also well known for regular sightings of spotted eagle rays (*Aetobatus narinari*). Behind the crest is a wide sand plain dotted with small coral heads which is home to garden eels and peacock flounders.

2 MAMA RHODA REEF
★★★★★★★★★

Location: South of Mama Rhoda Rock.
Access: By boat only.
Conditions: Almost always sheltered with no current.
Average depth: 2m (6ft)
Maximum depth: 4m (15ft)
Average visibility: 18m (60ft)
Mama Rhoda is one of the prettiest reefs in the Berry Islands, with large schools of snapper and grunt which shelter under big stands of elkhorn and staghorn coral. Hurricane Andrew dealt a severe blow to this reef, but it is recovering very well with acres of shallow snorkelling reef interspersed with sand patches. You will see nurse sharks, eagle rays, southern stingrays and golden rays, as well as colourful sea fans, sea plumes, lettuce sea slugs and flamingo tongues. This is a massive area, giving you the excuse to return time after time.

3 FISHBOWL
★★★★

Location: South of Mama Rhoda Rock.
Access: By boat only.
Conditions: Can be choppy, with an oceanic surge.
Average depth: 18m (60ft)
Maximum depth: Beyond 70m (230ft)
Average visibility: 50m (165ft)

This section of the wall is steeply sloping, but heavily built up along the crest with gullies, canyons and swim-throughs created by the well overgrown corals. Behind the reef there is a wide sand plain which becomes a massive band of high coral growth. Hanging vine algae are everywhere, adding a vivid green slash of colour to the orange elephant ear sponges (*Niphates erecta*), red and purple rope sponges (*Aplysina fulva*), and brown, antler-like tube sponges (*Agelas conifera*). There is very little black coral growth, but the fish life is good, hence the name. Large friendly grey angelfish (*Pomacanthus arcuatus*) are found here, as are longsnout butterflyfish (*Chaetodon aculeatus*).

4 CANYONS AND CAVES
★★★★★★

Location: Inshore from Fishbowl (Site 3) to the strip reef which runs parallel to the shore.
Access: By boat only.
Conditions: Often surge and choppy surface conditions, making it uncomfortable for snorkelling.
Average depth: 9m (30ft)
Maximum depth: 14m (45ft)
Average visibility: 25m (80ft)
Aptly named, this strip reef is interlaced with canyons and caves which are easily negotiated by divers. There are always regular sightings of Caribbean reef sharks (*Carcharhinus perezi*) and nurse sharks (*Ginglymostoma cirratum*) as well as eagle rays and the occasional manta ray (*Manta birostris*). There is some algal growth over the shallower corals, but there are also large schools of snapper and grunt. This is the most popular night dive in the area, when you can see large channel-clinging crabs, red night shrimps, slipper lobsters and spiny lobsters.

5 SHUTTERBUG REEF
★★★★★★

Location: Southeast from Caves and Canyons (Site 4), surrounded by white sand and therefore easy to find.
Access: By boat only.
Conditions: Choppy in the shallows, but little current.
Average depth: 6m (20ft)
Maximum depth: 12m (40ft)
Average visibility: 15m (50ft)
Although this is a large section of patch reef, it comprises fairly typical spur and groove formations with long gullies topped by coral blocks of most reef-building coral species. Everywhere you look there are damselfish including beaugregory (*Stegastes leucostictus*), yellowtail damsels (*Microspathodon chrysurus*), with their tell-tale fluorescent blue spots, and sergeant majors (*Abudefduf saxatilis*). The damselfish hover around guarding their

egg masses: sergeant majors choose to lay their eggs on a flat dead coral rock under an overhang; yellowtails prefer the insides of sponges; and beaugregory use the bases of sea fans and plumes.

The reef has large numbers of friendly angelfish, trumpetfish, snapper and grunt. Turtles are a common occurrence: they are known to breed in the Berry Islands and feed on the large turtle grass (Thalassia testudinum) plains as well as reef sponges.

6 HOLE IN THE ROOF
★★★★☆☆

Location: South of Chub Cay along the strip reef which runs towards the group of exposed rocks.
Access: By boat only.
Conditions: Choppy with surge on the surface only.
Average depth: 6m (20ft)
Maximum depth: 15m (50ft)
Average visibility: 25m (80ft)
This large circular hole in the top of a fairly flat section of reef can fit two people. The hole drops through the reef for about 80m (88yd), curving around to the right and exiting on the side of the sand patch under an overhang. There is a large friendly nurse shark here called Nurse Ratchett (!). Although there is a lot of algal growth on top of the corals, making it look rather untidy, there are nice groups of snapper, grunt and lots of small grouper and coney everywhere. The sand patch features garden eels, conch, sand tilefish and jawfish.

On deeper reefs in the Bahamas, tube sponges (Aplysina archeri) may be found.

7 WHALE POINT
★★★

Location: Southeast of Whale Point Lighthouse at the southwestern tip of Whale Cay.
Access: By boat only.
Conditions: Can be choppy with surge on the surface only.
Average depth: 18m (60ft)
Maximum depth: Beyond 70m (230ft)
Average visibility: 25m (80ft)
This steeply sloping wall is a classic spur and groove formation with quite wide gulleys between the coral fingers which rise over 6m (20ft) on either side of you. The reef becomes much more of a wide sandy plain as you swim deeper, with large coral heads covered in lots of algae. Gradually these individual coral bommies then become part of the structured reef, which drops way down into the depths of the northern lip of the Tongue of the Ocean. The area is good for spotting lobster and watching cleaning stations in operation – parts of the reef where larger fish come to be 'cleaned' of parasites and any diseased scales or skin by other reef inhabitants. Shrimp, wrasse and, most common of all, the cleaning goby (Gobiosoma genie) act as the cleaners.

How to Get There

There are two airstrips, one on Great Harbour Cay (which is primarily used by the private resort run by Tropical Diversions Resort), and the other on Chub Cay into which most of the air traffic flies on small charter flights from Nassau, Freeport and Fort Lauderdale. Live-aboard dive boats often call around the southern end of the island, but most tourists arrive by yacht.

Vehicle Hire

It is possible to hire a car from Great Harbour Cay, which can be useful as the island is well spread out, but both resorts have a shuttle service from the airport, which is all one really needs.

Where to Stay

Chub Cay Club, Chub Cay; US tel (800) 662 8555, local tel (242) 325 1490, fax (242) 322 5199. Lovely ocean view rooms

Squirrelfish (Holocentrus adscensionis) shelter in recesses.

with verandas in front of large marina. Good beach, swimming pool and excellent restaurant which features international cuisine with a Bahamian flair.

Tropical Diversions Resort, Great Harbour Cay; tel (242) 367 8838 or (800) 343 7256, fax (954) 921 1044. An exclusive resort with golf, bonefishing, snorkelling and long beaches.

Dive Facilities

Chub Cay Undersea Adventures, Chub Cay Club; US tel (800) 662 8555, local tel (242) 325 1490. This dive operation is booked from the USA through: Neil Watson's Undersea Adventures, PO Box 21766, Fort Lauderdale, Florida 33335; tel (954) 462 3400, fax (954) 462 4100; e-mail nealwatson@aol.com; www.neilwatson.com/chub.htm

Emergency Information

Government Clinic, tel (242) 367 8400.

The nearest **recompression chamber** is on Nassau, at Lyford Cay Hospital, Nassau, New Providence Island; tel (242) 362 4025.

Local Highlights

Bonefishing on the shallow sandbanks and deep-sea fishing are both popular activities in the Berry Islands.

Bush Medicine

Many of the Bahamas' indigenous plants, trees and shrubs have been used medicinally over the centuries, principally by the descendants of the African slaves brought to the islands in the 1600s. Combining African and ancient Arawak Indian knowledge, bush medicine is still used today. Some examples of its applications include aloe cactus for burns, cuts and bruises; banana leaf for fever; breadfruit leaves for high blood pressure; cerasee for fever, flu and cold; dill seed for infant stomach pain; Madeira bark for anaemia and loss of appetite; and periwinkle for diabetes and leukaemia.

ANDROS

Andros Island, otherwise known as 'The Big Back Yard', is the largest landmass in the Bahamas and the largest tract of unexplored land in the Caribbean at 3750 sq km (2300 sq miles). Located almost midway down the Bahamas, Andros is 50km (30 miles) southwest of Nassau across the deep Tongue of the Ocean trench. The island is approximately 160km (100 miles) long by 65km (40 miles) at its widest point, aligned in a north–south direction.

Although referred to as an island, Andros is actually a complex series of low-lying areas dissected by thousands of creeks and riddled with lakes. There are three major landmasses separated by two winding shallow 'bights'. Andros is dominated by thick impenetrable bush with mangrove-edged waterways and isolated lagoons, but to the north of the major landmass are pine forests of Andros pine, mahogany and lignum vitae.

Of special interest to divers is the eastern seaboard of Andros, which has reputedly the third longest barrier reef in the world, 268km (167 miles) long, running parallel to the coast. This is a massive, almost impenetrable inner barrier of elkhorn coral which takes the brunt of the bad weather and stormy seas, but it is the outer edge of the wall which divers come to see. Here it drops 1800m (6000ft) into the Tongue of the Ocean with spectacular canyons, sand chutes, caves, caverns and blue holes.

Andros has the highest concentration of blue holes anywhere in the Bahamas. For the most part, these are gigantic circular depressions in the limestone matrix which lead to impressive undersea caverns filled with stalactites and stalagmites. The Ocean Blue Hole (Site 4) in North Andros is particularly well known, with divers entering a gloomy world of suphurous, green-tinged water (you can even smell the sulphur underwater, through your face mask). There are shallow blue holes within the inner barrier reef as well as massive deep sink holes within the island, the majority of which are unexplored, with virtually all of them connecting. In the extreme conditions met during the exploration of

Opposite: *Andros has sites good for both snorkelling and diving.*
Above: *Fairy basslets (Gramma loreto) are vibrantly coloured, often found in numbers under overhangs.*

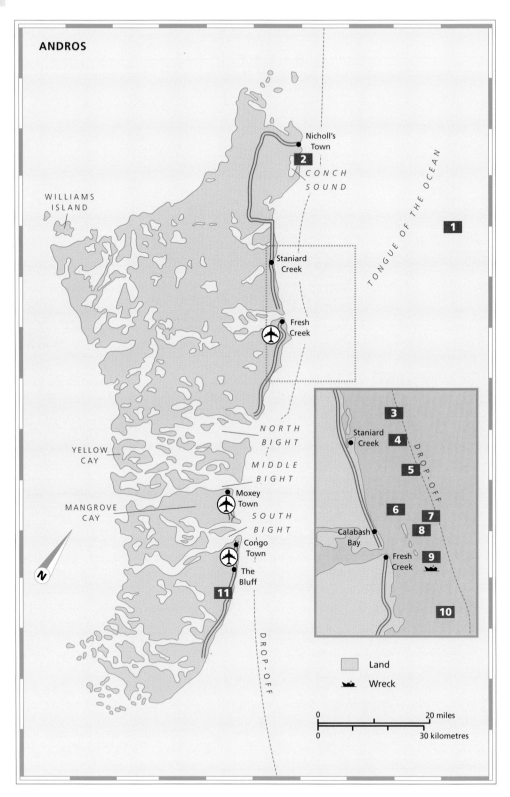

ANDROS

WILLIAMS ISLAND

Nicholl's Town

2

CONCH SOUND

TONGUE OF THE OCEAN

1

Staniard Creek

Fresh Creek

NORTH BIGHT

YELLOW CAY

MIDDLE BIGHT

Moxey Town

MANGROVE CAY

SOUTH BIGHT

Congo Town

The Bluff

11

DROP-OFF

N

Staniard Creek

3

4

DROP-OFF

5

6

7

8

Calabash Bay

Fresh Creek

9

10

Land

Wreck

0   20 miles
0   30 kilometres

these caverns, a number of divers have sadly lost their lives, and therefore it is imperative that proper instruction with qualified guides is undertaken before entering one. Rob Palmer's Blue Holes Foundation on Grand Bahama (see page 86) will be able to advise on any aspects of blue-holes diving.

There is only one dive resort on Andros, at Small Hope Bay just north of Fresh Creek. Small Hope Bay Lodge and Dive Resort is the oldest family-owned dive resort in the Caribbean, having been at the forefront of blue-holes exploration since 1960, and offers some of the most diverse diving available in the Bahamas. There is an emergency recompression chamber nearby at AUTEC (Atlantic Undersea Test and Evaluation Centre), a NATO facility testing sound variations on ships and submarines. It is at their buoys in the middle of the Tongue of the Ocean that divers are able to interact with silky sharks (see Site 1).

1 THE UNITED STATES NAVAL BUOY (Shark Buoy) (Tongue of the Ocean Buoy)

★★★★★

Location: Northeast from Small Hope Bay, midway between Andros and New Providence.
Access: By boat only.
Conditions: Can be choppy on the surface and current is always to be expected. This dive is only done when the sea is flat calm.
Average depth: 25m (80ft)
Maximum depth: Beyond 70m (230ft)
Average visibility: 45m (150ft)

This dive is under the United States Naval Buoy or DNM (Deployed Noise and Measurement) buoy, which is used for submarine tracking and exercises by NATO. The buoy is anchored to the seabed in 1800m (6000ft) of water – when you jump in off the side of the dive boat, you know that it is a long way down! The attraction of the dive is not only the open ocean experience, but also the very high probability of encounters with pelagic silky sharks (*Carcharhinus falciformis*).

The naval buoy is 6m (20ft) in diameter and the flat underside has become overgrown in algae; in addition small organisms land there during the planktonic stages of their lives. This attracts pelagic fish which eat the algae and which are further preyed upon by larger and larger fish until eventually the sharks show up. The sharks are also attracted by the vibrations of the buoy's cable as the current passes through this natural deep-water trench. This is a superb ocean encounter, but only for experienced divers. It is sometimes visited as a third dive by New Providence dive shops on a day trip to Andros.

2 CONCH SOUND BLUE HOLE

★★★★

Location: One hour's drive north to the beach in front of the settlement of Conch Sound, just south of Nicholl's Town. The hole is a few metres from the shore in the middle of a shallow bed of eel grass.
Access: From the shore.
Conditions: Only to be dived on an outgoing tide and current is always to be expected.
Average depth: 27m (90ft)
Maximum depth: 27m (90ft)
Average visibility: Variable with tidal flow in the hole.

British underwater cave explorer Martyn Farr set the world record for the longest distance explored in an ocean cave when he dived 1113m (1230yd) here in 1982. He had a support team of six divers with him to help stage the 14 tanks of air required to complete the dive, which went beyond Rob Palmer's previous record of 1km (1100yd). The record stood until 1996 when Brian Kakuk, whilst working at AUTEC, brought out Martyn Farr's Union Jack flag after replacing it with the American flag at 1340m (1470yd). Rob Palmer wrote in his book *Deep Into Blue Holes*, 'The way on was small and tight, and his air was low. But it was the way on . . .'

CORAL CUTS AND ABRASIONS

Care should always be taken underwater to avoid blundering into coral accidentally. Cuts or abrasions from old pieces of wreckage can be particularly nasty, especially if you are stung by fire coral at the same time. Wounds should be treated and sterilized immediately on exiting the water. Dive boats all have medical supplies on board, but in some instances a visit to the local hospital may be required due to the high amounts of planktonic bacteria to be found in warm water diving.

The Conch Sound blue hole is a speciality dive featured by Small Hope Bay; it is done only with one diver plus a guide due to the restricted access and difficulty of the dive. Even as an air dive only, this dive is still potentially very dangerous, starting at one of five separate entrances next to an old wooden wreck which is reputed to have been sucked down into the hole on an incoming tide. From here it is still a battle against the current and outgoing tide, though this way in is by far the safest way to negotiate the deeply sloping passageway fringed in sponges, algae and corals.

3 HOLE IN THE WALL
★★★★★

Location: Northeast of Staniard Creek to the outer wall.
Access: By boat only.
Conditions: Surface chop to be expected and some current.
Average depth: 60m (200ft)
Maximum depth: Beyond 70m (230ft)
Average visibility: 45m (150ft)
The Hole in the Wall was first dived over 25 years ago by Archie Forfar and Dick Birch (founder of the Small Hope Bay Dive Centre) but no-one could find it again until 1993 when the Small Hope Bay team finally re-located this unusual combination of wall, hole and tunnel. Starting at the edge of the drop-off in 36m (120ft), a wide vertical shaft drops down to 60m (200ft) and exits on the vertical wall. A secondary entrance at 48m (160ft) is located on the return back up to the surface. It is regarded as so spectacular that Jacques Yves-Cousteau sent a mini-sub captained by Albert Falco through this passage in the mid-1970s. It is an absolutely breathtaking dive, but only undertaken as a one-on-one speciality dive with a guide from the dive centre.

4 THE OCEAN BLUE HOLE
★★★★★★★★★

Location: Northeast of Small Hope Bay to the outer barrier reef almost opposite the town of Staniard Creek.
Access: By boat only.
Conditions: An exposed site which can be choppy on the surface but is calm in the blue hole except for tidal suction in some areas.
Average depth: 42m (140ft)
Maximum depth: Beyond 70m (230ft)
Average visibility: Variable due to sulphurous halocline at 25m (80ft)
This is a massive collapsed cavern, over 100m (110yd) across, which starts at 14m (45ft) around the edge and

drops in the centre to around 25m (80ft). The dive itself is around the outside perimeter of the collapsed roof, where depths drop rapidly to well beyond safe diving limits, but exploration has been done deep into the hole by a number of people. This potentially dangerous dive is led by an expert in the cave system with a maximum of two persons per guide to give a better level of safety. It is without doubt a spectacular site.

Three levels of the hole can be visited: level one is at the top of the vertical shafts at the edge of the fracture, which is best seen at the end of the dive. Level two is to 42m (140ft), where you drop down through a hole to a huge tunnel where the bottom is 98m (320ft) deep, then swim along the ceiling at 42m until you come to an area where vertical shafts of light come through from the surface. The third level is only for very experienced divers as the planned depth around the submerged structure is at 58m (190ft), coming up through a constricted tunnel at 33m (110ft) with a vertical deep blue light coming from above.

This site can be done many times and on each visit it is different, depending on the visibility, which is altered by tidal movements, and on the numbers of fish. Caribbean reef sharks and barracuda inhabit the upper levels, but never venture below to the smelly sulphurous levels. Around the upper levels at the edge of the drop into the hole are a large number of cleaning stations with huge numbers of grouper and jacks queuing up to be cleaned. The full scale of this site is best seen if you snorkel around the perimeter before the dive.

5 DIANA'S DUNGEONS
★★★★★

Location: Due east of Love Hill Bay to the outer wall.
Access: By boat only.
Conditions: Surface chop and a slight current.
Average depth: 36m (120ft)
Maximum depth: Beyond 70m (230ft)
Average visibility: 36m (120ft)
The wall starts in this area at around 18m (60ft) and quickly drops away into many twisting and winding

---

SEA FANS

Sea fans are a typical feature of virtually all Caribbean reefs. Some species are found as far north as Bermuda and all are located on the top of the reef crest. The fan is quite strong with a wide base of deep purple. Often, when fans have been damaged, they are overgrown with fire coral, which follows the existing branches of the fan.

canyons which lead through coral swim-throughs, small caverns and sand chutes to the outer wall at 30m (100ft). These gullies are superb, with excellent growths of sheet coral (*Agaricia lamarcki*), star coral (*Montastrea cavernosa*) and long sea whips (*Ellisella elongata*). Nassau grouper are common, as are spotted moray eels (*Gymnothorax moringa*) and oceanic triggerfish (*Canthidermis sufflamen*). The whole reef is alive with colourful sponges, but it is the magical caverns which make this dive so worthwhile.

6 PETER'S PLACE
★★☆☆☆

Location: Just north of and in a line with Goat Cay opposite Calabash Bay.
Access: By boat only.
Conditions: Surge experienced among the coral heads.
Average depth: 4m (14ft)
Maximum depth: 6m (20ft)
Average visibility: 15m (50ft)
Peter's Place is always done as a second safety dive after a first dive over the wall in very deep water. This is a huge shallow bank of small coral heads and gardens of elkhorn coral (*Acropora palmata* and *Acropora prolifera*) which stops the worst of the storms from reaching the eastern shores of Andros and offers shelter for snapper, grunt and squirrelfish. The curious

Stoplight parrotfish (Sparisoma viride) are common on all reefs.

pillars of coral make for some interesting exploration, and fish life is diverse, though numbers are low.

7 SKEEBO'S SURPRISE
★★★★

Location: Opposite the northern tip of Goat Cay on the drop-off, out from Calabash Bay.
Access: By boat only.
Conditions: Some surface surge and current can be expected, but normally calm below.
Average depth: 33m (110ft)
Maximum depth: Beyond 70m (230ft)
Average visibility: 45m (150ft)
This section of the drop-off starts quite deep, at 27m (90ft), and features an almost vertical slope. A small sand chute leads over the edge, and it is here, in the top few metres of the drop-off, that the marine life is most rewarding. A large and friendly barracuda is found here and small schools of Atlantic triggerfish and Bermuda chub appear to play tag with each other in the water column. The reeftop is rather uninspiring, but on the wall itself there are regular sightings of sharks and turtles.

8 KLEIN'S REEF
★★★★

Location: Directly east of the Middle Goat Cays.
Access: By boat only.
Conditions: Can be choppy with some surge.
Average depth: 15m (50ft)
Maximum depth: 15m (50ft)
Average visibility: 30m (100ft)
Klein's Reef is the name of the coral formations that wind here around a horseshoe-shaped sand strip in 15m (50ft). The best format for the dive is to stay on the sand patch and to explore all of the underhanging ledges under the corals, where you will find corkscrew anemones (*Bartholomea annulata*) with their resident cleaner shrimps (*Pereclimenes pedersoni*). This is extremely popular as a night dive as octopus and squid are common, along with spiny lobsters, sand dollars and moray eels.

9 THE MARION
★★★

Location: Southeast of Goat Cay, between the mid-level reef and the start of the slope to the drop-off.
Access: By boat only.
Conditions: Can be choppy on the surface.
Average depth: 21m (70ft)
Maximum depth: 21m (70ft)
Average visibility: 25m (80ft)
The *Marion* was a 30m (100ft) long by 12m (40ft) wide barge fitted with a construction crane which flipped over whilst under tow in 1987. Another crane was brought in to try and salvage the barge, but this crane was also destroyed by bad weather and the salvage of the *Marion* proved too difficult, so it was abandoned. Now resting on a sandy bottom dotted with small coral heads in 21m (70ft), it is slowly becoming colonized by marine algae and small corals. Sea fans appear to be some of the first colonizers after the algae, while the algae attracts wrasse and damselfish.

10 BRAD'S MOUNTAIN
★★★★

Location: South of the AUTEC cable winding station.
Access: By boat only.
Conditions: The boat trip can be a bumpy ride, but the dive itself is relatively calm.
Average depth: 15m (50ft)
Maximum depth: 15m (50ft)
Average visibility: 25m (80ft)
Brad's Mountain is a massive coral mound made up of thousands of corals and sponges all woven together in an intricate web of tightly packed gulleys and canyons. The tip of the mound comes to only 9m (30ft) below the surface. The dive is also well known for the huge numbers of Nassau grouper and red grouper which have been hand-fed by divers from AUTEC. These pesky fish are now quite large and act extremely aggressively towards divers, coming in very close to look for titbits, but do make for some great photographic subjects.

The mountain of coral also attracts large schools of fish (particularly in the afternoons), including big groups of horse-eye jacks (*Caranx latus*), permit (*Trachinotus falcatus*), Bermuda chub (*Kyphosus sectatrix*) and Atlantic spadefish (*Chaetodipterus faber*).

11 STARGATE
★★★★★

Location: South by air from Andros Town to Congo Town, then a taxi ride to this inland location near The Bluff.
Access: Difficult entry, hidden inside a grotto with stalactites where the water level is 3.5m (12ft) below the scrub-surrounded entrance.
Conditions: Only for very experienced cave divers.
Average depth: 36m (120ft)
Maximum depth: Beyond 70m (230ft)
Average visibility: Varies from 6m (20ft) to 30m (100ft) due to sulphurous exhaust water and fresh/saltwater halocline.
Stargate Blue Hole was the primary location of the 1987 Blue Holes Project, which was filmed by *National Geographic* and described the scientific collection of stalactites that helped date the Ice Ages by recording water levels. This is also the first blue hole where ROVs (Remote Operated Vehicles – with video) were used, along with closed circuit rebreather systems.

Once into the blue hole, the first drop is to around 25m (80ft) through the sulphur layers to where the cavers' lines make a 'Y' junction. Following one of the lines north there are incredible stalactite and flow stone formations. Once the 36m (120ft) level has been reached at the start of a collapse, about one third of your air will have been used: the second third is used to return safely back to the surface and the last third, as always, is kept as reserve in case of emergencies.

Stargate is one of the most incredible fracture zones in the world. A huge amount of research has been carried out within this massive and complex underground cave system, but there are still surprises, such as the rare blind cave fish (*Lucifuga speleotes*) and the ancient fossilized coral reef which forms the walls of the first cavern.

This dive is not for the faint-hearted and must be treated with great respect. Several of the world's most experienced cave divers have lost their lives during the exploration of these incredible underground traverses.

How to Get There

By air

Andros can be reached on daily Bahamasair flights from Nassau to San Andros, Andros Town/Fresh Creek, Mangrove Cay and Congo Town, or from Fort Lauderdale or Miami by private charter. Small Hope Bay also operate their own private charter airplane from Nassau, Fort Lauderdale and Miami.

By boat

Three ferries are sheduled each week from Nassau, with a travel time of around three hours. Most other visitors to Andros arrive in private yacht or on live-aboard dive boats, almost all of which include Andros in their scheduled dive excursions, primarily to dive the Ocean Blue Hole (Site 4).

Vehicle Hire

Enterprise Rent-A-Car, Fresh Creek, Andros; tel (242) 368 6229.
Ruthmae Oliver, Taxi No. 5, Love Hill, Andros; tel (242) 368 2377.

Where to Stay

Visiting divers coming to Andros have little choice of where to stay, especially since the only dedicated dive resort is Small Hope Bay Lodge. However, this resort is excellent.

Small Hope Bay Lodge, Andros Island; tel (242) 368 2013, fax (242) 368 2015; e-mail SHBinfo@SmallHope.com. US Booking office: PO Box 21667, Fort Lauderdale, Florida 33335; tel (800) 223 6961 or (954) 927 7096, fax (954) 927 7190.
Situated 2km (I mile) north of Fresh Creek, this family owned and operated resort has 20 cottages of coral rock and Andros pine lining the seashore, a hot-tub on the beach, superb views, excellent international food

ANDROSIA

Founded in 1973, Androsia is a batik factory in Andros Town which sells its vibrant fabrics and clothes throughout the Bahamas. The batik process is an ancient one, with stamps made out of foam and wire used to print the design on the fabric with hot wax. Once the wax has dried, the next process is to dip the fabric into coloured dyes; after this the fabric is boiled to remove the wax (which is re-used), leaving a latent print of undyed design on the fabric. Layers of designs may be built up in this way.

---

with a separate children's room and all-inclusive prices. One of the best all-inclusive resorts in the Bahamas.

Coakley House, Fresh Creek, Andros Island; tel (242) 368 2013, fax (242) 368 2015. A lovely old house which is fully equipped for self catering, though there is a maid who can prepare all of your meals if desired. It sleeps six and is located next to the waterfront at Fresh Creek. Allied to Small Hope Bay where meals can also be taken if required.

Where to Eat

Although there are local restaurants, most people never venture any further than Small Hope Bay.

Hank's Place, Fresh Creek, North Andros; tel (242) 368 2447. Old-fashioned island service, cool and spacious, for lobster, conch and crab.

Nakita's Restaurant & Lounge, Victoria Point, Mangrove Cay, South Andros; tel (242) 369 0025. Traditional Andros dishes of cracked conch, crab'n'rice, peas'n'grits, fried chicken.

Rosar's Restaurant, Nicholl's Town, Mid Andros, tel (242) 329 2072. Authentic Bahamian cuisine with dishes including bonefish steaks and conch salads.

Dive Facilities

Small Hope Bay Diving Centre is the oldest family owned and operated dive centre in the Caribbean, with around 40 years in the business. Small Hope Bay founder Dick Birch, along with Canadian physicist Roger Hutchins, set the world record for deep diving on compressed air at 139m (462ft) in 1963. Small Hope specializes in custom-tailored dive packages to explore the Andros blue holes or the deep-water caves and caverns in the Tongue of the Ocean. There is a chance to participate in the Jean-Michel Cousteau Snorkelling Adventure programme as well as speciality excursions to snorkel sites accessible from the shore. Details as for Small Hope Bay Lodge.

Emergency Information

Andromed Medical Centre, Nicholl's Town, Andros; tel (242) 329 2171

Johnson Bay Community Drug Store, Johnson Bay, Andros; tel (242) 369 4563

The nearest **recompression chamber** is at Lyford's Cay Hospital, Nassau. The AUTEC facility on Andros is only for extreme emergencies and is not available for general public use.

Local Highlights

The **Androsia Batik Factory** in Fresh Creek is worth a visit to see the batik fabric dyeing process in action; tel (242) 368 2080. Open Monday–Friday 07:30–16:00; tel: (242) 368 2080, fax (242) 368 2027. Small Hope Bay also offer nature walks, and kayak and jeep safaris into central Andros.

THE STORY OF THE ANDROSIAN PEOPLE

Following Columbus' landfall on San Salvador in 1492, subsequent Spanish expeditions 'discovered' Andros and made landfall in the north of the island in 1550. As with other islands, they came to Andros in search of slave labour. Of an estimated 40,000 Lucayans in the Bahamas all but a handful were wiped out by enslavement, disease, escape and suicide by the end of 1550.

By the 18th century, pirates had settled on Andros, which offered the perfect staging post for attacks on ships passing through the Northeast Providence Channel. Sir Henry Morgan made his headquarters at what is known today as Morgan's Bluff in North Andros, an area surrounded by huge Andros pine and mahogany forests.

During the 19th century freed slaves made their way to Andros and established fishing and farming settlements all along the eastern seaboard protected by the long barrier reef, their main crops being corn, plantains, yams, potatoes and peas. At Red Bay in the northwest some intermarried with Seminole Indians who had fled there from Florida and today many folk there have distinctly Indian features.

In the late 19th century sponging and sisal growing were important industries in Andros. The population is now around 10,000, and tourism, Androsia fabrics and the (US) AUTEC base provide employment.

Blue holes are entrances to underwater cave systems which are found scattered throughout the Bahamas. They take the form of deep circular sink holes on inland locations, or irregular entrances along a massive fracture zone which runs parallel to much of the eastern shores of the Bahamian islands. In the fracture zone, the caverns have developed within the carbonate platform and can extend laterally for many kilometres and vertically from 10m (33ft) to several hundred metres.

The entire Bahamas chain was completely underwater more than 250 million years ago. During the last ice age the sea level dropped and left four raised plateaus, now called the Bahama Banks. The bedrock of these banks is volcanic in origin, and it is only the top layers of coralline limestone that divers are able to explore. The limestone is susceptible to erosion, and severe tropical rainstorms over the centuries have created huge underground caverns and wells, to the extent that the Bahamas contain the largest number of blue holes in the world.

Blue holes are similar to the *cenotes* found in the Yucatán mainland of Mexico. One difference, however, is that in the Bahamas the blue holes have emerged where one of these vast caverns has collapsed, whereas in the Yucatán most of the caverns are in shallow water with little or no tidal movement.

For many years, ideas about the origin of blue holes have been mixed with local superstition and myth. Blue holes are often referred to by locals as 'blowing' or 'boiling' holes, a phenomenon supposedly created by the mythical creature Lusca, a belief still shared by many Bahamians today. The 'blowing' or sucking effect is largely caused by differences in water surface generated by tides, local wave action and ocean currents.

The blue holes of the Bahamas are extremely deep for the most part and are very tidal, making exploration of the caverns and subterranean passageways hazardous unless you are properly qualified and accompanied by experienced guides. It is essential that all divers wishing to partake in any cave exploration gain the proper qualifications.

ROB PALMER'S BLUE HOLES FOUNDATION

Rob Palmer and his wife Stephanie Schwabe set up the Blue Holes Foundation in 1994. Thanks to their work (and that of many others involved), the Bahamas have become the centre for a continuous scientific project on Blue Holes. Renamed Rob Palmer's Blue Holes Foundation after Rob's tragic death in a diving accident in the Red Sea in June 1997, its aims are to map and analyse scientific measurements from all over the Bahamas, co-ordinating teams of marine scientists, geologists, microbiologists and scores of dedicated and highly qualified enthusiasts.

In Stephanie Schwabe's words: 'It is important to realize that the underground caves and blue holes of the Bahamas are quite unlike any other cave system in the world. There is a tidal flow which can push water through the dangerous narrow passageways at more than three knots. Experienced cave divers have been killed here due to their lack of knowledge. One of the intentions of the Foundation is that all visiting cave divers register their dive plans with the Foundation to enable the safe collection and exchange of knowledge.'

Using a number of live-aboard dive boats, specialist cave-diving courses and expeditions are held throughout the year and interested cave divers can contact the Foundation at its headquarters in Freeport, Grand Bahama. A new addition to the programme is exploratory diving using kayaks to get to some of the more inaccessible coastal blue holes. The use of kayaks means that couples where one partner is not interested in cave diving can still enjoy some adventure, as participants learn about the ecology of the mangrove forests and are able to snorkel as a dive takes place.

Rob Palmer's Blue Holes Foundation: PO Box F-40579, Freeport, Grand Bahama Island, Bahamas; tel/fax (242) 373 4483, e-mail 100432.616@compuserve.com

Above: *Crab Cay Blue Hole (Site 9, The Exumas) is accessible only to qualified cave divers.*
Below: *Stephanie Schwabe leads the ongoing exploration of blue holes in the Bahamas.*

NEW PROVIDENCE

The capital of the Bahamas, Nassau, is located on the northeastern corner of New Providence Island and, together with adjoining Cable Beach and Paradise Island, is the most popular destination in the Bahamas, attracting upwards of a million visitors a year. It developed principally due to its superb natural harbour – its docks can now accommodate up to 12 cruise ships at any one time – and quickly became the commercial and banking centre of the islands. New Providence itself, which is around 34km (21 miles) long by 11km (7 miles) wide, is home to 150,000 people, about two-thirds of the Bahamian population.

To the west of Nassau, Cable Beach is a sandy stretch backed by a number of luxury hotels. Lying opposite Nassau is Paradise Island, which has a fine white sand beach. Originally known as Hog Island (after the wild boar which once roamed here), it was developed extensively in the 1980s to cater for a wealthy American clientele and, although possibly now over-commercialized, is considerably more upmarket than either Freeport/Port Lucaya or Cable Beach. Paradise Island has more than its fair share of glitzy nightlife, with casinos, Las Vegas-style cabaret shows and other entertainment. The island is connected to Nassau by a toll bridge ($2 per vehicle, including taxis).

On New Providence, most diving is off the southwest coast, which has a spectacular wall on the eastern edge of the Tongue of the Ocean and some mesmerizing shark dives. However, the north shore also has some incredible wrecks, kilometres of shallow coral reefs with spectacular forests of elkhorn and staghorn coral and amazing phenomena such as the Lost Blue Hole (Site 1). Travelling to the northeast from Paradise Island, a series of low cays have developed over the centuries into a massive barrier of reefs and shoals which stretches all the way up to North Eleuthera. North of these low cays is the edge of the continental shelf, which plunges down amidst a stretched-out line of ancient spur and groove reef. To the south of the cays lie enormous shallow sandbanks that stretch south to

Opposite: *The Abacos are famed for their clear, shallow waters.*
Above: *Peacock flounders (Bothus lunatus) love the shallow sand planes.*

the northwestern Exumas and are together known as the Middle Ground of the Great Bahama Bank. Although the north shores of New Providence are still little explored, there are fish in abundance and the diving is excellent.

The diving along the south shore of New Providence Island is incredibly diverse. Besides a huge number of wrecks (the majority of which have been used as film props at one time or another), this coastline offers divers one of the best chances in the world to dive with sharks in a relatively controlled situation. The sharks – primarily Caribbean reef sharks (*Carcharhinus perezi*) – are the backbone of the island's diving industry, but one should remember that they are wild animals and can exhibit aggressive and competitive behaviour.

Diving with sharks is so popular that it is easy to overlook the fact that the island has another compelling magnet, the continental shelf. This starts in relatively shallow water (around 12m/40ft), from where it drops 1800m (6000ft) into the depths. The wall dives here, where divers will encounter large schools of pelagic fish, are readily accessible, in contrast to other areas of the Bahamas where you have to undertake a deep dive with limited bottom time just to reach the drop-off.

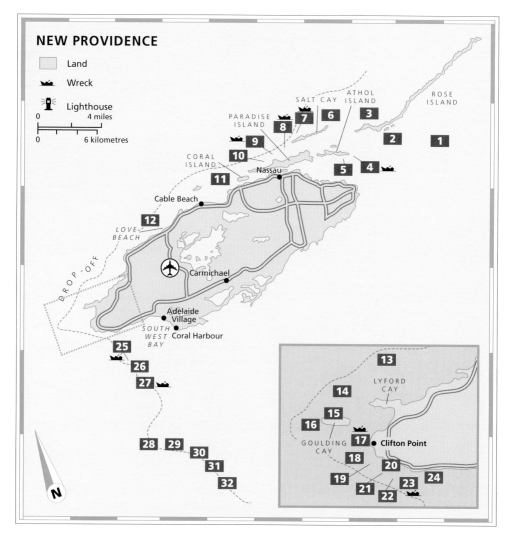

1 LOST BLUE HOLE
★★★

Location: 14km (9 miles) and a one-hour boat trip due east of Nassau and south of Rose Island.
Access: By boat only.
Conditions: Can be choppy on the surface as it is rather exposed.
Average depth: 25m (80ft)
Maximum depth: 60m (200ft)
Average visibility: 25m (80ft)

The Lost Blue Hole is one of the more unusual sites found in the Bahamas and is visited regularly by the experienced dive operation Bahama Divers. Best dived during the summer months of May through to July, this natural hole in the sandy sea floor is about 30m (33yd) in diameter and 60m (200ft) deep. The hole is in 12m (40ft) of water and the scattered coral heads around the rim are a natural focus of marine life, where you will see schools of sergeant majors (*Abudefduf saxatilis*), brown chromis (*Chromis multilineata*) and French grunt (*Haemulon flavolineatum*). As you descend into the hole, on the eastern side there is a small cavern in 18–27m (60–90ft) with a large ledge where nurse sharks and stingrays are common. During the summer, large numbers of reef sharks, Atlantic spadefish and barracuda will also congregate here.

2 BARRACUDA SHOALS
★★★★☆☆☆

Location: Southeast of Rose Island, about 20 minutes' boat ride to the northwest of the Lost Blue Hole (Site 1).
Access: By boat only.
Conditions: Can experience surge in the shallows.
Average depth: 6m (20ft)
Maximum depth: 9m (30ft)
Average visibility: 15m (50ft)

This is a fine dive site, consisting of three separate reefs in a triangular formation. The corals are in good order and extremely healthy, but there is also quite a lot of algal growth due to the lack of sea urchins in the area. Colourful sponges are intermingled with the corals and you can always find slender filefish (*Monacanthus tuckeri*) hiding among the porous sea rod and coral sea plumes (*Pseudoplexaura* spp.). Snapper, grunt, grouper and barracuda are common.

Above right: *The social featherduster (Bispira brunnea) is found on shallow reefs and wrecks.*

3 THUNDERBALL AND CANNONBALL REEFS
★★★☆☆☆☆

Location: North of Rose Island and undertaken as a second dive after the Lost Blue Hole (Site 1).
Access: By boat only.
Conditions: Can have surge in the shallows and is exposed to northerly swells.
Average depth: 6m (20ft)
Maximum depth: 8m (27ft)
Average visibility: 15m (50ft)

These two reefs next to each other have been filmed on numerous occasions, including for several James Bond movies. Running perpendicular to the island in a north-south formation, the coral growths start in only 2m (6ft) of water. Huge stands of elkhorn coral (*Acropora palmata*) stretch out their wide spans and offer shelter for numerous species of snapper and grunt. Large numbers of Nassau grouper, coney and angelfish are found all over, as well as roving groups of parrotfish and wrasse, which are common on these northern reefs due to the profuse growth of algae in some areas. The site is always popular with snorkellers because of its association with the 007 movies.

Above: *A spiny lobster (Panulirus argus) at night.*
Opposite: *Grey angelfish (Pomacanthus arcuatus) are common on wrecks along the north shore.*

4 THE LTC BARGE (LST) (Thunderball)
★★★☆☆

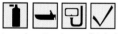

Location: Southeast of Athol Island.
Access: By boat only.
Conditions: An easy, sheltered site.
Average depth: 6m (20ft)
Maximum depth: 6m (20ft)
Average visibility: 15m (50ft)
This landing craft was used after World War II to ferry freight between Nassau and Exuma. While running out of Nassau harbour in the 1950s she started to take on water and the crew ran her aground on Athol Island in an attempt to save the cargo. The wreck is fairly intact and lies upright in 6m (20ft) of water with the top of the wheelhouse just a metre or so below the surface. Much of the ship is covered in fire coral (*Millepora alcicornis*), encrusting sponges and small sea fans, and there are numerous anemones, shrimps and other invertebrates in and around the wreck. It is popular with trainee divers and underwater photographers due to the fact that, though beginning to break up and covered in coral, the structure still resembles a ship.

5 ANGELFISH REEF
★★★☆☆☆☆☆

Location: Just to the southeast of the eastern tip of Athol Island.
Access: By boat only.
Conditions: Fairly sheltered, but can experience surge in the shallows.
Average depth: 6m (20ft)
Maximum depth: 6m (20ft)
Average visibility: 15m (50ft)
As the name indicates, there are numerous grey angelfish, queen angelfish, French angelfish and rock beauties all over this reef. The grey angelfish (*Pomacanthus arcuatus*) are well used to divers and appear to pose for photographs whenever you come near them; a couple are so tame that they will follow you about during the entire dive. The corals grow up fairly close to the surface, making the site perfect for snorkelling. Golden stingrays (*Urolophus jamaicensis*), conch (*Strombus gigas*) and flamingo tongues (*Cyphoma gibbosum*) can nearly always be found on this dive.

    Care, as always, should be taken when snorkelling during surge conditions as the giant elkhorn corals are very unforgiving. Fish life is always profuse under the corals, particularly snapper and grunt which like the protection the corals offer.

6 FISH HOTEL
★★★☆☆☆☆☆

Location: East of Salt Cay, northeast of Paradise Island.
Access: By boat only.
Conditions: Rather exposed, therefore best dived from March to November.
Average depth: 6m (20ft)
Maximum depth: 11m (36ft)
Average visibility: 18m (60ft)

This is a very lively, relatively flat, circular reef formation with thousands of schooling juvenile blue-striped and French grunt. With depths ranging from 3m (10ft) to 11m (36ft) and a natural oasis for many different species, it is a perfect site for spotting fish. Hard coral growth is fairly minimal, but this has made room for huge numbers of sea fans, sea plumes and whips.

7 THE DE LA SALLE
★★★

Location: Northwest of Salt Cay and due north of Paradise Island, about 25 minutes by boat.
Access: By boat only.
Conditions: Generally sheltered from March to November, but can be choppy on the surface.
Average depth: 17m (55ft)
Maximum depth: 21m (70ft)
Average visibility: 21m (70ft)

There are three wrecks all within a short distance of each other in this sandy area, which is well away from any good coral reefs. The first is the *De La Salle*, a 30m (100ft) island freighter which sits upright in 21m (70ft); the second lies just off its bow and is a former Haitian sloop called the *Grennen*, now lying in 18m (60ft); the third wreck is the *Miranda*, which was sunk as a dive attraction in 1980 – the first time an artificial reef of this kind was created in the Bahamas. Located closer in to Salt Cay, this 27m (90ft) former freighter now rests on her side in two sections in only 17m (55ft) of water. All three wrecks are home to large schools of snapper, grunt, blue tangs, barracuda, parrotfish and wrasse.

8 THE MAHONEY
★★★★☆

Location: Due north of Paradise Island.
Access: By boat only.
Conditions: Calm conditions from March to October, but some surge in the shallower sections of the wreck; current can be expected.
Average depth: 10m (33ft)
Maximum depth: 14m (45ft)
Average visibility: 25m (80ft)

There is some confusion over the name of this wreck, as she was never actually called the *Mahoney* while in service. Launched in 1887, the 63.5m (212ft) steel-hulled freighter was named four times before she was destroyed during the 1929 hurricane. The ship broke in two when she sank and, because she was a navigational

hazard, was dynamited. The two parts are now over 30m (100ft) apart on a flat coralline base dotted with small hard corals, sea fans and sea plumes. The main boiler is intact and smothered in fire coral and sponges.

9 THE SHIPYARD (The Graveyard)
★★★

Location: Due north of Paradise Island, about 20 minutes' boat ride from Nassau marina.
Access: By boat only.
Conditions: Slight current with some surface chop.
Average depth: 21m (70ft)
Maximum depth: 27m (90ft)
Average visibility: 25m (80ft)
This is another silty sand area which has been used as a scrapyard to sink ships that have come to the end of their lives. Sunk around 1985/86, the *Ana Lise* is a 45m (150ft) freighter which is intact and lying on her port side; nearby are the 28.5m (95ft) *Helena C* and the 27m (90ft) *Bahama Shell*, which was sunk in 1992. These last two are a bit crumpled together at the bows and all three can be briefly explored on a single dive. Close by is a wooden-hulled cargo ship called the *Adrian*, which was sunk in 1994, and a similar ship, the *Miss BJ*, but these are overlooked on most dives. Nurse sharks and stingrays are common, but generally these wrecks are uninteresting in terms of

marine life except around the shaded holds, which often have angelfish, wrasse and glassy sweepers in residence.

10 TRINITY CAVES
★★★

Location: Just inshore from The Shipyard (Site 9).
Access: By boat only.
Conditions: Some surge can be expected.
Average depth: 14m (45ft)
Maximum depth: 14m (45ft)
Average visibility: 18m (60ft)
The name of this site is a little misleading as it features caverns and ledges rather than actual caves. Carved out over the centuries by wave action, some of the ledges have formed into caverns and extend as far back as 9m (30ft), with three separate openings, the largest of which is 2.5m (8ft) wide by 1.5m (4¹/₃ft) high. The substrate is old coralline limestone with lots of sea fans and plumes and little hard coral, but this is an excellent night diving site with invertebrates such as red night shrimps (*Rhynchocinetes rigens*), spotted spiny lobsters (*Panulirus guttatus*) and brittle starfish (*Ophiothrix suensonii*) to be found.

At night brittlestars (Ophiothrix suensonii) perch on colourful sponges.

11 PIECE OF CAKE

★★★☆☆

Location: West of Coral Island and north of West Bay.
Access: By boat only.
Conditions: Can be rough from November to March, otherwise easy and sheltered.
Average depth: 8m (25ft)
Maximum depth: 8m (25ft)
Average visibility: 15m (50ft)

Normally done as a second dive to Traveller's Rest Wall (Site 12), this dive is, as the name implies, a piece of cake. It is on an extended ancient spur and groove reef of coralline limestone which has little hard coral growth but is profuse in sea fans, sea plumes and whips, along with a multitude of fish (mainly snapper, grunt, squirrelfish, blue tangs, parrotfish and wrasse). Nurse sharks and barracuda may also be seen here. There are many caves and caverns under the overhanging ledges where swim-throughs and gulleys can be negotiated.

12 TRAVELLER'S REST WALL

★★★★

Location: North of Love Beach, west of Nassau.
Access: By boat only.
Conditions: Very exposed site and best dived from March to October.
Average depth: 25m (80ft)
Maximum depth: Beyond 70m (230ft)
Average visibility: 30m (100ft)

Near the western end of New Providence, the wall starts in 15m (50ft), slopes gently to around 25m (80ft), and then drops vertically into the depths. The ridges of this deep-water spur and groove reef are cut by sand chutes which snake through high-sided coral canyons amidst large boulder star corals (*Monastrea annularis*), starlet corals (*Siderastrea siderea*) and symmetrical brain corals (*Diplora strigosa*). Above the coral and sea fans and sea plumes is a cloud of chromis and creole wrasse.

13 OASIS

★★★★

Location: Due north of Lyford Cay.
Access: By boat only.
Conditions: Exposed site; for experienced divers only.
Average depth: 33m (100ft)
Maximum depth: Beyond 70m (230ft)
Average visibility: 30m (100ft)

FIRE CORAL

For many first-time divers and snorkellers, an introduction to fire coral (*Millepora alcicornis*) can prove to be a painful and unforgettable experience. Fire coral is not actually a true coral but a member of the hydroid or sea fern family. It has a hard calcareous skeleton, either branching or in the form of bony plates (*Millepora complanata*). The coral polyps are armed with stinging cells and tiny barbed hooks which can penetrate the skin with ease and leave large irritations that may last for several days. Fire coral can be found in most areas of the reef and in shallow shipwrecks, and will often completely overgrow a gorgonian fan coral. If in doubt, do not touch.

It takes about 35 minutes to drive around from the south-shore dive marinas to this site and it is only done in exceptionally good weather, as so many good sheltered wall dives are found on the south coast. This is a deep, sloping wall with large sheet corals (*Agaricia* spp.) cut by deep grooves and gullies. Once the slope reaches 33m (100ft), it drops vertically with regular sightings of Caribbean reef sharks and even hammerhead sharks (*Sphyrna lewini*). An old telephone pole on the seabed marks the location of one of the best gullies.

14 LAMPTON'S WALL AND TUNNEL WALL

★★★★

Location: Due west of Lyford Cay to the edge of the drop-off.
Access: By boat only.
Conditions: Exposed site with generally choppy conditions on the surface.
Average depth: 9–25m (30–80ft)
Maximum depth: Beyond 70m (230ft)
Average visibility: 25m (80ft)

These are two walls running concurrently off the edge of the drop-off. Lampton's Wall is a mini-wall dropping from 9m (30ft) to around 25m (80ft) where it slopes much steeper to 33m (110ft) and then drops vertically into the blue. At Tunnel Wall, the reef slope starts at 12m (40ft) and just continues into deep water with a large cavern and swim-through at 21m (70ft). Depending on your diving experience, you can either stay on the mini-wall or venture over into much deeper water. The reef is mainly made up of soft corals with numerous swim-throughs and circular holes that have been formed under the main reef. Sea fans and sea plumes are common, but there are few big sponges or hard corals.

15 GOULDING CAY REEF AND THE FISH BOWL

★★★★★★

Location: North of Goulding Cay.
Access: By boat only.
Conditions: Exposed to tidal surge and slight current.
Average depth: 6m (20ft)
Maximum depth: 9m (30ft)
Average visibility: 25m (80ft)

There are opportunities for extensive snorkelling all along this huge coral reef area, which acts as an additional barrier reef to Goulding Cay. The section has been used as a backdrop for several movies, including *Flipper*, *Cocoon* and *Splash!* Elkhorn corals grow very close to the surface in some locations; large schools of snapper and grunt are common and virtually every coral head has at least one pair of damselfish.

16 GOULDING CAY WALL

★★★★

Location: Due west of Goulding Cay.
Access: By boat only.
Conditions: Fairly exposed, but little current.
Average depth: 21m (70ft)
Maximum depth: Beyond 70m (230ft)
Average visibility: 30m (100ft)

This site is known for its large black coral trees (*Antipathes* spp.), huge barrel sponges (*Xestospongia muta*) and antler sponges (*Ectyoplasia ferox*). Schooling pelagics are the norm, with Atlantic spadefish, Bermuda chub, horse-eye jacks and porgy (*Calamus calamus*). During June and July, thousands of breeding mutton snapper (*Lutjanus analis*) congregate.

17 WILLAURIE

★★★★

Location: South of Goulding Cay, west of Clifton Point.
Access: By boat only.
Conditions: Generally sheltered most times of the year.
Average depth: 18m (60ft)
Maximum depth: 21m (70ft)
Average visibility: 25m (80ft)

This is one of my favourite wreck night dives in the whole of the Caribbean. The *WiLLaurie*, originally christened the *Will Mary*, was built in Denmark in 1907. Working as a freighter between Rum Cay, San Salvador and Cat Island, she sank in Potters Cay in Nassau. Refloated, she was under tow when her lines snapped

during a storm and she ended up being washed against the rocks along the south shore near Clifton Pier. Stuart Cove salvaged the ship once more and sank her again as a dive attraction in 1988. At 45m (150ft) long and sitting upright, she is now heavily encrusted in all manner of marine growth. The sea fans are particularly colourful and all of them have filefish and large grouper nearby. The cargo holds are wide open and a large latticework of steel lines the top deck. A small wheelhouse is found at the stern. At night, the hull comes alive with the colours of golden cup coral (*Tubastrea coccinea*), arrow crabs, shrimps, hermit crabs, molluscs and snails. A resident turtle is also seen most nights. An old dive boat called the *Royal James*, also sunk in 1988, can be found near the stern of the *WiLLaurie*. It is usually smothered in silversides during the summer months.

18 BLACK FOREST WALL AND PALACE WALL

★★★★

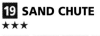

Location: South of the *WiLLaurie* (Site 17).
Access: By boat only.
Conditions: Mostly calm, but with some surface chop.
Average depth: 18m (60ft)
Maximum depth: Beyond 70m (230ft)
Average visibility: 30m (100ft)

These two sites are in essence a continuation of each other, as the whole of this southern wall makes up the eastern limit of the Tongue of the Ocean, which drops down to 1800m (6000ft). Sand and hard coral patches form the top of the reef, and then there is a slightly raised ridge of mixed coral growth before you get to the edge of the drop-off. As you pass over the lip of the wall, large orange elephant ear sponges (*Agelas clathrodes*) are everywhere, as well as lavender rope sponges (*Niphates erecta*) and brown tube sponges (*Agelas conifera*). Groups of horse-eye jacks (*Caranx latus*), black jacks and barracuda patrol these deeper reefs.

19 SAND CHUTE

★★★

Location: Southeast of Clifton Point.
Access: By boat only.
Conditions: Generally calm with no current.
Average depth: 25m (80ft)
Maximum depth: Beyond 70m (230ft)
Average visibility: 30m (100ft)

This is a wide sand chute which starts around 15m (50ft) and slides steeply off the wall at 25m (80ft).

Huge hermit crabs can be found on the sand plain along New Providence's south shore.

Heart urchins (*Meoma ventricosa*), garden eels (*Heteroconger halis*) and sand tilefish (*Malacanthus plumieri*) are found, as are yellowhead jawfish (*Opistognathus aurifrons*) and bridled gobies (*Coryphopterus glaucofraenum*). A small gulley and swim-through are on the west side of the chute (to your right going down the edge of the coral ledge).

20 THE JAMES BOND WRECKS
★★★★

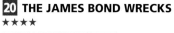

Location: South of Clifton Point, and close to shore.
Access: By boat only – about 15 minutes.
Conditions: Generally quite sheltered.
Average depth: 14m (45ft)
Maximum depth: 14m (45ft)
Average visibility: 15m (50ft)
There are two wrecks in this small area which have been used as props in James Bond movies. The former tugboat known as the *Tears of Allah* starred in *Never Say Never Again*. At 25m (80ft) long she sits upright on a sandy seabed and is gradually becoming overgrown with marine algae and small corals. Nearby is the wreckage of the *Vulcan Bomber*, a movie prop constructed of iron scaffolding which was used in the

film *Thunderball*. The *Thunderball* wreckage has now been underwater for over 30 years and is one of the best photographic sites in New Providence for invertebrates and tropical fish. This underwater 'jungle gym' is a maze of coral sea fans, sponges and clouds of fish, and makes an excellent dive.

21 WRECK ON THE WALL
★★★

Location: East of the Sand Chute (Site 19).
Access: By boat only.
Conditions: Sheltered with little or no current.
Average depth: 12m (40ft)
Maximum depth: Beyond 70m (230ft)
Average visibility: 30m (100ft)
This 12m (40ft) long wooden-hulled fishing vessel, originally named the *Spiyva*, was once involved in drug smuggling and, after being confiscated by the Bahamian government, was sunk as a dive attraction. She lies with her bows protruding slightly over the wall, making an excellent starting point for deeper exploration of the drop-off. There are large coral growths, sea fans, barrel sponges, rope sponges, schools of chromis, snapper and grunt on the drop-off.

Location: United States Naval Buoy, Tongue of the Ocean, 13km (8 miles) southwest of New Providence Island (see page 81).
Maximum depth: 1800m (6000ft)
Cast: Stuart Cove and some silky sharks (*Carcharhinus falciformis*)

Stuart Cove is the man Hollywood turns to when they require superb tropical settings, clear waters and sharks. Stuart Cove's diving operation Dive South Ocean, located on the southwest coast of New Providence Island, was remodelled as the Universal Studios film set for *Flipper*. What Stuart calls his back yard is actually one of the best scuba diving areas in the Caribbean, with fantastic drop-offs, an abundance of fish and beautiful coral reefs littered with wrecks.

When Stuart Cove told me that he and his cousin Graham were going out to the naval buoy to capture silky sharks by hand and remove fish hooks from their mouths, I went along with them to see how it was done. Forty minutes after leaving the dock at Dive South Ocean, we reached the massive United States Naval Buoy. The buoy, some 6m (20ft) in diameter, is used to track submarines but has developed its own open ocean ecosystem. The undersurface is covered by a film of algae which attracts small fish. Other species such as jacks and triggerfish seek shelter under the buoy, preying on the fish, and in turn these attract the larger and more efficient predators – the sharks.

This strategic spot was quickly discovered by sports and commercial fishermen who would catch the sharks, remove their fins and jaw and cast the carcass into the depths. Stuart, by contrast, came to see the potential here for an exhilarating diving experience.

That first dive under the buoy with 1800m (6000ft) of water fading to a deep indigo blue underneath him so captured Stuart's imagination that he returned time after time, unfortunately growing more despondent when he saw the resident population of sharks being depleted almost daily. 'The sharks were drastically reducing in number and at one point they had been completely fished out,' said Stuart. 'The location of the buoy is such that

sharks will continue to be attracted by the activity that is created around it.' After many discussions with commercial and sports fishing organizations in the Bahamas as well as individual sports fishermen, shark experts and conservation groups, an agreement was finally reached that there would be no long-line fishing around the buoy and that any sharks caught by sports fishermen would be set free.

TONIC IMMOBILITY
Another problem was then encountered: many of the silky sharks now had hooks, barbs and lures protruding from their jaws, obviously causing discomfort and in some cases proving a hindrance to feeding. Stuart had learned of a harmless way to immobilize the sharks called 'tonic immobility'. This involves grabbing hold of the tip of the shark's tail and bending it over; the shark immediately becomes dull, unresponsive and almost catatonic for between 30 and 90 seconds. It seemed this would be enough time to free a hook from a shark's mouth and let it free, with relatively little risk to the catcher. The problem was, however, how do you catch the shark? The answer is easy enough: just bait the water, attract the sharks to feed in front of you and, when one gets close enough, grab it by the tail!

Surprisingly, the scheme worked. Stuart and Graham learned to bait the silky sharks, bringing them closer until they were within reach. Stuart held the shark by the tail and supported the rest of its body whilst Graham moved in and removed the offending hook. The shark was set free immediately and would swim off with no side effects whatsoever.

'The smaller sharks are more of a problem as they move much faster and you only have a short time,' said Stuart. I asked Stuart if any other sharks appeared while the baiting and catching was going on. 'Yes,' he said, 'we have had tiger sharks, mako and Caribbean reef sharks, and once a hammerhead shark swam right through between us, just checking out what was going on.'

Opposite: *Stuart Cove (left) holds a silky shark whilst a hook is removed from its mouth.*

22 MV DAVID TUCKER
★★★

Location: East of the Wreck on the Wall (Site 21), southeast of Clifton Point.
Access: By boat only.
Conditions: Sheltered, but with some surface surge.
Average depth: 12m (40ft)
Maximum depth: Beyond 70m (230ft)
Average visibility: 25m (80ft)
The 17m (90ft) long *David Tucker* is a former Royal Bahamian Defence Force coastguard cutter. As part of a rescheduling strategy, three of these vessels were scuttled as dive attractions: one in this location; another, the *Edward Williams,* out beyond Southwest Reef near the Arena (Site 31); while the third was sunk in an area of flat sand – at present this is largely ignored as there is little life in the area, but it will no doubt be 'rediscovered' in a number of years when she has good coral coverage.

Below: *The small balloonfish (Diodon holocanthus) is a timid reef dweller.*
Opposite: *Hawksbill turtles (Eretmochelys imbricata) are seen off the Tongue of the Ocean.*

The *David Tucker* was sunk in 1997 with everything still on her, including kitchen equipment and utensils (divers are not allowed to remove anything from the wreck). Already there are early signs of algal colonization and small corals are found around the wheelhouse and hull. Some penetration of this wreck is possible, but most divers visit the ship after a trip over the wall and use her as a decompression stop.

23 THE CESSNA WRECK (Cessna Wall) (Hollywood Wall)
★★★★

Location: Southeast of the *David Tucker* (Site 22).
Access: By boat only.
Conditions: Calm and sheltered for the most part.
Average depth: 15m (50ft)
Maximum depth: Beyond 70m (230ft)
Average visibility: 25m (80ft)
The remains of a Cessna light aircraft were sunk here as a prop for the Hollywood movie *Jaws IV*. Lying in approximately 25m (80ft) near the edge of the wall, it is fairly well broken up and embedded in the reef. Much of the dive is spent at varying depths of the wall enjoying the massive coral formations, sea fans, barrel sponges and cruising pelagic fish.

24 THE DOLPHIN PENS (Porpoise Pens)
★★☆☆

Location: Southwest New Providence, west of Clifton power station.

Access: By boat or from the boat ramp along the south shore road, where a number of the island's instructor development courses are held.

Conditions: Generally calm and sheltered for the most part.

Average depth: 6m (20ft)

Maximum depth: 9m (30ft)

Average visibility: 18m (60ft)

Although this dive has a maximum depth of 9m (30ft), the seabed here does slope gently amidst varying heights of coral heads until it reaches the wall at around 12m (40ft). This site is where the original holding pens for the old television series *Flipper* were located. The remnants of the pens can be seen, as well as an old car, lying upside down. There is little good coral growth, but the area is a breeding ground for many reef fishes, and juveniles of most species can be found.

25 THE BAHAMA MAMA AND THE SHARK BOWL
★★★★

Location: South of Southwest Bay where the wall starts to turn due south.

Access: By boat only.

Conditions: Fairly sheltered for most of the year; no current.

Average depth: 15m (50ft)

Maximum depth: 15m (50ft)

Average visibility: 25m (80ft)

The *Bahama Mama* is a 33m (110ft) former party boat which was sunk as a dive attraction in 1995. She has a slight tilt to starboard and sand is beginning to pile up against the stern through tidal action. Dive boats make use of a mooring buoy about 18m (60ft) off the stern of the wreck, near one of the best low-lying strip reefs I have ever photographed. There were three species of moray eels, pufferfish, filefish, spotted drum, squirrelfish, snapper, grunt, grouper, hermit crabs, arrow crabs, anemones, Christmas tree worms and just about everything else in between.

Large schools of porkfish (Anisotremus virginicus) are deep reef denizens.

Nearby is the Shark Bowl, an alternative shark encounter site, which is used when other locations are blown out due to bad weather. You can usually see at least a couple of Caribbean reef sharks on every dive. The top of the wall at the Shark Bowl rises to only 11m (36ft) and the sharks are so used to divers that they come quite close even when not being fed.

 PUMPKIN PATCH AND KAREN'S REEF
★★★★

Location: Southeast of the *Bahama Mama* (Site 25).
Access: By boat only.
Conditions: Generally sheltered most of the year.
Average depth: 15m (50ft)
Maximum depth: Beyond 70m (230ft)
Average visibility: 25m (80ft)
This large section of reef is generally done as two separate dives, with Pumpkin Patch as the deep dive on the steeply sloping wall and Karen's Reef as the second, shallower dive. The dives feature large, immaculate blocks of star, brain and pillar coral, surrounded by low patches of coral and sandy areas, all of which are teeming with life. It is a favourite for fish watching, since the schools of horse-eye jacks, black jacks and blue tangs will come fairly close to you. Sharptail eels (*Myrichthys breviceps*) and chain moray eels (*Echidna catenata*) are found here, as well as several species of angelfish and permit (*Trachinotus falcatus*).

27 SEA VIKING WRECK
★★★★

Location: South along the reef from Site 26.
Access: By boat only.
Conditions: Fairly sheltered for the most part.
Average depth: 20m (66ft)
Maximum depth: Beyond 70m (230ft)
Average visibility: 25m (80ft)
The 20m (66ft) former sports fishing boat *Sea Viking* was a derelict hulk which had been left to rot in one of the canals in Coral Harbour. Bought by Nassau Scuba Centre, it was cleaned up and sunk as a dive attraction in 26m (85ft) on the edge of the wall. It is surrounded by an incredible array of barrel sponges, isolated coral heads and immaculate coral and sponge growths, all teeming with fish life.

28 RAZORBACK WALL (Razorback Ridge) AND THE PLAY PEN
★★★★★

Location: Due south of Adelaide Village.
Access: By boat only.
Conditions: Fairly sheltered with a slight current.
Average depth: 20m (66ft)
Maximum depth: Beyond 70m (230ft)
Average visibility: 30m (100ft)
Razorback is a raised ridge of coral which has formed at the edge of the wall. On the inward side is a sandy plain with garden eels (*Heteroconger halis*) and peacock flounders (*Bothus lunatus*). The ridge rises from a depth of 20m (66ft) to 12m (40ft) before it rolls over and plunges vertically into

the abyss. A narrow sand chute cuts through the ridge, which is covered in sponges and superb coral growth. Nearby, the Play Pen is a circular coral mound surrounded by sand: it attracts schools of chromis and creole wrasse. This reef is a massive cleaning station with thousands of gobies (*Gobiosoma genie* and *Gobiosoma oceanops*).

29 SOUTHWEST REEF
★★★★☆☆☆☆☆☆

Location: Due south of Nassau Scuba Centre.
Access: By boat only.
Conditions: Awash at extreme low spring tides. Generally sheltered, but there can be a slight surge.
Average depth: 8m (25ft)
Maximum depth: 14m (45ft)
Average visibility: 25m (80ft)
This is a huge expanse of healthy reef with massive elkhorn corals coming to the surface, making it perfect for snorkelling. There are also fields of blade fire coral (*Millepora complanata*) which can leave a nasty sting if brushed against accidentally. Lettuce leaf nudibranchs (*Tridachia crispata*) are common, eating the encrusting algae. The area is dotted with yellow and purple sea fans and schooling snapper and grunt are found, as are many pelagics.

30 SHARK VALLEY (The Valley) AND JACK'S JUMP
★★★★★

Location: South of Southwest Reef.
Access: By boat only, 40 minutes from the dive resorts.
Conditions: Sheltered, with little current or surge.
Average depth: 15m (50ft)
Maximum depth: Beyond 70m (230ft)
Average visibility: 30m (100ft)
This site is an unusual double wall formation at the end of a sloping sand plain. The first wall jumps from a depth of 20m (66ft) to 12m (40ft), then drops back down into a valley at 25m (80ft) before climbing back up to 15m (50ft) then falling away into the abyss. This is quite exhilarating, and can play havoc on your dive profile. The Valley is known for the numbers of sharks and southern stingrays (*Dasyatis americana*) which cruise along the

---

NIGHT DIVING TIPS

- Attend a night diving instruction course.
- Dive with someone aquainted not only with the dive site, but also with night conditions.
- At first, dive at dusk to become acclimatised to the dark.
- Carry a spare torch or two.
- When entering the water, take a compass bearing to the shore or mooring buoy.

---

reef. The corals are excellent and include a mass of sponges, sea fans, sea plumes and rods. Jack's Jump is the outer reef wall, which actually drops to a 15m (17yd) wide sandy plain at 33m (110ft) before falling into the depths. This site is great for cruising pelagics and some massive black grouper (*Mycteroperca bonaci*).

31 SHARK WALL AND THE ARENA
★★★★★

Location: Southeast from Jack's Jump (Site 30).
Access: By boat only.
Conditions: Fairly sheltered with no current.
Average depth: 20m (65ft)
Maximum depth: Beyond 70m (230ft)
Average visibility: 12–30m (40–100ft)
This dive is not for the faint-hearted and if you are not interested in sharks then do not dive. It is undertaken by Stuart Cove's Dive South Ocean, Nassau Scuba Centre and Dive Dive Dive. Divers are led down to a natural coral rubble amphitheatre and placed in a semi-circle, where they are quickly surrounded by sharks. The shark feeder comes into the centre of the arena with a large box filled with fish scraps, which are pulled out on the end of a blunt, short spear. Usually, around 20 Caribbean reef sharks (*Carcharhinus perezi*) cruise in and out of the arena between the divers, attacking the bait as it is presented to them. The feeding takes 20 minutes and after the bait has gone you can spend five minutes looking for shark tooth souvenirs.

One of three former coastguard cutters (see Site 22), the *Edward Williams*, was sunk in the immediate vicinity in April 1997. An intact shipwreck, it is becoming colonized by algae, corals, invertebrates and fish, and you are also likely to encounter sharks here.

32 HOLE IN THE HEAD
★★★★★

Location: The most southerly of the south-shore day trips.
Access: By boat only.
Conditions: Fairly sheltered with little current or surge.
Average depth: 33m (110ft)
Maximum depth: Beyond 70m (230ft)
Average visibility: 45m (150ft)
At this site there is a small mini-wall with a wide sand plain, before you reach the Tongue of the Ocean: in the sand plain stand two large coral pinnacles, the smaller of which is circular in shape and stands isolated on the sandy bottom, rising from 33m (110ft) to 18m (60ft). This is cut by a tunnel which runs under the pinnacle, where sharks are regularly seen sleeping. The second and much larger pinnacle stands against the edge of the wall and comes to within 12m (40ft) of the surface. Large schools of pelagic fish are always encountered and, of course, there are the sharks, thanks to the proximity of Site 31.

New Providence

HOW TO GET THERE

Nassau is serviced by numerous airlines with direct flights from Europe and all main US hub airports. Bahamasair has flights from Miami, Fort Lauderdale, Orlando, Puerto Rico, the Virgin Islands and Cuba, as well as linking the Bahamas chain with regular daily services. The airport is located 16km (10 miles) west of downtown, west of Lake Killarney. There is a much smaller airport on Paradise Island, into which Paradise Island Airlines has a daily non-stop service from Miami, West Palm Beach, Fort Lauderdale and Orlando. PanAm AirBridge offers daily seaplane flights from Miami to Paradise Island and Bimini; tel (242) 363 1687, fax (242) 363 3649.

VEHICLE HIRE

All car rentals are left-hand-drive US cars, but the driving is also on the left, British style, which causes no end of trouble between tourists and locals. Rates are from $50 per day. Scooters are an easy option, costing half the price of a car, but also twice the risk!

Avis, Downtown tel (242) 326 6380, Nassau International Airport tel (242) 377 7121, Paradise Island tel (242) 363 2061, and Cable Beach tel (242) 322 2889.
Budget, Nassau International Airport tel (242) 377 9000, Paradise Island Airport tel (242) 363 3095
Dollar Rent-A-Car, Nassau International Airport tel (242) 377 7231, Paradise Island tel (242) 325 3716.
Hertz, Nassau International Airport tel (242) 377 8684, Cable Beach tel (242) 377 8684.
Cycles Unlimited, Mackay St, Nassau, tel (242) 393 0155.

GETTING AROUND

Small buses known as Jitneys run on shuttle and circular routes around Nassau and its suburbs throughout the day until about 6pm. Other, free shuttles pick you up from your hotel to take you to the casino nearest your hotel either on Cable Beach or Paradise Island. All hotels have taxis nearby. Radio-dispatched taxis can be reached by calling (242) 323 5111/2/3/4.

WHERE TO STAY

There are a vast number of hotels, condominiums, villas, suites and apartments in and around Nassau, Paradise Island and Cable Beach, offering a total of some 10,000 beds. Cable Beach and Paradise Island have the largest hotels and all inclusive resorts such as Club Med, Breezes, Beaches and Sandals. New resorts are being constructed continually and large

areas of the island's south coast are also being reclaimed for private housing development.

Expensive
Atlantis Paradise Island Resort and Casino, PO Box N4777, Paradise Island, Nassau; tel (242) 363 3000, fax (242) 363 3524. This huge resort on a mile-long beach has over 1100 rooms, a 5.5ha (14 acre) waterscape, 12 restaurants, disco, night club, theatre, 18-hole golf course and full watersports facilities. A new tower will add 1200 rooms when completed in 1999.

British Colonial Beach Resort, PO Box N7148, Bay St, Nassau; tel (242) 322 3301, fax (242) 322 2286. Right downtown, with 3.25ha (8 acres) of tropical gardens and its own beach, this hotel overlooks the harbour and Bay Street's luxury shops. A landmark since 1922, the British Colonial is improving business facilities and adding executive suites. Tennis, swimming pool. Sun Divers Ltd are on the premises.

Nassau Marriott Resort & Crystal Palace Casino, PO Box N8306, East Bay St, Cable Beach; tel (242) 327 6200, fax (242) 327 6459 or 327 6801. The complex includes five high-rise towers, 12 restaurants, one of the largest casinos in the Bahamas, swimming pools, tennis and all watersports.

Nassau Beach, PO Box N7756, Cable Beach; tel (242) 327 7711, fax (242) 327 8829 or 327 7615. Built in the 1960s and recently restored, this old-style hotel is not as glitzy as some its neighbours, but it is popular with families thanks to children's facilities such as a fun camp. 400 rooms, six restaurants, tennis, pool, watersports.

South Ocean Golf & Beach Resort, PO Box N8191, South Ocean, New Providence; tel (242) 362 4391, fax (242) 362 4728. In a tranquil setting some 45 minutes from Nassau. Stuart Cove's Dive South Ocean is next door. The hotel is now under new ownership. Small pool, snack bar/BBQ grill next to a tiny strip of beach.

Radisson Grand Resort, PO Box SS6307, Paradise Island, Nassau; tel (242) 363 2011, fax (242) 363 3900. Set on a beautiful stretch of beach, this resort has 360 rooms (most with sea views), four restaurants, disco, tennis and watersports.

Moderate
Orange Hill Beach Inn, PO Box N8583, West Bay St, Nassau; tel (242) 327 7157, fax (242) 327 5186. A personal favourite and the diver's choice. Family owned and operated, it has a great atmosphere, a lively bar, good food and a pool.

Park Manor Guest House, PO Box N4164, 45 Market Street North, Nassau; tel (242) 356 5471, fax (242) 325 3554. Downtown Nassau, a few minutes from Bay Street. Nice apartments to various standards and prices with full self catering facilities.

WHERE TO EAT

Eating out in Nassau is generally good value and can be entertaining. Food styles range from finest international cuisine to traditional Bahamian with its emphasis on fresh-caught seafood. Hotel restaurants also offer a wide range of cuisine and ambience.

Although few restaurants actually require it, it is sensible to reserve in advance as Nassau can get very busy. Several will issue a menu on request prior to your making a reservation. There are also the usual fast food chains in Nassau, such as Dominos, Wendys, Pizza Hut, McDonalds, Dunkin Donuts, Kentucky Fried Chicken and Subway.

Expensive
Graycliff, West Hill St, Nassau; tel (242) 322 2796. Built over 200 years ago by the pirate Captain Graysmith, and later the home of an early governor of the Bahamas, Lord Dunmore, this now houses one of Nassau's finest restaurants.

Sun And . . ., Lakeview Drive off Shirley Street, east Nassau; tel (242) 393 1205. A converted old Bahamian home with probably the best food on the island, with a French/Bahamian combination. Famous for guava soufflés. Jacket required; closed Mondays.

Buena Vista, Delancy Street, downtown Nassau; tel (242) 322 2811. Colonial-style converted home with an unobtrusive pianist, great service and locally caught seafood. Smart-casual; jacket preferred but not essential.

Moderate
Rock 'n' Roll Café, Frilsham House, Cable Beach; tel (242) 327 7639. Seaside café in a former mansion house featuring the best steaks and burgers on the island. Frequented by celebrities and known for its great cracked conch. Casual dress.

Traveller's Rest, corner of West Bay Street and Gambier; tel (242) 327 7633. Bahamian cuisine in a relaxed friendly atmosphere; enjoy the spectacular sunsets while drinking the famous banana and strawberry daiquiris. Seafood specialities; dress casual.

Jitters Coffee House, Bay Street, above Girl's from Brazil, downtown Nassau; tel (242) 356 9381. Chalkboard menu which changes daily, great variety and scrummy milkshakes and deserts; casual dress.

Avery's Restaurant & Bar, Adelaide Village off Carmichael Road, South Shore; tel (242) 362 1547. Luscious old-time island dishes such as souse, peas'n'rice, soup'n'dumplings, chops and sandwiches. Offers free transport within a reasonable distance.

DIVE FACILITIES

Few of the larger resorts offer their own diving facilities, but the Nassau and New Providence diving operators offer a free pick-up service from any hotel or guesthouse on the island. It's worth contacting diving operations prior to your trip to check out the facilities and whether there are any special dive packages allied with hotels close by.

Bahama Divers, PO Box N5004, Yacht Haven Marina, East Bay Street, Nassau; tel (242) 393 5644, fax (242) 393 6078. A huge retail store which handles large numbers of divers and has excellent rental equipment, as well as multilingual staff.

Dive Dive Dive Ltd., PO Box N8050, Coral Harbour, Nassau; tel (800) 368 3483 or (242) 362 1143, fax (242) 362 1994. A large operation with a small shop on the south coast, shark feeding and dive instruction.

Divers Haven, PO Box N1658, East Bay Street, Nassau; tel (242) 393 0869, fax (242) 393 3695. A small dive shop with limited facilities.

Nassau Scuba Centre, PO Box CB11863, Coral Harbour, Nassau; US tel (888) 962 7728 or (954) 462 3400; local tel (242) 362 1964, fax (242) 362 1198, e-mail dive@nassau-scuba-centre.com. This operator can be booked through **Neil Watson's Undersea Adventures**, PO Box 21766, Fort Lauderdale, Florida 33335, USA; tel (954) 462-3400, fax (954) 462-4100, e-mail nealwatson@aol.com. Very professional, with mixed gas systems, shark feeding and training on the south coast, and a small shop.

Stuart Cove's Dive South Ocean, PO Box CB13137, Nassau; US tel (800) 879 9832 or (954) 524 5755, local tel (242) 362 4171, fax (242) 362 5227, e-mail scove1045@aol.com. A large, very professional operation on the south coast, with mixed gas systems, shark feeding, rebreather training, a large shop and E6 film and video. Also found at **Stuart Cove's Lyford Cay Watersports**, Clifton Inlet, Lyford Cay, Nassau; tel (242) 362 5227.

Dolphin Encounters, Fantasy Island; tel (242) 363 1003, fax (242) 327 5059, e-mail stm@mail.bahamas.net.bs. This is a small dive shop geared to take you diving with dolphins and stingrays in an enclosure only.

Sun Divers Ltd., PO Box N-10728, British Colonial Beach Resort, Nassau; tel (242) 325 8927, fax (242) 393 1630. A small operation and shop, with snorkelling and novice trips a speciality.

Sunskiff Divers Ltd., PO Box N142, Coral Harbour, Nassau; tel (800) 331 5884 or tel/fax (242) 362 1979, e-mail tbhv89a@prodigy.com. A small operation specializing in more personalized trips for small groups of divers and snorkellers.

FILM PROCESSING

Full E6 Processing is available from:
Stuart Cove's Dive South Ocean; tel (242) 362 5186 or 362 4171, fax (242) 362 5227.

Nassau Scuba Centre, tel (242) 362 1964, fax (242) 362 1198.

Colour Masters, Rosetta & Patton Stréets, Palmdale, Nassau; tel/fax (242) 356 3414.

Mr Photo, (four outlets in Nassau); tel (242) 323 8146 / 322 3000 / 322 6557 / 356 3306.

EMERGENCY INFORMATION

Doctor's Hospital, corner of Shirley and Collins avenues, Nassau; tel (242) 322 8411.

Princess Margaret Hospital, Shirley Street, Nassau; tel (242) 322 2861.

Recompression chamber:
Lyford Cay Hospital, Nassau; tel (242) 362 4025 or contact channel 16 by radio to any of the island's diving operators.

Police tel 919 or (242) 322 4444
Fire tel 919
Ambulance tel (242) 322 2221

LOCAL HIGHLIGHTS

Local free publications – *Bahamas Tourist News*, *What To Do*, *What's On* – are available everywhere and have excellent information on all of the attractions.

At **Dolphin Encounters** on Blue Lagoon Island, just a 20-minute scenic boat ride from Nassau, you can enjoy a close-up encounter with a friendly bottlenose dolphin. This comes in various degrees of intimacy, including paddling, standing waist-deep in water, swimming and playing, and a 45-minute scuba dive.

Costs start at around $30 for a paddle and rise to $100 for a swim or dive. Blue Lagoon is also home to the Bahamian version of the Cayman Islands' Stingray City; tel (242) 363 4324 (dolphins), (242) 363 3577 (stingrays).

Powerboat Adventures runs fast day-trips to the Exuma Cays, taking visitors to several unspoilt islands (one with large iguanas), with opportunities for excellent snorkelling over pristine reefs. Lunch is included; tel (242) 327 5385, fax (242) 328 5212.

Crystal Cay Marine Park has an underwater observatory almost identical to that found in Eilat, Israel, and allows landlubbers to travel down underwater to view the living coral reef and its inhabitants in a 360° panorama. There are also the usual touristy bits with pet sharks, turtles, stingrays, beaches and souvenirs; tel (242) 328 1036.

Golf: There are three championship golf courses on New Providence. The Cable Beach Golf Club Course, allied with the Radisson Cable Beach Resort, is the oldest course on the island, tel (242) 327 6000; Paradise Island Golf Course is another, tel (242) 363 3925; the third is attached to the South Ocean Golf and Beach Resort, tel (242) 359 3670.

Forts: Be sure to fit in a tour of Nassau's historical past with a visit to Fort Montague, Fort Charlotte (whose cannon were never fired in anger) and Fort Fincastle, next to the Water Tower, which is shaped like a paddle-wheel steamer. You can walk or take the lift to the top of the Water Tower for some spectacular views of Nassau and its environs. Whilst here, climb up the Queen's Steps, cut into the ancient limestone by slaves many centuries ago.

The Junkanoo Expo on Prince George Wharf, Woodes Rogers Walk, depicts the incredible creative talent surrounding the Junkanoo parades held on Boxing Day and New Year's Day; tel (242) 356 2731.

ELEUTHERA

The northeastern corner of the Great Bahama Bank is bordered by the island of Eleuthera (from the Greek for 'freedom'). Located 95km (60 miles) east of Nassau, halfway between the Abacos to the northwest and Cat Island to the southeast, the island is over 160km (100 miles) long and only 5km (3 miles) across at its widest point.

Eleuthera is known as the birthplace of the Bahamas and was the site of the first proper New World settlement in the islands. Originally called Cigatoo by the local Arawak Indian population, the island was used as a staging post by Spanish ships laden with treasure from the Americas. Stopping briefly at the northern tip of the island, they would rest and and fill their casks with fresh water before sailing north to Bermuda, turning to starboard and making the homeward journey across the Atlantic. Then, in 1648, a group of British settlers arrived, seeking religious freedom and calling themselves the 'Elutherian Adventurers'.

The new settlers split up into groups, some of them using Preacher's Cave for worship and shelter from the periodic hurricanes which passed through the islands. (A more recent example of these storms, Hurricane Andrew, caused considerable damage to the island in 1992.) With the arrival of further settlers, townships were established at Spanish Wells and at Dunmore Town, on Harbour Island – now known locally as 'Briland' (a contracted pronunciation of Harbour Island) and often described as the prettiest of the Bahamian islands. Dunmore Town came in effect to be the first capital of the Bahamas, and the town is rich in examples of old colonial-style buildings with open verandas and beautiful gardens.

After the establishment of the Bahamas as a British Crown Colony, the Brilanders were granted land on the mainland of Eleuthera in 1783, much of which is still farmed today by the early settlers' descendants. The inhabitants of Spanish Wells and nearby St George's Cay are largely descendants of the early English farmers and Scottish shipbuilders. Among

Opposite: *Harbour Island off northern Eleuthera boasts an idyllic setting.*
Above: *Slender filefish (Monacanthus tuckeri) hide amidst sea plume branches.*

the lingering traditions on Eleuthera are that the islanders still catch turtles for food and, although illegal, turtle shell is on open display. In an odd contrast to all this history, in which the locals take great pride, most folk use electric golf carts to get around.

Much of the diving and snorkelling takes place on the more exposed Atlantic side of Eleuthera and inside the protective barrier reef off the north of the island. This reef is 11km (7 miles) long and known as the Devil's Backbone due to the fearsomely jagged coral ridges which come close to the surface in many areas, and have been responsible for the destruction of many ships.

Travelling south down the island, the main settlement is Governor's Harbour, which has its own airstrip, a superb sheltered cove, a Club Med and a few other fully inclusive resorts in the area. The best diving to be found this end of the island is in the extreme south off the vertical drop-offs south of Bannerman Town. The reef here stretches southeast past Little San Salvador and then on to Cat Island. Little San Salvador itself, however, has been sold to the Princess Cruise Line and other visitors are discouraged from the island. Live-aboard dive boats are therefore the best way to travel the pristine reefs and fabulous virgin walls.

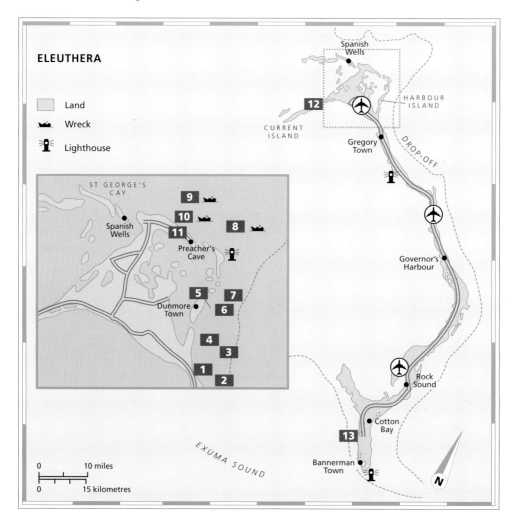

1 GLASS WINDOW BRIDGE
★★★★

Location: 15 minutes by boat from Valentine's Dive Centre on Harbour Island to the land bridge (known as the Glass Window Bridge) on Eleuthera.
Access: By boat only.
Conditions: Can experience strong surge.
Average depth: 15m (50ft)
Maximum depth: 20m (66ft)
Average visibility: 25m (80ft)

Over the years, this section of the Eleuthera coastline has been pounded by the Atlantic surf, knocking down massive limestone boulders which now litter the seabed. Corals have never had a chance to gain a foothold, but there are encrusting algae and burrowing sponges such as *Siphonodictyon coralliphagum* on their surfaces. The tumbled boulders have created swim-throughs, caverns and shallow caves where extremely large supermale parrotfish can be found as well as the usual snapper, Nassau grouper (*Epinephelus striatus*) and small hunting schools of very large tarpon (*Megalops atlanticus*).

2 THE PLATEAU
★★★★★

Location: 20 minutes by boat southeast from the harbour mouth and 1.6km (1 mile) south of Glass Window Bridge (Site 1).
Access: By boat only.
Conditions: Choppy on the surface from October through to March, and therefore best dived from March to September.
Average depth: 18m (60ft)
Maximum depth: 41m (136ft)
Average visibility: 30m (100ft)

The Plateau is one of the finest examples of classic spur and groove reefs in the Caribbean. It has very clearly defined coral spurs leading off into the depths with sand and coral rubble chutes between: so precisely defined are the reefs that *National Geographic* published a special feature on their formation and inhabitants. The spurs are made up of plate, elkhorn and staghorn corals, and have abundant fish life. It is very common to see large pelagics here such as eagle rays (*Aetobatus narinari*), amberjacks (*Seriola dumerili*) and Atlantic spadefish (*Chaetodipterus faber*). The reeftops feature creole wrasse, blue chromis, and all of the representative angelfish, butterflyfish, parrot-fish and wrasse. This is an intermediate dive, not for beginners.

3 THE PINNACLE
★★★★

Location: 16km (10 miles) southeast of the harbour mouth on Harbour Island and 9km (5 miles) off the coast.
Access: By boat only.
Conditions: Can experience serious current with surface chop.
Average depth: 38m (127ft)
Maximum depth: Beyond 70m (230ft)
Average visibility: 45m (150ft)

A blue water dive, this is for experienced divers only. The mooring line is attached to the top of the pinnacle at 30m (100ft) and divers descend this line before continuing down the pinnacle until they reach an archway which bisects the pinnacle. There are big stands of black coral (*Antipathes* spp.) in the cavern and on the outer edges you can find massive barrel sponges standing over 2m (7ft) tall. The mooring line appears to make a vibrating resonance underwater in the current and this attracts large barracuda, amberjacks, wahoo and tons of yellowtail snapper. Sharks are found on every dive, principally blacktip and bull sharks. Time is limited due to the depth of this dive.

4 SEA GARDENS
★★★☆☆☆☆

Location: 10 minutes by boat south of the harbour mouth, off Whale Point.
Access: By boat only.
Conditions: Can experience surge during November to March and surface chop and current.
Average depth: 5–7m (17–24ft)
Maximum depth: 11m (36ft)
Average visibility: 18m (60ft)

This is one of the best snorkelling sites in the area, with beautiful stands of elkhorn coral (*Acropora palmata*), which have flourished due to movement of water through the sound between the islands. From June to August, schools of silversides congregate in the shallow caverns. There are yellowtail snapper, Bermuda chub, barjacks, spotted eagle rays and green turtles (*Chelonia mydas*).

TIPS FOR DEEP DIVING

- attend a deep diving course
- recognize the early symptoms of nitrogen narcosis
- increase depth slowly
- dive only with experienced deep divers
- do not put yourself or others at risk
- plan your dive and dive your plan
- when symptoms appear, ascend until symptoms are relieved

5 THE CAVE
★★★★★

Location: 1.6km (1 mile) due east of the harbour mouth, between Harbour Island and Eleuthera.
Access: By boat only.
Conditions: Not suitable for beginners and best dived from March to September.
Average depth: 19m (63ft)
Maximum depth: 38m (126ft)
Average visibility: 25m (80ft)
This is a cavern dive on the outer edge of Miller's Reef, a spur and groove formation where a mini-wall has been created due to the vertical profile of the reef. The wall is covered in blackcap basslets (*Gramma melacara*) and squirrelfish (*Holocentrus adscensionis*). The 6m (20ft) by 5m (17ft) cavern is at the bottom of the reef and runs straight into the ledge for approximately 23m (25yd). There is good plate coral as well as lots of small fluorescent green cactus corals (*Mycetophyllia lamarckiana*).

6 THE ARCH
★★★★

Location: 0.5km (¼ mile) north of Site 5.
Access: By boat only.
Conditions: Can be choppy with some surge.
Average depth: 33m (110ft)
Maximum depth: 39m (130ft)
Average visibility: 30m (100ft)
Miller's Reef is a classic spur and groove formation and a natural coral arch is located at 33m (110ft), which runs 15m (17yd) through the coral spur headland. A huge barracuda (*Sphyraena barracuda*) is always found in this cavern as well as fairy basslets (*Gramma loreto*) and bigeye snapper (*Priacanthus arenatus*). Migrating humpback whales are also seen by the edge of the reef during October. The Arch is for experienced divers only.

7 PINK HOUSE REEF
★★★★☆☆☆☆

Location: 1km (¾ mile) north of the harbour mouth.
Access: By boat only.
Conditions: Some surge in the shallows with slight northerly current to be expected.
Average depth: 1.5–5m (5–17ft)
Maximum depth: 6m (20ft)
Average visibility: 18m (60ft)

This is almost identical in reef layout and marine life to Sea Gardens (Site 4), except for the huge number of tunnels which cut under the reef structures, making this spot unique along Miller's Reef. From June to September virtually every tunnel is filled with schooling silversides, attended by trumpetfish (*Aulostomus maculatus*), lizardfish (*Synodus saurus*), bar jacks (*Caranx ruber*), southern sennet (*Sphyraena picudilla*), tarpon and barracuda. The coral life is good and, although the area is prone to hurricanes, the reefs have never been damaged.

8 THE CARNARVON
★★★☆☆

Location: North of Eleuthera, east of the northerly barrier reef known as the Devil's Backbone.
Access: By boat only.
Conditions: Surge and surface chop to be expected; best dived in May to July.
Average depth: 5m (17ft)
Maximum depth: 11m (36ft)
Average visibility: 18m (60ft)
The 57m (186ft) *Carnarvon* was a steam-powered, steel-hulled Welsh freighter which foundered on the Devil's Backbone during a hurricane in 1910. Now totally broken up and completely underwater, the ship is spread over a large area of reef with her boilers, pistons, drive shaft, stern and four-blade single propeller still clearly visible. This is a popular area for fishermen and consequently there are few fish in the vicinity. The shallower parts of the wreck are covered in fire coral (*Millepora alcicornis*).

9 CIENFUEGOS WRECK
★★★☆☆☆☆

Location: 1.6km (1 mile) west of the *Carnarvon* (Site 8) on the Devil's Backbone.
Access: By boat only.
Conditions: Rather exposed to any northeasterly storms, so surface chop and surge can be expected.
Average depth: 1–9m (3–30ft)
Maximum depth: 10m (33ft)
Average visibility: 18m (60ft)
The dive boat anchors on the sheltered inside of the reef and divers swim under the reef through various swim-throughs, past a huge pile of ballast stones from a 17th-century wreck, until they reach the *Cienfuegos*. This was a beautiful Ward Line passenger liner built in Chester, Pennsylvania in 1883. She was 88m (292ft) long and weighed 2332 tons, and became stranded on the Devil's Backbone on 5 February 1895. She is now

Above: *On the reeftop saddled blennies (Malacoctenus triangulatus) nestle among algae.*
Below: *The fireworm (Hermodice carunculata) should never be handled.*

totally wrecked but is still loaded with brass, dishes, silverware and other interesting artefacts. There is good fish life on the reef itself, but very little on the wreck due to overfishing. There are several more wrecks within the immediate vicinity, but it is important to note that it is illegal to remove any artefacts from shipwrecks in Bahamas waters.

10 THE TRAIN WRECK
★★☆☆☆

Location: Just north of Preacher's Cave, on the inner barrier reef before the Devil's Backbone.
Access: By snorkelling from the shore or by boat.
Conditions: Rather exposed to any northerly storms, so surface chop and surge can be expected.
Average depth: 1–9m (3–30ft)
Maximum depth: 9m (30ft)
Average visibility: 18m (60ft)
Although known as the Train Wreck, this was in fact a barge which was carrying a steam locomotive when it was destroyed during a violent storm in 1865. There is no evidence of the barge remaining, although some of the train's undercarriage and wheels can still be seen, as well as brass spikes, rail track, coal and ballast stone. The remains are covered in fire coral (*Millepora alcicornis*) and small sea fans. Sergeant majors (*Abudefduf saxatilis*) and damselfish are common here.

11 BAT CAVE AND THE BONE SINK HOLE
★★★★☆

Location: Inland site on North Eleuthera, close to Preacher's Cave, between Bridge Point and North Bar.
Access: By water taxi from Harbour Island and then a taxi down to the inland caverns, where you can enter directly from the edges of the sink hole and cavern.
Conditions: Brackish water, so should be dived only by experienced cave divers.
Average depth: 30m (100ft)
Maximum depth: 30m (100ft)
Average visibility: 60m (200ft)
These are undertaken as a speciality dive with Valentine's Dive Centre. Unlike the Mexican *cenotes* where the visibility drops during the summer months, in these caverns the visibility is crystal clear all year round. The caverns are just a small walk through the brush from the parking area at Preacher's Cave, where the early Elutherian Adventurers sought shelter from hurricanes. Bat Cave has a permanent line installed and is treated as a cavern dive, where you stay within eyesight of the surface.

The Bone Sink Hole is some 12m (40ft) below ground level and equipment must be man-handled down a narrow path. This sink hole is some 30m (100ft) across and is only for much more experienced divers. There is not much life except for some peculiar blind cave fish and shrimps.

12 CURRENT CUT
★★★★★

Location: Between Current Town and Current Island.
Access: By boat only. It is not advisable to try to snorkel from the shore.
Conditions: Current flow up to 10 knots.
Average depth: 9m (30ft)
Maximum depth: 15m (50ft)
Average visibility: 3–25m (10–80ft), dependent on prevailing winds
Regarded as one of the top ten drift dives in the world, this is essentially a race along the seabed on what is possibly the strongest localized tidal current in the Bahamas. Divers are dropped into the water at the peak of the tidal race approximately 2½ hours either side of high or low water. There are no corals in the current cut between the two islands, but there are large numbers of fish, particularly those which like fast tidal streams such as eagle rays and blacktip reef sharks. The current moves so fast and the dive is essentially so short that guests of Valentine's Dive Centre are given two or three exhilarating shots at the current.

13 BAMBOO POINT
★★★★★

Location: Off the drop-off along the southernmost shore of Eleuthera.
Access: By water taxi from Harbour Island and then a taxi or bus ride down to Bannerman Town on the south coast of Eleuthera, then by local boat to the reef wall.
Conditions: Little current, fairly sheltered.
Average depth: 30m (100ft)
Maximum depth: Beyond 70m (230ft)
Average visibility: 45m (150ft)
This is one of the most pristine dives anywhere in the Bahamas, with a sudden drop reef wall which starts at 12m (40ft) and drops vertically into the depths off the edge of the continental shelf. The reef wall stretches to the southeast to Little San Salvador Island and then on to Cat Island. There are superbly structured hard and soft corals, with huge sponges and clouds of fish. This site is dived only occasionally, by land-based operations and adventurous live-aboard dive boats.

HOW TO GET THERE

Eleuthera has three international airports, one in the south at Rock Sound, one midway down the island at Governor's Harbour and one called North Eleuthera International Airport, near Harbour Island. Bahmasair serves all three with daily flights from Nassau. American Eagle flies into Governor's Harbour from Miami. US Air Express and Continental Connection serve North Eleuthera from Miami and Fort Lauderdale respectively, while Sandpiper offers charters from Nassau. Charters to North Eleuthera are also available from Miami and Fort Lauderdale. Taxis meet all flights and a $5 fare gets you to the nearby ferry dock for the short trip to Harbour Island, also $5.

Keva Water Taxi operates between North Eleuthera and Harbour Island; tel (242) 333 2287, VHF Channel 16.

VEHICLE HIRE

Motorbikes, cycles and boats can be hired from **Michael's Cycles**; tel (242) 333 2384. Cars, golf carts and boats can be hired from **Ross Garage**; tel (242) 333 2122.

WHERE TO STAY

Valentine's Yacht Club & Marina, Dunmore Town, Harbour Island; tel (242) 333 2142, fax (242) 333 2135. Small apartments set back from the marina. Has a pool and a small restaurant, but is closed August to November.

Romora Bay Club, PO Box ELH 27146, Harbour Island; tel (242) 333 2325, fax (242) 333 2500. Cottage and apartment style; serves great food.

Landing Hotel and Restaurant, PO Box 190, Harbour Island; tel (242) 333 2707, fax (242) 333 2650, e-mail tbarry@batelnet.bs Built in 1800 and still with a colonial feel; with a verandah setting for sunset cocktails. Situated opposite the harbour jetty.

GLASS WINDOW BRIDGE

The island of Eleuthera narrows to a slender limestone isthmus towards its northern part. At one spot, a small bridge spans a partial rift in the limestone, allowing passing sailors a glimpse of the calm Caribbean on one side or the much rougher Atlantic on the other side. Known as the Glass Window Bridge, this formation is all that keeps Eleuthera as a single island.

The green moray (Gymnothorax funebris) is particularly large.

Pink Sands Hotel, Harbour Island; tel (242) 333 2030, fax (242) 333 2060. Situated on the Atlantic side of Harbour Island with 5km (3 miles) of pink sand beach. Fancy rooms with CD/cassette radios.

Coral Sands Hotel, Harbour Island; tel (800) 468 2799, fax (242) 333 2368. Informal family style, with a beach-side terrace.

Club Méditerrané Holiday Village, PO Box 25080, Queens Highway, Governor's Harbour; tel (242) 332 2270, fax (242) 332 2855. Has a good reputation for couples holidaying with children.

Rainbow Inn, PO Box 53, Waterside, Governor's Harbour; tel/fax (242) 335 0294. Friendly small seaside villas with self catering and maid service. Snorkelling available.

Cove Eleuthera, Gregory Town, North Eleuthera; tel (242) 335 5142, fax (242) 332 2691; e-mail covlutra@bahamas.net.bs. Ocean view, superb setting, pool, restaurant and tennis court, and great snorkelling.

WHERE TO EAT

Most visitors to Harbour Island eat in hotels, though everyone seems to visit the Dunmore Deli at least once during their stay.

Dunmore Deli, Princess St, Harbour Island; tel (242) 333 2644. Excellent international deli with patés, fresh cut meats, exotic cheeses and a duty-free liquor store. Popular veranda-style restaurant.

DIVE FACILITIES

Valentine's Dive Centre, Valentine's Yacht Club and Marina, PO Box 1, Harbour Island, Bahamas. US tel (800) 383 6480, local tel/fax (242) 333 2309, e-mail vdc@batelnet.bs. A professional, conservation-oriented operation, with a small shop. Runs trips to blue holes.

Romora Bay Club Dive Shop, Romora Bay Hotel, PO Box 146, Harbour Island; tel (242) 333 2323, fax (242) 333 2500. Small operation catering for hotel guests.

Clear Water Dive Shop, Bayfront Plaza, Queen's Highway, Governor's Harbour; tel (242) 332 2146. A relatively small operation with a limited selection of rental equipment.

EMERGENCY INFORMATION

Police, Harbour Island, tel (242) 333 2919; Rock Sound Airport Police, tel (242) 334 2052.

Medical Clinic, Dunmore Town, Harbour Island, tel (242) 333 2227; Medical Clinic, Governor's Harbour, tel (242) 332 2001.

The closest **recompression chamber** is a short flight away at Lyford Cay Hospital, Nassau; tel (242) 362 4025.

LOCAL HIGHLIGHTS

The spectacular **Glass Window Bridge** in the northern part of Eleuthera (see box) is well worth a visit.

Dunmore Town is one of the oldest settlements in the Bahamas. Stroll around the town and look into the local galleries where handicrafts work and paintings are for sale.

The **pink sand beach** on the Atlantic side of Harbour Island is a pleasant walk, and you can always take some sand home as a souvenir.

TOURIST INFORMATION

Bahamas Tourist Office
Bay St, Harbour Island; tel (242) 333 2621 (irregular hours)
Sunset House, Queen's Highway, Governor's Harbour; tel (242) 332 2142 (normal office hours)

THE EXUMAS

Just 20km (35 miles) southeast of New Providence lie the Exuma Cays, some of the prettiest and least visited islands of the Bahamas. For the most part these 365 islands, which stretch over 65km (100 miles) from Sail Rocks in the north to Great Exuma and Little Exuma in the southeast, are uninhabited. Many are very exposed to easterly storm fronts and, as they are so low-lying, there has been little development. However, wherever there is a sheltered bay or an additional protective island, you will find a small settlement, and there are actually hundreds of safe anchorages around the islands, which make them popular with live-aboard dive boats and yachtsmen.

Although most visitors to the Exumas arrive on passing yachts – which are able to anchor anywhere along the east coast – in reality few people stay at sea, preferring the resorts on Staniel Cay in the north and Great Exuma, the largest of the islands, in the south. The capital of the Exumas is George Town, situated on the north of Great Exuma. Here, many visitors (including the Duke of Edinburgh) stay at the Club Peace & Plenty. Until recently there was another resort nearby, but it was shut down by the Bahamian government following the discovery that it was a front for an illegal drug cartel. The Exumas were once a major stop-over point for the illegal drugs trade en route to the USA.

Directly opposite George Town is Stocking Island, which has an adjacent barrier reef that stretches over 4km (7 miles). Although the reef diving here is pristine, the islands are best known for their blue holes. Angelfish Blue Hole (Site 7), lying in the shelter of Stocking Island, is a wonderful vertical shaft which drops to 29m (97ft) before branching off at right angles. Nearby are Mystery Cave (Site 8), a site which has been explored thousands of metres underground, and Crab Cay Blue Hole (Site 9) which starts in only 4m (17ft) of water.

Opposite: *The Exuma Cays are very popular with both sailors and divers.*
Above: *Nassau grouper (Epinephelus striatus) are found on reefs everywhere in the Bahamas.*

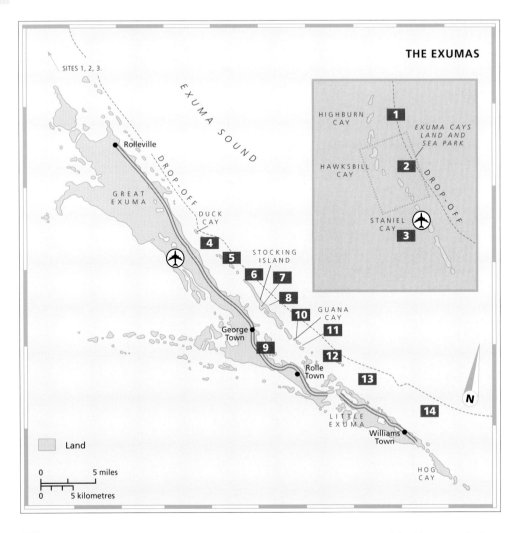

THE EXUMAS

SITES 1, 2, 3.

EXUMA SOUND

DROP-OFF

Rolleville

GREAT EXUMA

DUCK CAY

4

5

STOCKING ISLAND

6 **7**

8

10

GUANA CAY

11

George Town

9

12

Rolle Town

13

LITTLE EXUMA

Williams Town

N

HIGHBURN CAY

EXUMA CAYS LAND AND SEA PARK

1

HAWKSBILL CAY

2

DROP-OFF

STANIEL CAY

3

HOG CAY

Land

0   5 miles

0   5 kilometres

1 HIGHBURN CAY WALL
★★★★

Location: Northeast of Highburn Cay on the edge of Exuma Sound.
Access: By boat only.
Conditions: Can be choppy, with surge on the surface only.
Average depth: 33m (110ft)
Maximum depth: Beyond 70m (230ft)
Average visibility: 45m (150ft)
This massive wall, which stretches all the way down the eastern reaches of the Exuma Cays, is probably one of the least explored areas of the Bahamas due to the physical scale of the drop-off. A steeply sloping coral reef interspersed with sandy patches drops to 33m (110ft) where it then rolls over and drops vertically into the abyss. The edge of this wall has huge barrel sponges (*Xestospongia muta*), boulder star corals, sheet corals and whips. Large bushes of rare black coral can be found and all along the edge there are chromis, snapper and grunt. Be sure to keep a watchful eye out into the blue, as sharks are quite common.

2 EXUMA LAND AND SEA PARK
★★★★★★★★★★★

Location: Northern group of the Exumas, south of New Providence Island.
Access: By boat only.
Conditions: Sheltered bays and inlets with mostly undived virgin reefs.
Average depth: 12m (40ft)
Maximum depth: 21m (70ft)
Average visibility: 30m (100ft)

The Exuma Land and Sea Park was set up by the Bahamas government to protect one of the most pristine areas of coral reefs in the entire island chain. Covering 285 sq km (176 sq miles), the park includes acres of staghorn and elkhorn coral, important mangrove forests that serve as essential fish nurseries, and numerous blue holes, caverns and caves. The islands of the park are bordered to the west by a massive shallow sandy bay which is famous for bonefishing and conch collecting. On the eastern shores, the edge of the continental shelf comes close in, offering spectacular and unspoiled diving at sites only rarely visited by live-aboard dive boats.

3 THUNDERBALL REEF
★★★★

Location: Staniel Cay on the northern range of the Exuma Islands.
Access: By boat only.
Conditions: Sheltered, but the cave should be dived only when the current is flowing out of it.
Average depth: 6m (20ft)
Maximum depth: 12m (40ft)
Average visibility: 15m (50ft)
This reef has been used as the backdrop for a number of Hollywood films including the James Bond movie *Thunderball*, after which it is named. The shallow cave's roof is dissected by hundreds of small open holes, allowing shafts of sunlight to cut into the gloom. The water is quite shallow and the inside of the cave varies from a sandy bottom to hard rock, undulating as you penetrate further. The outer reef features sparse but healthy corals, and lots of fish life.

4 DUCK CAY
★★★☆☆

Location: South of Duck Cay and southeast of Ramsey on Great Exuma.
Access: By boat only.
Conditions: Can be choppy on the surface with some surge.
Average depth: 6m (20ft)
Maximum depth: 14m (46ft)
Average visibility: 21m (70ft)
This is a meandering type of reef which has formed a mini-wall with overhanging ledges and numerous swim-throughs. There are quite large sea fans over 1m (3ft) across and lots of rope sponges and sea plumes. A small school of barracuda tends to hang around the shallows, usually accompanied by juvenile jacks of various species.

5 FLAT CAY WALL
★★★

Location: Northeast of Flat Cay and Channel Cay.
Access: By boat only.
Conditions: Quite exposed during bad weather, but it is a deep dive and below the surge.
Average depth: 25m (80ft)
Maximum depth: Beyond 70m (230ft)
Average visibility: 25m (80ft)
On the inside this site is rather uninteresting with very little good coral growth, but once over the lip of the wall it gets much better. This steeply sloping wall is well covered in soft and hard corals with large tube sponges, sea fans and sea plumes predominating. Large redmouth grouper are common, as are solitary barracuda. This is a popular site to observe angelfish and butterflyfish.

The shallow reefs are riddled with caves, canyons and caverns.

6 STINGRAY REEF
★★

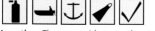

Location: The ocean side or northeast of Conch Cay.
Access: By boat only.
Conditions: Choppy surface conditions and can experience oceanic surge.
Average depth: 10m (33ft)
Maximum depth: 15m (50ft)
Average visibility: 21m (70ft)
The inshore side of the reef is mainly a thin sandy covering over an ancient spur and groove reef dotted with small sea plumes and fans, with little coral growth except in sheltered areas. As you go further into deeper water, however, the spur and groove system becomes much more obvious with good coral growth, rope sponges, sea fans and sea plumes. Many of the brain corals are covered in Christmas tree worms (*Spirobranchus giganteus*) and under the overhangs large Nassau grouper can be seen waiting at cleaning stations.

7 ANGELFISH BLUE HOLE
★★★

Location: Inside Hurricane Bay on the west of Stocking Island, opposite George Town.
Access: By boat only 5 minutes from Exuma Dive Centre's dock in George Town, but can be accessed by the houses on Stocking Island.
Conditions: Sheltered, but the cave should be dived only when the current is flowing out of it.
Average depth: 28m (95ft)
Maximum depth: 28m (95ft)
Average visibility: 9m (30ft)
Inside the shelter of Hurricane Bay, Angelfish Blue Hole is named after the large queen angelfish (*Holocanthus ciliaris*) which inhabit the lower regions. The blue hole is marked by two mooring buoys which are attached to a chain that goes into the hole and eventually joins up with a line that follows the roof of the inner passageway. Circular in shape, the hole drops rapidly to 28m (95ft), where nurse sharks are usually found resting during the day. From October to

---

SLIPPER LOBSTERS

Slipper lobsters are members of the Scyllaridae family and resemble the more common spiny lobster, but without the extended antennae or claws. The shell or carapace has a rough knobbly texture and is mottled in colour. Slipper lobsters are quite timid and are able to swim backwards quickly by rapid flicks of their tail. They are more commonly seen at night.

March a large group of spotted eagle rays (*Aetobatus narinari*) live in the bay and swim around the blue hole's entrance.

8 MYSTERY CAVE
★★

Location: Opposite Angelfish Blue Hole (Site 7) at the entrance of the lagoon in Hurricane Bay, Stocking Island.
Access: By boat only.
Conditions: This site should be explored only on an outgoing tide and under the guidance of qualified cave experts.
Average depth: 6m (20ft)
Maximum depth: 25m (80ft)
Average visibility: 6m (20ft)
The cave system runs for at least a couple of thousand metres and splits off into many different passageways. It was here that Jacques-Yves Cousteau first discovered the links between the inland and offshore reef blue hole systems with the use of dye compounds in the water. Although the dye theory proved correct over several kilometres, the underground system is only partly accessible to divers and the navigable passages do not extend as far as was first thought. The entrance of the cavern is semi-circular in shape with a sandy bottom, and is patrolled by groups of dogtooth snapper and barjacks.

9 CRAB CAY CREVASSE (Crab Cay Blue Hole)
★★★

Location: Directly in the sailing route through the inner passageway of small cays south of George Town on Great Exuma.
Access: By boat only.
Conditions: Sheltered, but can be dived only on an outgoing tide.
Average depth: 25m (80ft)
Maximum depth: 36m (120ft)
Average visibility: 9m (30ft)
This is a large semi-circular depression in an otherwise flat sandy seabed, with a vertical lip on one side starting at 6m (20ft) and, on the other side of the blue hole, a steeply sloping bank. There are three different entrances to the hole and, as always, care must be taken around these entrances. Divers are advised not to go any further than the outer cavern without proper cave-diving qualifications and additional safety requirements. The top of the blue hole is filled with snapper and grunt.

Of the 80 or so species of parrotfish found in the world's tropical oceans, 14 are found in the Caribbean, all belonging to the family Scaridae. Found around all the Bahamian reefs, they are an elongated fish with a blunt head and deep body, in the bright, gaudy colours which give the parrotfish their common name. Their powerful jaws have fused teeth, or 'beaks'; these are used to scrape algae and softer coral polyps from reef or wrecks and are strong enough to leave noticeable scars on hard stony corals. The fish grind their food and bits of coral with plate-like teeth located in their throats. In the process, large amounts of chalky, limestone residue are excreted at regular intervals – parrotfish are a major source of sand in the tropics.

Although they are edible, parrotfish are very rarely caught commercially. Sizes range from the large 1.25m (4ft) rainbow parrotfish (*Scarus guacamaia*) to the tiny 20cm (7in) greenbloch parrotfish (*Sparisoma atomarium*). Rainbow parrotfish are very distinctive, with an orange/brown head, brilliant emerald-green rear body and golden brown fins. Older supermales will also have a fringe of algae growing above their upper lip, resembling a moustache, and can weigh over 20kg (45lb). The best locations in the Bahamas to see rainbow parrotfish are in the Bimini Islands and on Theo's Wreck (see page 45) off Grand Bahama Island.

Another rare species also found on Theo's Wreck at night is the blue parrotfish (*Scarus coeruleus*), which rests in the wreckage. Further species are known to secrete a mucus cocoon around themselves at night, as a protection against hunting moray eels.

Many of the parrotfish species are solitary, such as the stoplight parrotfish (*Sparisoma viride*) and the redband parrotfish (*Sparisoma aurofrenatum*), but others join into loose aggregations roving over the reefs, such as the princess parrotfish (*Scarus taeniopterus*) and the striped parrotfish (*Scarus croicensis*), which quite often mix with other species. They swim by flapping their pectoral fins (like shortened wings) and only use their tails for sudden bursts of propulsion.

The identification of parrotfish is hindered by the fact that most varieties have up to four distinct phases as they reach maturity, undertaking dramatic changes in shape, colour and markings. The first stage is known as the Juvenile Phase, the next the Initial Phase; a few species have an Intermediate Phase; then on full maturity, when the fish change into supermales, they reach the Terminal Phase. Some parrotfish are hermaphrodites and change sex from female to male. Others mature without going through a sex change.

The blue parrotfish (Scarus coeruleus) rests amidst colourful sponges at night.

10 GUANA REEF
★★☆☆

Location: Between Guana Cay and Elizabeth Island.
Access: By boat only.
Conditions: Quite exposed to westerly winds, when choppy surface conditions can be expected.
Average depth: 4m (14ft)
Maximum depth: 8m (27ft)
Average visibility: 21m (70ft)
This is a large area filled with huge sections of patch coral made up of many different species. Five of these giant coral heads rise 4m (14ft) from the sandy seabed. The tops of the coral mounds are fairly flat, with little coral growth, but the sides form mini-walls where squirrelfish (*Holocentrus adscensionis*) hide and large numbers of fairy basslets (*Gramma loreto*) can be found. Stingrays are common in the area, especially the smallest – the golden stingray (*Urolophus jamaicensis*).

11 FOWL CAY REEF
★★★★

Location: Between Guana Cay and Fowl Cay.
Access: By boat only.
Conditions: Fairly sheltered from most bad weather conditions.
Average depth: 2m (6ft)
Maximum depth: 6m (20ft)
Average visibility: 15m (50ft)
A popular snorkelling site, this very pretty protected reef features three distinct coral heads that rise up very close to the surface. The reef is covered in Christmas tree worms and featherduster worms (*Bispira brunnea*). Unfortunately the shallowest parts of the reef are smothered in fire coral (*Millepora* spp.), so great care must be taken when exploring these sections.

12 ANCHOR REEF
★★

Location: East of Man of War Cay, opposite Rolle Town at the southern part of Great Exuma.
Access: By boat only.
Conditions: Can be choppy on the surface, making entry and exit from the dive boat difficult.
Average depth: 12m (40ft)
Maximum depth: 12m (40ft)
Average visibility: 15m (50ft)

This is a strip reef formed in part by the top end of an old spur and groove formation with a hard rocky substrate. A very old ship's anchor with a shaft 3m (10ft) long is wedged by one of its flukes under a coral block. The anchor is heavily encrusted in corals and sponges and always has an attendant swarm of rainbow wrasse picking off the algae which grows amongst the coral. The reef is rather untidy due to the pervading approach of the various species of algae, which now grow unchecked in many areas due to a lack of sea urchins – which suffered a catastrophic blight a few years ago.

13 PIGEON CAY
★★☆☆

Location: Northeast of Forbes Hill off Little Exuma.
Access: By boat only.
Conditions: Rather exposed with surface chop.
Average depth: 6m (20ft)
Maximum depth: 14m (47ft)
Average visibility: 21m (70ft)
This site is similar to Stingray Reef (Site 6) with an old, worn-down spur and groove reef formation, and small scattered corals on the top. However, this reef forms more of a mini-wall with lots of brain corals, gorgonian sea fans and large plate corals. Caribbean reef sharks (*Carcharhinus perezi*) and nurse sharks (*Ginglymostoma cirratum*) are common along these southern reefs.

14 BLACK ROCKS
★★

Location: Opposite Williams Town, north of Little Exuma.
Access: By boat only.
Conditions: Weather-dependent, with choppy waves possible on the surface.
Average depth: 15m (50ft)
Maximum depth: 21m (70ft)
Average visibility: 21m (70ft)
This dive is around twenty or so separate coral heads which are scattered over a sandy bottom, where you can find sand tilefish (*Malacanthus plumieri*), peacock flounders (*Bothus lunatus*) and stingrays (*Dasyatis americana*). Each of the coral heads is about 4m (14ft) high and 7m (8yd) in diameter. There is good sponge growth and quite a lot of the older dead coral surfaces are covered in sargassum weed (*Sargassum natans*). Fish life is not abundant but there are spotfin butterflyfish (*Chaetodon ocellatus*), large numbers of stoplight parrotfish (*Sparisoma viride*) and the usual attendant wrasse, snapper, grunt and grouper species.

How to Get There

Bahamasair has a daily service from Nassau and Miami to Exuma International Airport on Great Exuma, 5km (8 miles) north of George Town. The flight takes 45 minutes from Nassau and travels the length of the Exuma Cays, giving wonderful aerial views of the reefs. Island Express flies to Staniel Cay and Great Exuma from Fort Lauderdale. Peace & Plenty Hotel offers a private charter service from Nassau, as do a number of independent charter services. Taxis meet all flights; the fare to the hotels is around $22

Vehicle Hire

Thomson's Rental in George Town, tel (242) 336 2442, has a choice of cars or vans. Scooters are available from Exuma Dive Centre in George Town, tel (242) 336 2390.

Taxis

Luther Rolle, George Town, Exuma, tel (242) 345 0641 or VHF Channel 16.

Junior Strachan, Taxi No. 4, George Town, Exuma, tel (242) 345 0641 or VHF Channel 16.

Where to Stay

Club Peace & Plenty, Queens Highway, George Town, Exuma; US tel (800) 525 2210, local tel (242) 336 2551, fax (242) 336 2093. A delightful hotel on the ocean front with its own dock and swimming pool. Its 35 deluxe rooms all have a great view and the restaurant is superb (especially the local fish and steaks). Free ferry service to nearby Stocking Island for snorkelling.

Peace & Plenty Beach Inn & Bonefish Lodge, George Town, Exuma; US tel (800) 525 2210, local tel (242) 336 2551, fax (242) 336 2093. The lodge, which caters for fishing parties, has 16 rooms with great views and a nice restaurant, although it also has a reciprocal dining arrangement with its sister hotel.

Two Turtles Inn, George Town, Exuma; US tel (800) 688 4752, local tel (242) 336 2545, fax (242) 336 2528. Small, quaint inn in George Town overlooking Elizabeth Harbour. Its 14 rooms are furnished in island style.

Staniel Cay Yacht Club, Staniel Cay, Exuma; US tel (954) 467 8920, local tel (242) 355 2011/2024, fax (242) 355 2044. Individual lodges located in the heart of the Exuma Cays chain. The club has its own marina and is located near to a small airstrip which is used by private air charters. Also has an excellent restaurant.

Where to Eat

Most visitors to the islands eat in their respective resort hotels, as the food tends to be good. There are local eating houses serving traditional Bahamian dishes such as fresh fish, conch and peas'n'rice.

Dive Facilities

Exuma Dive Centre, Queens Highway, PO Box Ex-29238, George Town; tel (242) 336 2390, fax (242) 336 2391. A new operation with all new rental equipment.

Staniel Cay Yacht Club & Dive Centre, Staniel Cay, Exuma; tel (954) 467 8920 or (242) 355 2011, fax (242) 355 2044. A small operation catering for club members, with limited selection of rental equipment.

Emergency Services

Police, tel 919 or (242) 336 2666

Government Clinic, George Town, tel (242) 336 2088.

IslandMed Clinic and Pharmacy, Great Exuma, tel (242) 336 2220.

The closest **recompression chamber** is at Lyford's Cay Hospital, Nassau, New Providence Island; tel (242) 362 4025.

Tourist Information

Bahamas Tourist Office – Exuma
Cousins Building, Queens Highway, George Town, Exuma; tel (242) 336 2430, fax (242) 336 2431.

Huge sponges adorn virtually all the deeper reefs.

CAT ISLAND

Cat Island is midway down the Bahamas archipelago, 210km (130 miles) southeast of Nassau and northeast of Long Island. It is 80km (48 miles) long and has been described as one of the most beautiful islands of the Bahamas, with the highest point of land in the whole chain at Mount Alvernia at 62m (206ft). On top of Mount Alvernia is the Hermitage, a monastery built by an Anglican priest who converted to Roman Catholicism, Father Jerome (John Hawes). The 2000 or so inhabitants of Cat Island revere his memory.

The island may have received its present name from a contemporary of the infamous pirate Edward 'Blackbeard' Teach called Arthur Catt, who used the island as a base for his piratical raids. However, the name may also have come from the fact that large numbers of feral cats were left on the island when the Spaniards abandoned their settlements here in the 1600s. Cat Island was convenient for Spanish ships as a staging post between the Old and New World, and ships would stop off for fresh water and supplies before continuing on their way.

Due to the shape of the island, the settlements are all spaced far apart, often making a long taxi ride necessary to get anywhere. Most of the existing resorts are in the south of the island, with further large tracts of southern and central land being sold by property developers to private investors for holiday homes. Though it is one of the least populated islands in the Bahamas, the facilities are gradually improving with the influx of new investment.

The entire west coast is unnavigable due to shallow sandbanks, while the east coast is very rugged and exposed to Atlantic storm fronts. This is one of the least dived areas in the Bahamas, with the majority of the diving done along the south coast in Cutlass Bay between Columbus Point in the east and Devil's Point in the west. Here the reef wall starts at only 15m (50ft) and plummets down with gulleys, canyons, chimneys and swim-throughs. This is virgin territory at its best.

Opposite: *Cat Island has some of the best dive sites in the Family Islands.*
Above: *Small cactus corals are found principally on shallow reefs.*

1 GREENWOOD REEF
★★★★

Location: Directly opposite the Greenwood Inn, southeast Cat Island.
Access: From the shore.
Conditions: Can experience surge and is rather choppy during the winter months.
Average depth: 4m (14ft)
Maximum depth: 8m (27ft)
Average visibility: 9m (30ft)
This is a patch reef system directly in front of the Greenwood Inn. Because this is the Atlantic side of the island the 10km (8 mile) beach gets all the flotsam and jetsam imaginable. However, the reefs have good stands of elkhorn coral growing close to the surface. A resident pair of grey angelfish (*Pomacanthus arcuatus*) are quite friendly. The seagrass beds are alive with wrasse, hermit crabs and sand gobies.

2 BLACK CORAL WALL
★★★★

Location: Southeast of Martin Bluff at the west of Big Winding Bay, at the edge of the drop-off.
Access: By boat only.
Conditions: Can experience surge on the surface making boat trips rather choppy, but calm underwater.
Average depth: 25m (80ft)
Maximum depth: Beyond 70m (230ft)
Average visibility: 30m (100ft)
Along the edge of the drop-off, this site features massive buttresses of coral forming huge individual

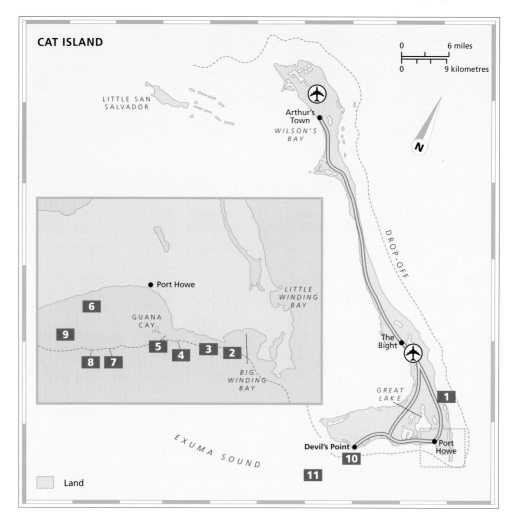

CAT ISLAND

LITTLE SAN SALVADOR

Arthur's Town
WILSON'S BAY

0   6 miles
0   9 kilometres

N

DROP-OFF

Port Howe

LITTLE WINDING BAY

GUANA CAY

6

9

5

4

3

2

8   7

BIG WINDING BAY

The Bight

GREAT LAKE

1

EXUMA SOUND

Devil's Point

10

Port Howe

11

Land

heads. Deeply cut, there are gulleys and canyons which wind down through the reef, with narrow sand chutes everywhere. Large black coral bushes (*Antipathes* spp.) can be found under shaded overhangs. As you travel deeper, the longer and more plentiful wire corals (*Ellisella barbadensis* and *E. elongata*), which come in a number of colours, can be found. Large tiger grouper (*Mycteroperca tigris*) are seen in large breeding aggregations during December and January. Off the wall, Caribbean reef sharks (*Carcharhinus perezi*) are common, as are turtles, barracuda and eagle rays.

3 THE MAZE
★★★★

Location: West of Black Coral Wall (Site 2), midway to Guana Cay.
Access: By boat only.
Conditions: No current, but occasional surface chop.
Average depth: 25m (80ft)
Maximum depth: Beyond 70m (230ft)
Average visibility: 30m (100ft)
This is a drop-off dive with numerous cuts through the huge coral heads creating swim-throughs, small caverns and narrow canyons. The marine landscape here is breathtaking, with huge coral spurs jutting out off the wall. Very large sheet corals hang down over underhanging walls where nurse sharks rest during the day. Black coral bushes are present, as are large venus sea fans (*Gorgonia flabellum*), bright purple in colour. Flamingo tongue shells (*Cyphoma gibbosum*) are

Opposite: *The shallow barrier reefs consist partly of elkhorn coral (Acropora palmata).*

common on the sea fans. Creole wrasse and blue chromis hover along the reef edge at 15m (50ft) with numerous snapper, grunt and parrotfish present all along the wall.

4 VLADY'S REEF (The Chimney)
★★★★

Location: 10 minutes by boat east from Guana Cay.
Access: By boat only.
Conditions: Quite exposed; can be choppy on the surface.
Average depth: 18m (60ft)
Maximum depth: Beyond 70m (230ft)
Average visibility: 25m (80ft)

CORAL NUTRITION

Corals receive their food nutrition from three separate sources: from plankton captured by their tentacles, through organic nutrients absorbed from the water column and from organic compounds formed from the microscopic algae which grows on the coral. It is this last algae which gives the corals their colouration. When rising sea temperatures occur (due to phenomenon such as El Niño), one of the first aspects of the marine ecosystem to be affected is coral, as in overly warm water coral will expel its symbiotic algae, causing 'bleaching'. To divers, this phenomenon is marked by huge patches of brilliant white coral, but if the warming of the water continues, the coral will die.

At this site one massive coral head near the mooring buoy comes to within 6m (20ft) of the surface before dropping down to 25m (80ft) on the outer edge of the wall. Just to the left of this reef crest is a chimney which is easily negotiated and brings you out onto the wall. Nearby is a massive black coral tree and deep-water gorgonians. The coral heads have created hundreds of gulleys and canyons where large stingrays (*Dasyatis americana*) can be found. Atlantic spadefish (*Chaetodipterus faber*) are common here, mixing with Bermuda chub (*Kyphosus sectatrix*). This is a nice reef with good coral growth.

5 THE ANCHOR
★★★☆☆

Location: Off the shallow reef in front of Guana Cay.
Access: By boat only.
Conditions: Choppy on the surface with some surge in the shallows.
Average depth: 8m (27ft)
Maximum depth: 21m (70ft)
Average visibility: 25m (80ft)
At this site there is a very old iron anchor completely overgrown by corals and sponges and embedded in the reef next to a sandy patch. Difficult to spot at first, it has obviously been underwater for a great many years. Continuing south, the old spur and groove patch reef forms a mini-wall to another sand plain before much larger coral formations can be found. In shallower water, large stands of elkhorn coral (*Acropora palmata*) reach almost to the surface where snapper and grunt always seem to be present. In the larger gulleys, horse-eye jack (*Caranx latus*) and crevalle jack (*Caranx hippos*) form large schools just keeping out of reach of divers. The sandy patches have sand tilefish (*Malacanthus plumieri*), yellowhead jawfish (*Opistognathus aurifrons*) and sand divers (*Synodus saurus*).

6 THE CUT
★★☆☆☆

Location: West of Port Howe opposite the large white markers on the beach.
Access: From the shore.
Conditions: Generally sheltered due to the proximity of the shallow barrier reef.
Average depth: 5m (17ft)
Maximum depth: 8m (27ft)
Average visibility: 12m (40ft)
Popular with snorkellers and divers, the Cut is also used as the principal night diving site along the south coast due to the sheltered reef being so close to shore. The elkhorn and staghorn coral is all in good order and lobsters are very common. Look closely amongst the

gorgonian sea fans and you will find slender filefish (*Monacanthus tuckeri*). Nurse sharks (*Ginglymostoma cirratum*) are seen hunting here at night and large eagle rays are often seen foraging in the sand with their strong snouts looking for marine molluscs and crabs. At night time the common reef fishes are asleep on the reef, making them much more approachable. Red night shrimps (*Rhynchocinetes rigens*) can be spotted by their luminous green eyes, and various species of hermit crabs are everywhere.

7 THE CAVE
★★★★

Location: At the drop-off in front of the Cut (Site 6).
Access: By boat only.
Conditions: Surge on the surface can make the boat trip rather choppy, but expect calm underwater.
Average depth: 25m (80ft)
Maximum depth: Beyond 70m (230ft)
Average visibility: 30m (100ft)
Part of the standard spur and groove reef that runs back from the wall, this 'cave' is in fact a deep channel. As you swim down the smooth-sided valley, a second passage branches off to the left with four different exits out onto the vertical drop-off. This is a spectacular dive with large black coral bushes, sheet coral, sea fans and sea plumes, hundreds of strands of wire coral, rope sponges and barrel sponges. Caribbean reef sharks are always seen here, but they are rather skittish.

8 BIG BLUE
★★★★

Location: On the drop-off directly opposite the mooring buoys on the shore at Port Howe.
Access: By boat only.
Conditions: Current can be expected along the wall.
Average depth: 30m (100ft)
Maximum depth: Beyond 70m (230ft)
Average visibility: 30m (100ft)
There is a 99% chance of seeing sharks at the point where this drop-off becomes more vertical and the coral buttresses flatten out as they extend out into the blue. Due to the depth, it is only for experienced divers. There are huge sea fans, barrel sponges (*Xestospongia muta*) and massive purple stove-pipe sponges (*Aplysina archeri*); barracuda are common and there are the usual shoals of blue chromis and creole wrasse (*Clepticus parrai*).

Opposite: *A balloonfish (Diodon holocanthus) senses the approach of a diver overhead.*

9 PRIMA DONNA
★★★☆☆

Location: Opposite the mooring buoys at Port Howe.
Access: By boat only.
Conditions: Surge can be expected.
Average depth: 6m (20ft)
Maximum depth: 9m (30ft)
Average visibility: 15m (40ft)
This well-formed upper edge of a spur and groove reef runs all along the mouth of the wide bay known as Reef Harbour. Coming close to the surface in many locations, the crest of these coral ridges is topped with good-quality elkhorn coral (*Acropora palmata*). All the various species of brain coral at this site have Christmas tree worms (*Spirobranchus giganteus*) growing on them as well as cleaning gobies (*Gobiosoma genie*) hanging around waiting for fish. Stoplight parrotfish and numerous wrasse species can be found everywhere.

10 DEVIL'S POINT
★★★★★

Location: On the drop-off southeast of Devil's Point.
Access: By boat only.
Conditions: Current can be expected.
Average depth: 21m (70ft)
Maximum depth: Beyond 70m (230ft)
Average visibility: 30m (100ft)

Tiny blennies can be found on top of numerous hard corals.

The edge of the wall starts in 14m (47ft) and drops off rapidly into the depths. Large grouper are very common, particularly black grouper (*Mycteroperca bonaci*) and the much smaller bicolor coney (*Cephalopholis fulvus*). Soft corals predominate on the upper slopes with sea plumes and sea fans everywhere. Sheet corals, wire corals and large tube sponges cover the lower slopes, and the whole area is a mass of fish.

11 TARTAR BANK
★★★★★

Location: 10km (16 miles) southwest of Cat Island.
Access: By boat only, 45 minutes from the beach.
Conditions: Current can be expected around the plateau.
Average depth: 30m (100ft)
Maximum depth: Beyond 70m (230ft)
Average visibility: 45m (150ft)
This offshore submarine pinnacle is definitely the top dive in Cat Island, but is very difficult to reach due to the distance involved and the fact that it often experiences rough weather. Large schools of spadefish, pelagic triggerfish and many sharks are to be expected, particularly from November to January. Turtles are common, as are barracuda, big jacks and eagle rays. Corals are not as good as might be imagined but everything appears so much larger, especially the tube sponges.

HOW TO GET THERE

By air
There are daily Bahamasair flights from Nassau to either Arthur's Town Airport or The Bight Airport. It is better to get your flight into The Bight if you are staying at the Greenwood Inn for scuba diving, as it takes around two hours by taxi (and costs around $75) from Arthur's Town to the deep south. The Greenwood Inn also offer a private charter from Nassau. There are four airstrips on Cat Island for use by private charter.

By boat
The mail boat MV *North Cat Island* leaves Potter's Cay in Nassau every Wednesday for Bennett's Town and Arthur's Town on Cat Island and takes around 14 hours.

WHERE TO STAY

Hotel Greenwood Inn, Port Howe; US tel (800) 661 3483, local tel /fax (242) 342 3053. Colourful and friendly family atmosphere, with only 20 rooms. Freshwater swimming pool on the beach. Bahamian-style food with fresh fish daily. (Packed lunches are also made up for picnics and all-day diving trips.)

Fernandez Bay Village, New Bight, Cat Island; US tel (800) 940 1905 or (305) 474 4821, fax (305) 474 4864, local tel (242) 342 3043. Upmarket brick and self catering stone cottages, though also with a restaurant and small grocery store in the resort.

Hawk's Nest Resort and Marina, Hawk's Nest Creek, Cat Island; US tel (800) OUT-ISLAND, local tel /fax (242) 357 7257. Overlooking Bight Bay, this resort has a relaxed, friendly and informal atmosphere. All rooms have a sea view.

WHAT TO WEAR

The Bahamian lifestyle is very informal and dress is most definitely casual to the point of slobbishness. You will spend your days in swimming costumes, shorts and T-shirts, but please bear in mind that bathing suits are not acceptable in restaurants or shops. In outdoor restaurants, slacks, shorts and shirts are the norm, though in some of the smarter resorts men are expected to wear long trousers and possibly a jacket.

The golden coney (Epinephelus fulvus) is quite rare.

DIVE FACILITIES

Greenwood Dive Centre, Port Howe; tel/fax (242) 342 3053. A relatively small, personal but very experienced operation, with two dive boats handling 20 divers in total. Facilities include 12 full sets of equipment and courses run to suit most diving levels, in German and English. There is no shop.

Fernandez Bay Village Dive Resort, New Bight; US tel (800) 9401905 or (305) 474 4821, fax (305) 474 4864, local tel/fax (242) 342 3043. Limited equipment for the use of its own guests. No shop, and uses Greenwood's air compressor and dive boat.

Hawk's Nest Resort and Marina, South Cat Island; US tel (800) OUT-ISLAND, local tel/fax (242) 357-7257. Another small operation which uses Greenwood's facilities.

EMERGENCY INFORMATION

The main **Government Clinic** on Cat Island is located at the Bight, tel (242) 342 4049, and there is another at Orange Creek, tel (242) 354 4050.

District Medical Officer, tel (242) 342 3026 or 342 3062.

The nearest **recompression chamber** is at Lyford Cay, Nassau, New Providence Island; tel (242) 362 4025.

LOCAL HIGHLIGHTS

Visit **The Hermitage** on the top of Mount Alvernia, the highest point in the Bahamas at 62m (206ft). This famous, but tiny monastery was built by Father Jerome (see box). A rough road and steep path lead you up to the monastery past the Stations of the Cross. The hike is well worth the effort.

At Port Howe, named after an English admiral who fought in the American Revolution, you will find the remains of **Deveaux Mansion**, once the grand house of Col. Andrew Deveaux, who took Nassau from the Spaniards in 1783.

Beachcombing along the miles of empty beaches is a favourite pastime for many visitors: not only are exotic shells washed up, but an incredible array of flotsam is borne here by the Atlantic.

FATHER JEROME

John Hawes, an Anglican priest who took the name Father Jerome on his conversion to Catholicism, came to Cat Island to rebuild the churches which were destroyed in the 1906 hurricane. He fell in love with the eastern Bahamas and decided to make his home on Cat Island.

During his time here, he built two fine churches on nearby Long Island, St Paul's and St Peter's. The Moorish-style church on the hill above Clarence Town on Long Island is superb and well worth a visit. You can climb the narrow twin towers for spectacular views of the surrounding countryside. He also founded the St Augustine Monastery in Nassau before retiring to Cat Island to live the remainder of his life as a hermit.

As a final act of religious devotion Father Jerome carved steps up to the top of Mount Alvernia, the highest point in the Bahamas at 62m (206 ft). Along the way, he also carved the 14 Stations of the Cross, representing events from the Passion of Christ. On reaching the summit, he built a scaled-down, child-sized replica of a European monastery – The Hermitage – complete with small chapel, bell tower and three closet-sized rooms which he used as living quarters, Father Jerome lived here the last dozen years of his life. When he died at the age of 80 in 1956, he was reputedly buried with his arms outstretched in the shape of a cross.

LONG ISLAND GROUP

L ocated southeast of the Exumas chain, Long Island is reputed to have been the third island discovered in 1492 by Christopher Columbus, who is said to have described it as the most beautiful island he had ever seen. The explorer is commemorated by a cross on the headland at Columbus Point, the northern tip of the island.

Long Island is 106km (66 miles) long, with 35 small communities linked by the newly paved Queen's Highway, which runs its full length. The island has rolling hills that drop down to crashing surf on the exposed eastern side, while in the west it slopes down gradually to a massive shallow sandy bank which stretches over to the Exumas. In Clarence Town in the south, Father Jerome built a beautiful Moorish-style church on the hill. Arawak and Lucayan Indian artefacts can be seen around Deadman's Cay, while, in the south of the island, ancient salt pans can also be found.

Two other islands normally included within the Long Island Group are Rum Cay and the uninhabited Conception Island, both northeast of the main island. Originally called *Santa María de la Concepción* by Christopher Columbus, Rum Cay owes its present name to the rum-running years of the early 1900s. Located 34km (20 miles) east of Columbus Point on Long Island, the island is around 16km (10 miles) long and has a population of around 100, all centred on the main town of Port Nelson in the south. Northwest of Rum Cay is uninhabited Conception Island, lying almost in the centre of a deep-water trench with Long Island on one side, Cat Island to the north and San Salvador to the east. Now declared a National Nature Reserve, Conception Island is home to many different species of endemic and migratory birds, as well as nesting green and hawksbill turtles.

Much of the diving on Long Island is done along the northern stretch of the island along the shallow reefs which connect westwards to the Exumas. It is here (Site 3) that Stella Maris first started feeding sharks on a regular basis over 30 years ago. Other notable sites include Dean's Blue Hole (Site 2) and the Big Green Hole (Site 1) at Lochaber, south of

Opposite: *Cape Santa Maria on northern Long Island has miles of empty beaches.*
Above: *Fire coral (Millepora alcicornis) should be avoided by divers.*

Clarence Town, both on the Atlantic side of the island. Rum Cay has suffered badly from periodic hurricanes on its inner southern shore, but, to the northwest of the island, Pinder's Reef has some excellent snorkelling. The waters north of Flamingo Bay are tinged green from fresh-water outfalls, where huge grouper creep up on unsuspecting snorkellers and frighten the life out of them. Along the main road north on Rum Cay a couple of blue holes can be found, but little or no exploration has been done in them.

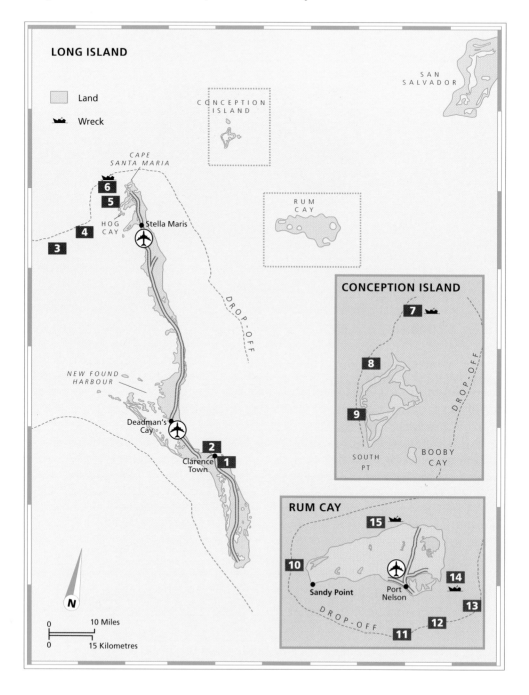

1 BIG GREEN HOLE
★★★★

Location: Southeast of Clarence Town at Lochaber.
Access: From the shore.
Conditions: Very clear in the shallows; slight current.
Average depth: 3m (10ft)
Maximum depth: 20m (66ft)
Average visibility: Variable from 30m (100ft) in the shallows to 6m (20ft) in the green hole.
This idyllic lagoon is situated along quite a rough track, but is well worth the effort to reach it. Access to the beach is next to the Lochaber Beach Lodge: owners Dick and Dawn Meehan will also escort you to some of the outer reefs on the Atlantic side of the island if you are interested. The Big Green Hole is an ancient sink hole, but the shallow nature of the lagoon gives the water a greenish tinge instead of the deep blue associated with most Bahamas blue holes.

To the north of the lagoon (travelling left from the lodge), you come across an old fisherman's boat which has sunk on a sandbar. The snorkelling in this area is lovely and you will find yourself followed constantly by a small school of palometa (*Trachinotus goodei*) and even a couple of spotted eagle rays which live in this corner.

2 DEAN'S BLUE HOLE
★★★★★★

Location: East of the Queen's Highway at the entrance to a new residential housing development, along a wide road and then a narrow track along the clifftop to the wide entrance to the blue hole on the beach.
Access: From the shore.
Conditions: Very clear in the shallows, so best dived in the morning when the sun is high.
Average depth: 25m (80ft)
Maximum depth: Beyond 70m (230ft)
Average visibility: Variable from 30m (100ft) in the shallows to 60m (200ft) through the cavern.
Dean's Blue Hole was successfully dived and mapped by an expedition led by Jim King in August 1992. With a depth of 200m (660ft), Dean's Blue Hole is one of the largest in the Bahamas and has over 1200m (1320yd) of survey line laid, in an area approaching the size of a sports stadium. Open to the sea, the top of the hole is a steeply sloping sand slope dotted with coral heads, all smothered in snapper and grunt. Visibility is often superb, allowing divers and snorkellers to see each other in the clear water. However, although the cavern is massive, divers can explore only the upper layers, which makes the dive quite short.

3 STELLA MARIS SHARK REEF
★★★★

Location: 20 minutes west of Stella Maris Marina, midway between Long Island and Sandy Cay.
Access: By boat only.
Conditions: Choppy surface conditions, but little or no surge or current.
Average depth: 11m (36ft)
Maximum depth: 11m (36ft)
Average visibility: 15m (50ft)
The Stella Maris Dive Resort started shark feeding here over 30 years ago. Originally finding a patch reef which had a family of Caribbean reef sharks (*Carcharhinus perezi*), divers visited the reef regularly and continued to encounter the sharks. Slowly, by introducing some fish bait into the arena, they induced more sharks to appear and gradually, over the years, the engine noise of a boat has become enough to attract the sharks. Even without feeding, the sharks come very close to the divers, making for excellent photographic opportunities. A small amount of bait in the form of friendly fish harpooned on the nearby reefs was eaten by the 12 to 16 sharks, but I have the word of the resort's owners that spearing fish is now totally banned and that this bait is no longer used.

4 THREE SISTERS
★★★

Location: Due west of Hog Cay.
Access: By boat only, about 15 minutes from the dock.
Conditions: Choppy on the surface; slight current.
Average depth: 12m (40ft)
Maximum depth: 15m (50ft)
Average visibility: 20m (66ft)
These three coral patches, or bommies, all have a split canyon running through them and are home to small schools of horse-eye jacks, snapper and grunt. Sea fans can be found on the top of the reef and thousands of fairy basslets under the overhangs, their vivid neon bodies flashing in the sunlight. These reefs are also home to one of the sharks which attends the feeding at Site 3,

recognizable by the cut in its dorsal fin and several large parasites. Extremely territorial, this shark will buzz divers, considerably heightening the experience of the dive.

5 FLAMINGO TONGUE REEF
★★★★★★

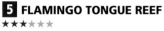

Location: Due west of the Stella Maris beach *cabañas*.
Access: By boat only, but snorkelling can be done on the patch reef directly out from the *cabañas*.
Conditions: Little or no current.
Average depth: 6m (20ft)
Maximum depth: 10m (33ft)
Average visibility: 15m (50ft)
This shallow strip and patch reef is named after the large numbers of flamingo tongue shells (*Cyphoma gibbosum*) on the sea fans and sea plumes. All of the small coral patches have overhangs, under which lobsters sit and wave their antennae. Golden stingrays (*Urolophus jamaicensis*) can be seen flitting over the sand as well as spotted moray eels and large numbers of snapper and grunt.

6 THE COMBERBACH
★★★★

Location: West of the Cape Santa Maria Resort beach.
Access: By boat only, about 20 minutes from the dock.
Conditions: Surface chop and a slight northerly current.
Average depth: 25m (82ft)
Maximum depth: 31m (104ft)
Average visibility: 23m (75ft)
The *Comberbach* was a 30m (100ft) steel-hulled coastal freighter which was deliberately sunk by Stella Maris in 1989. Completely intact and sitting upright, the ship has now become home to large numbers of snapper, grunt and parrotfish that graze on the algae, corals and sponges which have now completely covered the wreck. The engine room is accessible, as are the holds, the forward part of which contains a wrecked Volkswagen van. About 30m (100ft) south of the *Comberbach* are the remains of a yacht destroyed during a recent hurricane.

7 SOUTHAMPTON REEF
★★★★★★

Location: Northwest of Conception Island.
Access: By boat only, two hours from Stella Maris.
Conditions: Generally rough waters, but sheltered in amongst the coral heads.
Average depth: 9m (30ft)
Maximum depth: Beyond 70m (230ft)
Average visibility: 23m (75ft)

Southampton Reef is a huge barrier reef system which stretches off to the northwest of Conception Island. The reef was badly damaged during the last major hurricane and the safe entry into the inner lagoon was blocked by fallen elkhorn coral, so little diving is now done, except on an exploratory basis. A smashed-up, unknown wreck can be found to the northwest, which is home to large numbers of snapper, grunt, parrotfish and wrasse.

8 CONCEPTION ISLAND REEF
★★★★★

Location: A few minutes from the shore of Conception Island.
Access: By boat only, two hours from Stella Maris.
Conditions: Sheltered lagoon, no current.
Average depth: 6m (20ft)
Maximum depth: 9m (30ft)
Average visibility: 15m (50ft)
This delightful snorkelling reef is in excellent condition, with only a small handful of divers arriving each week from Stella Maris or from live-aboard dive boats. The underhanging coral heads are cut with small holes under which live the largest numbers of fairy basslets (*Gramma loreto*) I have ever seen. There are moray eels, the rare golden variety of the coney, and plentiful numbers of queen triggerfish.

9 CONCEPTION ISLAND WALL
★★★★★★★

Location: Southwest of Conception Island.
Access: By boat only, two hours from Stella Maris.
Conditions: Surface chop, slight surge and current.
Average depth: 18m (60ft)
Maximum depth: Beyond 70m (230ft)
Average visibility: 45m (150ft), but can be reduced in rainy season.
Conception Island Wall has about ten mooring buoys placed along the southern wall to avoid any anchor damage to this national park and bird and turtle sanctuary. The island is actually an atoll with a large, sheltered, shallow inner lagoon where dive boats often anchor up for the night. Unfortunately, during the rainy season the lagoon can flood and spew its muddy discharge over the south wall, reducing the visibility.

The drop-off starts at around 18m (60ft) and drops vertically in many places into the abyss. The whole of the south shore wall is cut by numerous sand chutes forming fascinating gullies and canyons, most of which have horse-eye jacks schooling around the various cleaning stations. Blacktip sharks and turtles are seen on most dives, as is a huge barracuda which hangs out under the dive boat and can be approached to within a few centimetres of its nose. This site has some wonderful diving.

10 SNOWFIELDS
★★★☆☆☆☆☆☆

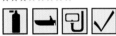

Location: West around Sandy Point on Rum Cay, then north to the large patch reef.
Access: By boat only, 25 minutes from the marina.
Conditions: Can experience surge and slight southerly current, but protected from the prevailing winds.
Average depth: 5m (17ft)
Maximum depth: 6m (20ft)
Average visibility: 25m (80ft)
Snowfields is better suited to snorkelling than diving due to the consistently shallow depth of this large patch reef system. The last major hurricane which swept through here destroyed much of the larger elkhorn coral (*Acropora palmata*), allowing several species of algae to colonize the damaged areas. Though there are never enough sea urchins and algae grazers to keep the rapid algal growth

---

Hanging vine algae carpet large portions of the deeper overhangs off the reef wall.

at bay, there are excellent small boulder and brain corals, pillar corals and star corals. You can find most varieties of wrasse here as well as parrotfish, angelfish, butterflyfish, small grouper and coney (*Epinephelus fulvus*), particularly in its rarer golden phase coloration.

11 GRANDPA GROUPER
★★★★

Location: Virtually due south of Port Nelson on Rum Cay, at the corner of the drop-off.
Access: By boat only.
Conditions: Surface chop and current can be expected.
Average depth: 20m (66ft)
Maximum depth: Beyond 70m (230ft)
Average visibility: Over 30m (100ft)
This is a typical deep wall site with lots of swim-throughs, holes and coral canyons. The top of the reef crest is quite deep at around 18m (60ft), and, as all this section of the reef involves deep diving to over 30m (100ft), it is generally beyond the scope of novice divers. There are some huge boulders which rise from the sand at 21m (70ft) and come to within 6m (20ft) of the surface, plus many cracks, holes and fissures created by fresh-water run-off and overlapping sheet

corals. The undersides of all these overhangs have delicate small sponges, black corals, fan leaf algae (*Lobophora vareigata*) and hanging vines (*Halimeda* spp.). Black jacks (*Caranx lugubris*) always patrol this reef, along with several large barracuda.

12 THE CHIMNEY
★★★★

Location: Northeast from Grandpa Grouper (Site 11).
Access: By boat only.
Conditions: Experiences surface swell, shallow surge and current; can be blown out in rough weather.
Average depth: 30m (100ft)
Maximum depth: Beyond 70m (230ft)
Average visibility: Over 30m (100ft)
The top of the reef along this section is almost flat coral substrate; beyond, a vertical shaft drops down from 21m (70ft) to 30m (100ft), then travels out to the wall another 10m (11yd). The shaft makes a spectacular start to the dive and, with the hole only 3–4m (10–15ft) in diameter, you must be very careful not to touch the sides or dislodge any of the fragile corals or sponges. Horse-eye jacks, turtles and barracuda are common along the wall, as are wire corals, barrel sponges and elephant ear sponges.

13 BARRACUDA JUNCTION
★★★★

Location: Northeast from The Chimney (Site 12).
Access: By boat only.
Conditions: Experiences surface swell, shallow surge and current; can be blown out in rough weather.
Average depth: 30m (100ft)
Maximum depth: Beyond 70m (230ft)
Average visibility: Over 30m (100ft)
This is a deep section of reef which starts at around 21m (70ft) and drops vertically over the wall. There are several underhanging coral ledges created by sheet corals at around 33–45m (110–150ft). There are always large schools of horse-eye jacks (*Caranx latus*) and big

---

TUBE WORMS

Tube worms come in a number of varieties and sizes. All are sensitive to light and pressure and to observe them closely you must approach them very slowly. They are topped with colourful radioles, often spiral in shape. When taking photographs, it is better to use a longer-focusing lens so as not to disturb them. You may get only one chance, as the light from any flash will cause the worm to react and retreat rapidly back into its protective tube.

---

red grouper (*Epihephelus morio*); the latter are very similar to Nassau grouper, except that they have a smooth-topped dorsal fin and no black spot at the start of the tail. This site is popular with photographers due to frequent sightings of large barracuda. Looking down and away from you as the sandy slope starts at around 50m (165ft), you may also catch sight of the resident nurse shark (*Ginglymostoma cirratum*).

14 HMS CONQUEROR
★★★★★

Location: East of Rum Cay, opposite Sumner Point on the shallow fringing reef.
Access: By boat only.
Conditions: Can be choppy with surge due to shallow water conditions and exposed location.
Average depth: 6m (20ft)
Maximum depth: 9m (30ft)
Average visibility: 15m (50ft)
HMS *Conqueror* was a 101-gun British man-o'-war which sank on New Year's Day 1862. Lying in only 9m (30ft), the wreck is visible from the air and has been declared a historical site by the Bahamas government. A wooden-hulled, three-masted steam sailing vessel with a single screw propeller, she is now completely broken up with cannon, cannonballs, winches, anchors and bronze spikes scattered all over the reef amidst good stands of elkhorn coral. The site is not visited that often due to its exposed nature and the need for near-perfect conditions before it can be dived or snorkelled.

15 TATOO EXPRESS WRECK
★★★★★

Location: To the north of Rum Cay, on the barrier reef opposite Gin Hill.
Access: By boat only.
Conditions: Generally experiences surface swell, shallow surge and current; can be blown out in rough weather.
Average depth: 8m (27ft)
Maximum depth: 12m (40ft)
Average visibility: 15m (50ft)
This Haitian coastal freighter, which was carrying three motor cars, 150 bicycles and hundreds of pairs of shoes, collided with the reef after experiencing engine failure on its way from Miami to Haiti in 1995. Now completely wrecked, the ship's remains are quickly becoming overgrown in algae and small coral growths. Parrotfish, wrasse, sergeant majors, Bermuda chub, snapper and grunt have all made this unfortunate ship their home. It is a popular snorkelling site, but worth it only if you are in the general area.

How to Get There

By air
There are four runways on Long Island for private aircraft, of which Stella Maris is the only point of entry and by far the most popular. Bahamasair has a daily service from Nassau which is routed through Deadman's Cay. Island Express operates from Fort Lauderdale in Florida to Stella Maris from Thursday to Sunday. Stella Maris also have their own private service which operates around the islands and from Nassau. Rum Cay has its own point-of-entry airport and Bahamasair flies here twice weekly. Charter flights are also available from San Salvador to Rum Cay. Normal return fares from Nassau to either Rum Cay or Stella Maris are around $150 return with a 44lb weight restriction.

By boat
The mail boat MV *Abilin* makes a weekly trip from Nassau to Clarence Town in the south of Long Island on Mondays and takes around 18 hours. The cost of the service is around $45. You can reach Rum Cay by boat from Stella Maris, which takes around four hours. Conception Island is uninhabited and can be reached only by charter boat, live-aboard dive boat or private yacht.

Vehicle Hire

Stella Maris Resort has a few vehicles for hire as well as bicycles. There are no car hire facilities on any of the other islands in this group.

Long Island is the only place that you will find taxis, as you will either be picked up at the local airstrip by a hotel representative (if they know that you are coming), or may catch a lift from one of the locals who tend to hang around looking for tips. The cost from Stella Maris airport to the Stella Marais Resort is $3, but it will cost you $100 if you land at Deadman's Cay and need to get to Stella Maris.

Where to Stay

Long Island
Stella Maris Resort Club, PO Box LI30105, Stella Maris, Long Island; US tel (800) 426 0466 or (305) 359 8236, fax (305) 359 8238, local tel (242) 336 2106, fax (242) 338 2052; e-mail smrc@stellamarisresort.com. The divers' resort on Long Island, with two pools and reasonable but pricey food. The rooms are

in need of some renovation, and there are no telephones, except at reception.

Cape Santa Maria Beach Resort, Long Island; US tel (800) 663 7090, fax (604) 598 1361, local tel/fax (242) 357 1006. A luxury upmarket resort catering to sports fishermen, with no telephones or TV, except at reception.

Lochaber Beach Lodge, PO Box N30330, Clarence Town, Long Island; no telephone. Two delightful, self-contained beach apartments away from it all.

Rum Cay
At the time of going to press, the Rum Cay Club was closed and up for sale, so no accommodation was available. Some live-aboard dive boats may venture this far.

Where to Eat

As with most of the Family Islands, the hotels generally have good-quality restaurants and divers tend to remain in their hotels to eat. However, meals can be expensive and local restaurants offer much better value as well as some excellent fresh seafood. The township supermarkets all have everything that you need if you want to save money.

Harbour Restaurant, Dock Side, Clarence Town, Long Island. Local specialities such as blackened grouper and guava duff are excellent.

Da Danz Club and Restaurant, Morrisville, Long Island. Serves native mutton, wild boar and great breakfasts.

Dive Facilities

Stella Maris Dive Resort and Marina, Stella Maris Resort, Long Island; tel (242) 338 2051 or 336 2106, fax (242) 338 2052. Originator of the shark-feeding dive, a fairly professional operation with weekly ventures to blue holes and Conception Island.

Rum Cay Dive Centre, Rum Cay; no telephone. Limited facilities and open only on request, but due to be expanded.

Emergency Facilities

There are a couple of small clinics on Long Island, but in general terms, if

there are any serious medical emergencies, or potential problems, you must arrange for the fastest and safest possible airlift to Nassau or Miami.

Doctor's residence, Long Island, tel (242) 337 0555.

Nurse's residence, Long Island, tel (242) 337 0666.

The nearest **recompression chamber** is at Lyford Cay Hospital in Nassau on New Providence Island, tel (242) 362 4025.

Local Highlights

Long Island
The **churches** near Clarence Town built by Father Jerome are beautiful, and one offers splendid views of the southern end of the island from its bell tower. Open all the time.

Paul Constantakis is a Greek sponge fisherman who harvests local sponges and exports them to the USA as well as back to Greece. He can be found behind the supermarket in Pettis.

Deadman's Cay is the main town and has **Arawak paintings** in some of the local caves, many of which have still not been fully explored.

Beaches

All beaches in the Bahamas are open to the public and free of charge. Charges may be made to enter a marine park or biosphere reserve. Topless sunbathing is usually forbidden, although it is now tolerated in some beach areas of Nassau. Resorts such as Small Hope Bay on Andros have a screened, segregated area for those who want to go topless. Few of the beaches have lifeguards and many are often affected by heavy sea swell and undercurrents.

If you get caught in an undertow or are being pulled out to sea, do not panic. The golden rule is to swim parallel to the shore and after 15m (17yd) conditions should have changed to allow you easier access back to shore. Water-condition flags are posted at many beaches. Pay attention to them.

Several species of mangrove tree are found in the Bahamas, for the most part forming extensive impenetrable tracts of shrubbery where few people venture. In Bimini, for example, the most common is the red mangrove (*Rhizophora mangle*) which grows over 6m (20ft) high and extends all around the inner Bimini lagoon from the high tide level on the island into the shallow flats. The black mangrove (*Avicennia marina*), the largest of the species, growing to over 9m (30ft), is more commonly found in the southern Bahamas. Areas such as the Marls off Abaco are a maze of shallow winding channels with mangrove 'islands' that play home to West Indian tree ducks, frigate birds, egrets and pelicans. Indeed, virtually all the sheltered western bays of the Bahamas are swathed in mangroves, with the largest areas being found on Andros.

A pioneering plant, the mangrove is able to survive in salt water and extend its roots deep into softer coral and mud substrates. The black mangrove (*Avicennia marina*) has offshoot respiratory or knee roots (pneumatophores) which project above the water level. These have numerous holes (lenticels) through which air enters, passing through soft spongy tissue down to the roots beneath the mud.

The red mangrove (*Rhizophora mangle*) produces adventitious roots that descend into the muddy substrate in an arched fashion, offering maximum strength and support for the parent plant that produces the fruit. As soon as these roots strike the mud, often some distance from the parent, they produce a new shoot, quickly forming a thick stem and new trunks, thus rapidly colonizing sheltered lagoons.

MANGROVE FORESTS

As the mangrove forest grows, accumulated debris from fallen leaves, birds' nests, droppings and flotsam becomes tangled in the roots. This collects and gradually builds into dry land, extending and altering the shape of the island.

It is around the water-bound root systems that major fish hatcheries and nurseries are found, with huge numbers of snapper and grunt always found in the shallows, quite often surrounded by fry. Looking closely amongst the mangrove roots you will find that they also host many other marine species,

such as sponges, tunicates, small anemones and hydroids. The surrounding muddy banks are host to several species of eel grass or turtle grass (such as *Thalassia testudinum* and *Syringodium filiforme*), which further anchor the muddy bottom.

Whilst diving from Great Exuma, I noticed that the interior of Elizabeth Harbour was filled with upside down jellyfish (*Cassiopea xamachana*), which clustered around the shore and under the dense fringing mangrove forest. These jellyfish would lift off and 'pulse' their way amongst the mangroves, resting on the bottom from time to time with their arms raised upwards, often resembling small plants. They raise their arms upwards to

Above: *Mangrove roots are home to many species of invertebrates and juvenile fish.*
Opposite: *Upside-down jellyfish (Cassiopea frondosa) are associated with mangrove beds.*

speed the growth of the symbiotic single-celled algae, or zooxanthellae, from which they receive nourishment.

Largely ignored, mangrove forests are an essential part of the Bahamas, as they are responsible for the present-day shape of much of the coastline. They are also an important ecosystem, offering a safe haven for many different species of fish and invertebrates and their young, all of which will eventually move out to populate the nearby reefs.

SAN SALVADOR

L ocated 320km (200 miles) southeast of New Providence, San Salvador is said to have been the original landfall of Christopher Columbus in 1492. In 1986, however, a *National Geographic* article put his landfall 90km (60 miles) to the southeast at Samana Cay. Controversy raged for years, but today the consensus among scholars is that San Salvador is still the most likely island, and that Columbus landed at Long Bay on the sheltered western side, where a large stone cross now stands – site of a local celebration on the anniversary each year.

Later, Captain John Watling, a notorious English pirate, used the island as a base. From the 17th century onwards the island became known as Watling's Island, until the Bahamian legislature changed the name back to San Salvador in 1926.

The island is 20km (12 miles) long by 8km (5 miles) wide and can be circum-navigated on a single road. The few settlements and individual houses are located along this road, circling the island and its swampy interior. The main township is Cockburn Town, south of the airport, where most of the local services can be found, as well as a small museum.

Famous for its crystal clear and flat calm waters, San Salvador is known as the top wall diving destination in the Bahamas. The walls are for the most part pristine and vertical in many areas, though hurricanes do take their toll and there is evidence of damaged corals on the reeftop. All the dive sites have mooring buoys to prevent anchor damage and divers are lectured on reef etiquette and buoyancy control by their dive masters before each dive.

The diving operators on the island have placed 48 mooring buoys in total around the island, and a further 20 sheltered sand holes, clear of any reefs, are used as anchor drops, primarily for snorkelling on the shallower patch reefs which are protected from the worst of the weather.

Opposite: *The Riding Rock Inn dive boat leaves its marina for one of San Salvador's superb dive sites.*
Above: *Painted tunicates (Clavelina picta) are often found attached to coral plumes.*

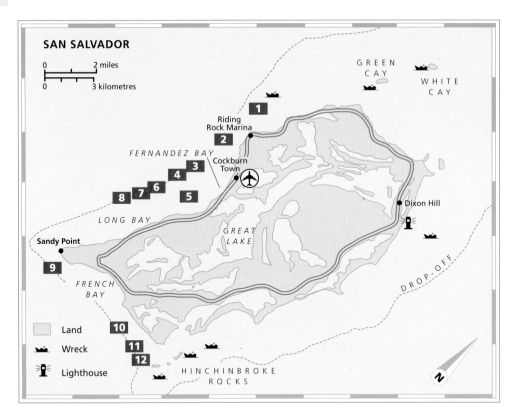

SAN SALVADOR

0 | 2 miles
0 | 3 kilometres

GREEN CAY
WHITE CAY

1

Riding Rock Marina
2

FERNANDEZ BAY
Cockburn Town
3
4

6
7
8
5

Dixon Hill

LONG BAY

GREAT LAKE

Sandy Point

9

FRENCH BAY

DROP-OFF

Land
Wreck
Lighthouse
10
11
12
HINCHINBROKE ROCKS

N

---

1 FRASCATE WRECK

★★☆☆☆☆

Location: North of the airport, opposite Club Med.
Access: By boat, seven minutes from Riding Rock Marina.
Conditions: Surge can be expected as it is so shallow.
Average depth: 2m (6ft)
Maximum depth: 5m (17ft)
Average visibility: 9m (30ft)

This steel-hulled coastal freighter was en route from England to Jamaica when she came to grief on this shallow reef on 1 January 1902. The 80m (262ft) vessel broke up quickly in a number of subsequent storms and, after being deemed a navigational hazard, salvagers moved in with explosives and stripped her of her copper and brass, as well as the propeller. The *Frascate* now lies strewn over 2000m^2 (half an acre) of seabed. The boilers are lying on their sides and you can actually snorkel through one of them, although this is not recommended as there is encrusting fire coral (*Millepora alcicornis*) everywhere. Winches, propshaft and tons of overlapping steel plate are now home to schools of parrotfish, wrasse and surgeonfish.

2 RIDING ROCK WALL

★★★☆☆

Location: Opposite Riding Rock Marina.
Access: By boat only, five minutes from the dock.
Conditions: Slight surge and current; can be choppy.
Average depth: 14m (47ft)
Maximum depth: Beyond 70m (230ft)
Average visibility: 30m (100ft)

The wall here runs parallel to the shore, directly in front of the hotel. The depth at the mooring is 12m (40ft) but, as you travel north, the edge of the wall drops down to around 20m (66ft), so be careful of your dive profile as this site is usually done as a second or third dive of the day (or a night dive).

Turtles are present, and can be approached quite easily. Small groups of horse-eye jacks buzz divers and there are large overhanging stands of wire coral, black coral and deep water gorgonians. At night, the reef crest is topped with different coloured basket starfish (*Astrophyton muricatum*), clinging to sea fans and sea plumes, their multi-jointed arms stretched out into the slight current.

3 TELEPHONE POLE

★★★★★★☆☆

Location: Opposite Hill Landing, about seven minutes south from Riding Rock Marina.
Access: By boat only.
Conditions: Slight surge on the reeftop, but calm over the drop-off.
Average depth: 12m (40ft)
Maximum depth: Beyond 70m (230ft)
Average visibility: 30m (100ft)

This is the closest good site to the marina. On entering the water you are likely to be met by a very gregarious Nassau grouper (*Epinephelus striatus*) called Oscar. If ever you want a grouper in your face, this is the spot, and, well used to being handled, Oscar will pose for the queuing photographers. The dive itself is down through a dropping sand chute which has formed a cavern and channel, cutting through the vertical drop-off. The site is named after a telephone pole that has broken in two: one half stretches across the mouth of the main part of the cavern entrance, while the other half is wedged in the outer cave next to the entry point on the wall at 25m (83ft).

Clouds of creole wrasse (*Clepticus parrai*) hover mid-water, picking off passing planktonic morsels. Just to the north of the crevice where the sandy plain abuts the reef crest, a huge purple sea plume (*Pseudopterogorgia americana*) can be found. Also at the edge of the sand plain there are golden stingrays and peacock flounders. This is a dive not to be missed for the sheer quality of the canyon and the pristine marine life.

4 VICKY'S REEF

★★★★☆

Location: Directly out to the drop-off from the Snapshot reef (Site 5).
Access: By boat only.
Conditions: Can be choppy on the surface, with slight surge and current.
Average depth: 17m (57ft)
Maximum depth: Beyond 70m (230ft)
Average visibility: 30m (100ft)

The mooring buoy is set into a huge sandy area which runs from Snapshot (Site 5) all the way out to the lip of the coral reef. There are huge numbers of garden eels (*Heteroconger halis*) on the sandy floor, amidst mounds of sand which have been created by lugworms. As you reach the edge of the wall, the stony corals rise up to 12m (40ft) before dropping precipitously on the other side.

> ### SILVERSIDES
>
> Silversides are actually juveniles of four separate species which group together in large aggregations for protection. From early summer through September several areas around the Bahamian islands are host to literally thousands of these fish. Inhabiting some of the deeper recesses in shipwrecks, caves and canyons, they prefer areas with several exits. When you are swimming through them, they move as a single entity, ever changing shape and form. Jacks, tarpon and barracuda are always seen within the vicinity of these massive shoals and can be observed attacking in what appears like very strategic planning, surrounding, herding and then rushing in for the kill.

The wall has a vertical and underhanging drop down to about 33m (110ft), where the first of several indented lips is formed. Huge orange elephant ear sponges (*Agelas clathrodes*) are found in profusion as are wire corals (*Ellisella barbadensis*). It is worth looking closely at the wire corals, as you may spot the extremely rare whip coral shrimp (*Pereclimenes amboinensis*), only previously recorded in Indo-Pacific waters. Turtles and Caribbean reef sharks are common in this area of the wall.

5 SNAPSHOT

★★★★☆☆☆☆☆

Location: Midway down Fernandez Bay opposite Hill Landing, ten minutes' ride from the Riding Rock Marina.
Access: By boat only.
Conditions: Can experience slight surge, but generally sheltered.
Average depth: 3m (10ft)
Maximum depth: 5m (17ft)
Average visibility: 30m (100ft)

This is a wonderful shallow site, perfect for photography and snorkelling. A favourite with many people, Snapshot is a series of coral patches amidst a white powder sand basin. It acts as a natural oasis for large schools of squirrelfish, snapper and grunt. Rock beauties (*Holacanthus tricolor*) are everywhere, as are saddled blennies (*Malacoctenus triangulatus*) and masked gobies (*Coryphopterus lipernes*), the only goby which tends to school in large numbers.

There are yellowhead jawfish in the sand patches and damselfish laying eggs on the stalks of seawhips and fans. This location is also home to a large number of anemones (*Condylactis giganteus*) and Pederson's cleaner shrimps can be found all over. There is no shortage of photographic subjects and, with over one hour of permitted bottom time, it is a great place to explore and photograph the animals away from the deeper walls. It is also the only place I know where schools of squirrelfish can be found during the day.

6 SHANGRI-LA
★★★★☆☆

Location: Opposite Hill Landing, about 15 minutes south from Riding Rock Marina.
Access: By boat only.
Conditions: Slight surge on the reeftop, but calm over the drop-off.
Average depth: 12m (40ft)
Maximum depth: Beyond 70m (230ft)
Average visibility: 30m (100ft)

Shangri-La is a huge amphitheatre-shaped indentation in the edge of the wall. The wall has a vertical face until about 24m (80ft) and then undercuts; here larger whip corals, orange sponges and barrel sponges are found. Every small hole on the reef wall has a longfin squirrelfish (*Holocentrus rufus*) at its entrance. Again, just as at other sites in this area, tiny shrimps of Pereclimenes genus can sometimes be found on the olive-green whip corals. The shrimps are similar to a species found in the Indo-Pacific, and it is a mystery how they came to be in the Bahamas.

7 DEVIL'S CLAW
★★★★★☆☆

Location: 10 minutes south of Riding Rock Marina on the outer wall.
Access: By boat only.
Conditions: Can be choppy on the surface, with slight current running south to north.
Average depth: 15m (50ft)
Maximum depth: Beyond 70m (230ft)
Average visibility: 30m (100ft)

Devil's Claw is named after three deep slashes in the outer wall, down which divers can descend from 15m (50ft) and come out at around 30m (100ft). All three canyons meet together at a single huge coral head which, when viewed from above, looks like the pad of a hand with the gullies being the three fingers.

There are hundreds of wire corals spiralling into the depths here. Small groups of black jacks (*Caranx lugubris*) intermingle with big Bermuda chub (*Kyphosus sectatrix*) – keeping just out of arm's length, they will accompany you for most of the dive. Keep looking out to sea and below you as there are always sightings of sharks along this wall, as well as turtles, barracuda and the occasional tarpon. This area is also home to a large number of diamond-backed blennies (*Malacoctenus boehlkei*), as well as arrow blennies, whip coral shrimps and schools of black durgon (*Melichthys niger*). This is an excellent site, not to be missed.

8 GARDENER'S REEF
★★★★★☆☆

Location: Opposite the Columbus Monument, Long Bay.
Access: By boat only.
Conditions: Surface chop and northerly current.
Average depth: 15m (50ft)
Maximum depth: Beyond 70m (230ft)
Average visibility: 30m (100ft)

This is a deeper, barely defined spur and groove reef which runs perpendicular to the shore. The spurs and grooves are low-lying, and merge in and out of each other, with few or no sand patches, until they reach the edge of the drop-off. Here they cut almost vertically into the wall as if they had been scooped out by an ice cream scoop, with perfectly rounded sides, disappearing into the depths. The lip of the reef has rounded and indented edges tumbling into overhangs and caves in clearly defined steps at 10m (33ft) intervals. Sheet corals such as *Agaricia lamarcki* and *Agaricia undata* are common, as is the venus sea fan (*Gorgonia flabellum*).

The top of the reef is fringed by a constantly moving shoal of blue chromis (*Chromis cyanea*) and bluehead wrasse (*Thalassoma bifasciatum*). Solitary barracuda are always lingering, as are the ubiquitous schools of yellowtail snapper, black durgon and Bermuda chub.

9 DOUBLE CAVES
★★★★★

Location: Round from Sandy Point at French Bay.
Access: By boat, 30 minutes from Riding Rock Marina.
Conditions: Surge on the reeftop; calm at the drop-off.
Average depth: 15m (50ft)
Maximum depth: Beyond 70m (230ft)
Average visibility: 30m (100ft)

One of the best dives on the island, Double Caves is much more than the name implies. The dive is generally conducted through one cave system to the outer wall, returning back to the inner reef through another, and is not just two clearly defined caves. The winding channels of the caves are open to the reeftop in many cases and have vertical sides, encrusted in coral 15m (50ft) high. As you enter the outer area of the wall at 33m (110ft), look directly down to a white sloping sandy area where you will usually see hammerhead sharks.

The caverns and swim-throughs are an absolute delight and, although the reef crest was badly damaged by hurricanes, the walls and crevices are teeming with life. Huge black coral trees (*Antipathes* spp.) are everywhere, as are deep-water gorgonian sea fans (*Iciligorgia schrammi*), sheet corals and star corals.

Above: *The Frascate was wrecked in January 1902 on a very shallow reef (Site 1).*
Below: *Snorkellers can swim through the massive boilers of the Frascate.*

10 LA CREVASSE
★★★★★☆☆

Location: East of French Bay.
Access: By boat, but can be done from the shore.
Conditions: Surge and chop on the reeftop; current.
Average depth: 12m (40ft)
Maximum depth: Beyond 70m (230ft)
Average visibility: 30m (100ft)

This site is very similar to Double Caves (Site 9) but multiplied in size several times over, with some huge crevasses over 15m (50ft) deep. The outside wall has a near vertical face which then undercuts where the larger corals and sponges are found. The convolutions of the interconnecting gullies and caverns will keep the most avid underwater explorer happy.

Sponges are everywhere, but perhaps the most obvious differences between the southern French Bay sites and the Fernandez Bay/Long Bay sites is the fact that there is much less algae on the corals. Hanging vine (*Halimeda goreaui*) can be found under most of the overhangs, but by comparison many of the west coast sites are being smothered by network algae (*Microdictyon marinum*).

11 GREAT CUT
★★★★★☆☆

Location: East from La Crevasse (Site 10).
Access: By boat or a lengthy swim from shore.
Conditions: Surface swell and current to be expected.
Average depth: 18m (60ft)
Maximum depth: Beyond 70m (230ft)
Average visibility: Over 30m (100ft)

This is a deep gulley which starts at around 11m (36ft) and bisects the wall. Following a swim-through to the outer wall, under a coral dome, you appear on the outer wall at around 33–45m (110–150ft). There are always large schools of horse-eye jacks (*Caranx latus*), big Nassau grouper (*Epihephelus striatus*), and several species of snapper and grunt which prefer the reef crest. Wire corals spiral out into the blue and huge barrel sponges and orange-coloured elephant ear sponges predominate. Fairy basslets (*Gramma loreto*) are everywhere, as are several types of cleaning goby and wrasse.

12 DR JOHN'S
★★★★★☆☆☆

Location: At the eastern end of the island.
Access: Generally by boat, but can be a shore dive.
Conditions: Generally surface chop and slight current.
Average depth: 15m (50ft)
Maximum depth: Beyond 70m (230ft)
Average visibility: Over 30m (100ft)

This is a near vertical wall which starts at around 12m (40ft) and plummets to 40m (130ft), where you will encounter a sloping sand ledge. Deeply cut with fissures, the wall features deep-water gorgonians (*Iciligorgia schrammi*) as well as good stands of black coral (*Antipathes* spp.); look closely at this fine coral for arrow blennies (*Lucayablennius zingaro*), which flit amongst the fronds with a rapid flick of their coiled tail. There is not as much fish life as on other sections of the reef, but there is less algae.

Brittlestars (Ophiothrix suensonii) are only seen at night, when they crawl onto sponges.

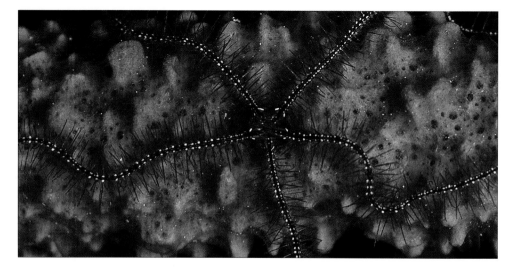

HOW TO GET THERE

By air
Bahamasair fly into San Salvador from Nassau every day except Saturday, but the schedule can be somewhat erratic and delays are to be expected. American Eagle fly from Miami and Nassau direct to San Salvador. Club Med offers charter flights on Saturdays and Sundays to their resort from Miami, while Riding Rock Inn offers charters from Fort Lauderdale. You can also arrange your own charters to San Salvador from Nassau and some Family Islands.

By boat
The mail boat MV *Maxine* leaves Potter's Cay in Nassau each Tuesday for both San Salvador and Rum Cay. The trip takes around 18 hours and costs $40; tel (242) 393 1064.

VEHICLE HIRE

Riding Rock Inn has vehicles for hire from **C&S Car Rental** at $85 per day and bicycles at $10 per day; tel: (242) 331 2631 or 331 2714.

Dorett's Car Hire and Grocery Store has jeeps and cars for hire, also at $85 per day; tel (242) 331 2184.

WHERE TO STAY

Riding Rock Inn Resort, San Salvador; tel (242) 331 2631/2 or (800) 272 1492, fax (242) 331 2020. Fort Lauderdale Booking Office tel (305) 359 8353, fax (305) 359 8254, e-mail RidingRock@aol.com. The oldest resort on the island, with a sea view from most rooms. Dive packages available.

Club Med–Columbus Isle, San Salvador; tel (242) 331-2000 or (800) 258 2633, fax (242) 331 2222. Said by some to be the best Club Med in the world, this resort has an upmarket design, imported antique fittings and expansive layout, and often runs at full occupancy. There are 250 rooms, but only one swimming pool.

WHERE TO EAT

Club Med–Columbus Isle has the best food on the island. It costs non-residents around $35 for dinner and show, which includes wine on the table, beer or soft drinks, making it the most economical meal on the island. It is possible to stay at Riding Rock Inn and eat at Club Med.

Riding Rock Inn has a restricted menu, with only fish or meat. Their conch chowder is reckoned to be the best on San Salvador. Conch is a staple food of the islands and is offered in one form or another every day.

Three Ships Restaurant in Cockburn Town has Bahamian-style cooking, with steaks, fresh fish and conch dishes; tel (242) 331 2787.

Charlie's Sunrise Lounge, south of Cockburn Town overlooking the ocean, has a similar menu to the Three Ships; tel (242) 331 2012.

DIVE FACILITIES

Guanahani Dive Ltd., Riding Rock Inn, San Salvador; tel (242) 331 2631/2 or (800) 272 1492, fax (242) 331 2020. Fort Lauderdale Booking Office tel (305) 359 8353, fax (305) 359 8254, e-mail RidingRock@aol.com Has three dive boats and full diving instruction classes to all levels and includes underwater photography as its main speciality. There is a very large retail shop, weekly slide shows and a great club atmosphere catering for dive clubs, small groups and single divers.

Club Med–Columbus Isle Dive Centre, San Salvador; tel (242) 331 2000 or (800) 258 2633, fax (242) 331 2222. All diving costs are included in the Club Med price except hire of wetsuits and computers. Their four dive boats are able to handle around 170 divers per day and 50 snorkellers. It is a more impersonal operation and has only a small shop, but it has the latest equipment and a safety recompression chamber.

FILM PROCESSING

Full E6 slide processing, as well as video editing, camera hire, photography courses and slide shows, is available from **Chris McLaughlin's Underwater Photo Center** at Riding Rock Inn, tel (242) 331 2631, fax (242) 331-2020, e-mail hafleuss@aol.com.

EMERGENCY INFORMATION

Club Med has a recompression chamber on site. Although they are affiliated to DAN, it is important to contact DAN first as the chamber at Club Med should be used in emergency only. The treatment costs $600 per hour and your insurance company might hesitate about covering it. Treatment, including airlift to Mercy Hospital in Miami, is free to all Club Med guests.

Club Med operate on VHF Channel 69 during diving hours and on Channel 10 for a 24 hour emergency service. Riding Rock Inn Dive Centre operates standby on Channel 6 for any such emergencies.

Other than the Club Med facility, the closest recompression chambers are at UNEXSO in Freeport, Grand Bahama, or Nassau, New Providence.

There is a small **Government Clinic** in Cockburn Town, tel (242) 331 2105, which is not equipped for major emergencies, although a new clinic and small island hospital are nearing completion. The medical facilities at Club Med are much better at present.

COLUMBUS

Columbus' pioneering voyage on the *Santa Maria* in 1492 was plagued by superstition, near mutiny and, finally, a lack of water and supplies. Then, after ten weeks at sea, a lookout on an accompanying caravel, the *Pinta*, gave the cry for land. Columbus' log stated, 'This island is quite large and very flat, with very green trees and many waters and with a very large lake in the centre, without any mountain' – a fairly accurate description of present-day San Salvador. The local Lucayan Indians called the island Guanahani (Land of Many Lakes), but Columbus gave it the name San Salvador (Our Saviour). He wrote that the local inhabitants were a simple and humble people who offered help in exchange for goods such as flour, nails, shovels and glass.

J's Discount Drugs in Cockburn Town stocks certain medical supplies; tel/fax (242) 331 2750.

LOCAL HIGHLIGHTS

The Columbus Monument on Crab Cay is a trek of about a kilometre along a bushy path. The monument was erected in 1892 by the *Chicago Herald*.

The Columbus Cross Monument south of Fernandez Bay was erected in 1956, and supposedly stands at the location of Columbus' first landfall in the New World. Nearby another monument commemorates the passage of the Olympic flame on its way to Greece from Mexico City in 1968.

The Dixon Hill Lighthouse is one of only a handful of manually operated lighthouses left in the world. Placed on a bed of mercury and powered by kerosene, the light can be seen for 31km (19 miles) out to sea.

The San Salvador Museum has an interesting mix of early Lucayan artefacts and exhibits on the history of the island, including displays on Christopher Columbus. If it is closed, you can collect the key from Miss Malthina Bastian at the BATELCO offices.

Columbus Isles Horse and Riding Ranch, south of Cockburn Town, has a number of well-kept horses and offers trekking along the uninhabited east coast; tel (242) 331 2760, fax (242) 331 2761.

THE UNDISCOVERED BAHAMAS

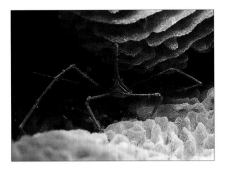

Known as the Undiscovered Bahamas, the southern islands just northeast of Cuba and northwest of the Turks and Caicos Islands are a wide-ranging group of largely unpopulated islands and cays. The Jumento Cays stretch west from Long Island to Columbus Bank, while Samana Cay lies to the east. A possible candidate as the original landfall of Columbus, Samana Cay is now deserted, with its village in ruins, and is only rarely visited by any of the live-aboard dive boats. It is surrounded by an almost continuous ridge of coral reef.

Most popular of these islands is probably Crooked Island (Sites 2–4), where the drop-off comes close to the northwest point between Bird Rock Light and Pitts Town Point. There are sheltered moorings around Crooked Island and, when weather permits, the continuous reef along the north shore is spectacular. Nearby is Acklins Island, which forms the eastern part of the Crooked Island District triangle. Here, the reef north of Atwood Harbour is a classic wide-ranging spur and groove system with good coral growth, though quite exposed. Southeast of Acklins and midway to Great Inagua is Hogsty Reef (Site 5), which has a horseshoe-shaped outer reef, similar to a true coral atoll. A large freighter stranded in the central north part of the reef is used as a staging post for boats following humpback whales and dolphin migrations.

Beyond Hogsty Reef and just above the Windward Passage which separates Haiti from Cuba is Great Inagua Island, the third largest of the Bahamian islands and home to large numbers of West Indian pink flamingoes. The Bahamas National Trust has earmarked a reserve here around Lake Windsor and Lake Rosa, where over 60,000 birds can be seen. North of Matthew Town on Great Inagua, a 60m² (200 sq ft) man-made harbour offers safe anchorage, with three wrecks lying just outside on the inner reefs. A million tonnes of salt are harvested each year in this area by the Morton Salt Company. The deep-water wall (Sites 6–7) comes in to Great Inagua around all its shores, but dive boats tend to concentrate on the reef off South Bay and Statira Shoals to the southeast. To the northeast, the diamond-shaped, uninhabited Little Inagua Island is surrounded by a fringing reef and offers excellent snorkelling and diving.

Opposite: *Great Inagua has a wonderfully scenic coastline.*
Above: *The arrow crab (Stenorhynchus seticornis) tends to hide in coral recesses during the day.*

North of Little Inagua is the most easterly of the Bahamian islands, Mayaguana. Somewhat off the beaten track, Mayaguana is the same size as Bermuda. The island came to life during NASA's Mercury and Apollo space programmes when a new airstrip and missile-tracking station were built here. Now, with NASA gone, the Environmental Research Group Bahamas Ltd. and the Bahamian government are developing an eco-tourism park with experimental farms, botanical gardens and trails. Devil's Point at the southwest corner of Mayaguana is one of the most popular dive sites with the live-aboard dive boats that venture this far.

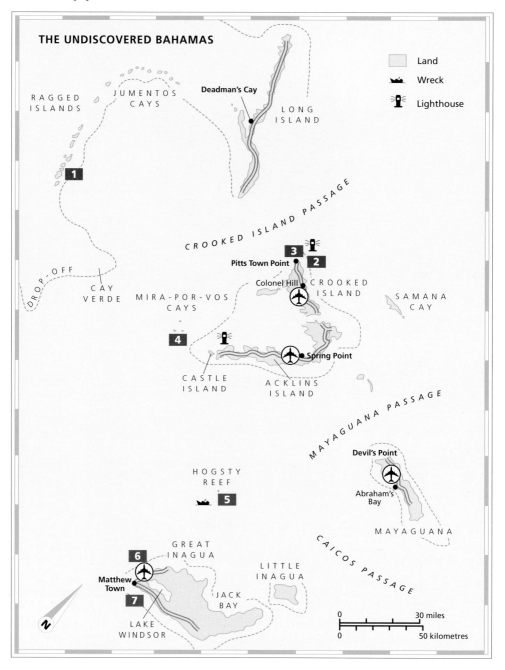

THE UNDISCOVERED BAHAMAS

Land
Wreck
Lighthouse

RAGGED ISLANDS

JUMENTOS CAYS

Deadman's Cay

LONG ISLAND

1

CROOKED ISLAND PASSAGE

3
2
Pitts Town Point

Colonel Hill
CROOKED ISLAND

SAMANA CAY

DROP-OFF

CAY VERDE

MIRA-POR-VOS CAYS

4

Spring Point

CASTLE ISLAND

ACKLINS ISLAND

MAYAGUANA PASSAGE

Devil's Point

HOGSTY REEF

5

Abraham's Bay

MAYAGUANA

GREAT INAGUA

6

Matthew Town

7

JACK BAY

LITTLE INAGUA

CAICOS PASSAGE

LAKE WINDSOR

N

0   30 miles
0   50 kilometres

1 JUMENTOS CAYS (Ragged Islands Fringing Reef)

★★★★☆☆☆

Location: The southern islands of the long chain stretching south from Long Island to the shallow Columbus Bank.
Access: By boat only.
Conditions: Can be exposed and is rarely visited.
Average depth: 15m (50ft)
Maximum depth: Beyond 70m (230ft)
Average visibility: 30m (100ft)

The Ragged Islands' fringing reef forms the southern part of the Jumentos Cays. Over 80km (50 miles) long, it is a mass of coral platforms, single huge coral heads, strip reef and enormous shallow elkhorn coral gardens. There are literally thousands of virgin dive sites all along this eastern coastline where tunnels, caverns and swim-throughs are the norm on every dive. Nurse sharks, turtles and rays are seen on most dives and the shallow-water reefs are home to masses of fish.

2 CROOKED ISLAND DROP-OFF

★★★★★

Location: The northwest point of Crooked Island on the edge of the wall.
Access: By boat only.
Conditions: Rather exposed with some surface chop and slight current.
Average depth: 30m (100ft)
Maximum depth: Beyond 70m (230ft)
Average visibility: 45m (150ft)

This is a spectacular wall dive similar to the vertical and underhanging drops found on Cat Island, San Salvador and southern Eleuthera, except that here the wall starts at around 9m (30ft). It is a vertical, almost flat wall which plummets into the abyss amidst soft coral sea plumes, wire coral, gorgonian sea fans and massive colourful sponges. There are lots of large grouper, particularly red grouper (*Epinephelus morio*), yellowfin grouper (*Mycteroperca venenosa*) and tiger grouper (*Mycteroperca tigris*). Above the reef are massive schools of yellowtail snapper (*Ocyurus chrysurus*).

3 SEAVIEW REEF

★★★★☆☆☆

Location: Southeast from Bird Rock Lighthouse along the northern shore of Crooked Island.
Access: By boat only.
Conditions: Can be exposed and is best dived from April to September.
Average depth: 30m (100ft)
Maximum depth: Beyond 70m (230ft)
Average visibility: 45m (150ft)

This long fringing reef is a well-structured spur and groove formation, quite shallow in a number of places, and then forming deep sand chutes and coral gulleys which drop over into the depths. Well-formed hard corals fringed with gorgonian sea fans and sea plumes adorn the walls. Huge barrel sponges and convoluted rope sponges of various colours are everywhere. Creole

Spotted morays (Gymnothorax moringue) are small inquisitive eels.

wrasse and blue chromis are in constant movement above you and there are schools of most of the snapper and grunt species.

4 MIRA-POR-VOS ISLETS
★★★☆☆☆☆

Location: Southwest of Castle Island, the southernmost tip of the Crooked Island triangle.
Access: By boat only.
Conditions: Quite rough in the Mira-por-Vos passage with surge around the shallow corals.
Average depth: 9m (30ft)
Maximum depth: 25m (80ft)
Average visibility: 25m (80ft)
The name, coined by Christopher Columbus, means 'keep an eye about you' and is fitting, as this shallow sandbank is studded with hundreds of coral heads and low fringing reefs with a number of small cays breaking the surface. Tidal surge tends to be from the southwest so most of the shallow diving and snorkelling takes place amongst the scattered coral heads to the east of the largest rock, known as South Cay. The corals are in good order and are fringed by various species of algae and small sea fans. Damselfish like this type of community best of all, where they cultivate small gardens of algae and are voracious defenders of their property against incomers.

5 HOGSTY REEF (Los Corrales)
★★★★★★☆☆☆

Location: Midway between Crooked Island and Great Inagua.
Access: By boat only.
Conditions: Rather exposed with submerged coral heads everywhere.
Average depth: 12m (40ft)
Maximum depth: 25m (80ft)
Average visibility: 30m (100ft)
Hogsty Reef is known as one of the staging points between Puerto Rico and the Turks and Caicos Islands

---

NITROGEN NARCOSIS

Deep diving is common in the Bahamas, and the possibility of being affected by nitrogen narcosis is high. If you are planning to dive deep, first take a deep diving course, then increase your depth gradually 3m (10ft) at a time. The effects of nitrogen narcosis (also known as the 'Rapture of the Deep') are akin to euphoria and drunkenness. See page 169 for more details.

---

for live-aboard dive boats which follow the migrating humpback whales from late November through to early March. The reef is also well documented by seafarers over hundreds of years as a place to avoid, due to the treacherous nature of the reef shoals, which come very close to the surface in many locations. The entire bank is littered with the remains of many shipwrecks, now well encrusted in marine growths including sea fans, small hard corals and fire coral.

6 DEVIL POINT, GREAT INAGUA WALL
★★★★★

Location: Due east of Devil Point, north of Matthew Town, Great Inagua.
Access: By boat only.
Conditions: Some current to be expected.
Average depth: 33m (110ft)
Maximum depth: Beyond 70m (230ft)
Average visibility: 30m (100ft)
This area of the Great Inagua Wall is dominated by a massive sand slope drop-off which has huge coral heads scattered all over it. The sandy areas have thousands of garden eels (*Heteroconger halis*), and sand tilefish, peacock flounders and razorfish are common all over. The coral heads act as an oasis for marine life, with superb coral growths, sponges, sea fans and many fish.

7 SOUTH BAY, GREAT INAGUA WALL
★★★★★

Location: East of Southwest Point, Great Inagua, along the wall opposite Saltpond Hill.
Access: By boat only.
Conditions: Mainly sheltered with little or no current.
Average depth: 33m (110ft)
Maximum depth: Beyond 70m (230ft)
Average visibility: 45m (150ft)
This is a much more vertical wall, but is cut by winding passageways, gulleys, canyons and caves which bring you out from 15m (50ft) onto the wall at around 25m (80ft). Sheet corals, wire corals and star corals are found all over. Sponge life on these southern reefs is particularly prevalent, with rope sponges (*Aplysina caulifrons*), brown tube sponges (*Agelas conifera*) and stove-pipe sponges (*Aplysina archeri*). Spiny lobster are in most of the crevices and the shallower areas have giant anemones (*Condylactis gigantea*) with their usual array of cleaner shrimps waiting for lunch to swim by. Shade-loving fish such as squirrelfish and bigeye appear to inhabit every nook and cranny, often lying on the rock with their mouths open being cleaned.

HOW TO GET THERE

You can fly into Great Inagua, Mayaguana, Crooked Island, Little Ragged Island and Acklins Island with Bahamasair on a fairly regular schedule from Nassau. The mail boat also cruises the islands weekly from Cooper's Town, Nassau. Most visitors to the island come by boat, whether by private yacht, charter or live-aboard dive boat.

WHERE TO STAY

Again, most visitors stay on their respective boats, but there are some small places offering accommodation on the islands. Guests also tend to eat where they stay, as there is little else.

Crooked Island Beach, Cabbage Hill, Crooked Island; tel (242) 344 2321. Six rooms and a restaurant.

Pitts Town Point, Landrail Point, Crooked Island; tel (242) 344 2507. Fourteen rooms and a restaurant, with diving equipment available for rent.

Crystal Beach View Hotel, Gregory Street, Matthew Town, Great Inagua; tel (242) 339 1550.

Walkine's Guest House, Gregory Street, Matthew Town, Great Inagua; tel (242) 339 1612. Five homely rooms next to the beach.

For more details contact the Bahamas Ministry of Tourism, Market Plaza, Bay Street, PO Box N3701, Nassau, Bahamas; tel (242) 322 7501 or 356 7591/2/3, fax (242) 328 0945 or 322 4041.

WHERE TO EAT

All of the main settlements have small restaurants serving Bahamian food, principally freshly baked corn bread, johnny cakes, fresh-caught fish, peas'n'rice, conch and local meat. As elsewhere in the Family Islands, the shops, restaurants and guest houses all operate on VHF Channel 16.

Last Stop Take Away, Russell & Meadow Street, Matthew Town, Great Inagua; tel (242) 339 1740.

DIVE FACILITIES

The only land-based diving facility on any of these islands is at Pitts Town Point on Crooked Island. There are no air compressors anywhere else and no recompression chambers. For all practical purposes, the only diving done around the islands is from live-aboard dive boats.

Pitts Town Point, Landrail Point, Crooked Island; tel (242) 344 2507. Has no shop and only a limited supply of rental equipment, and is really only an extra service for the hotel's guests.

EMERGENCY SERVICES

Great Inagua Hospital, Matthew Town, Great Inagua; tel (242) 339 1249.

Police, Matthew Town tel (242) 339 1444.

The closest **recompression chambers** are at UNEXSO in Freeport, Grand Bahama, tel (242) 373 1244, fax (242) 351 9740, and **Lyford Cay Hospital**, Nassau, New Providence Island; tel (242) 362 4025 or emergency radio Channel 16.

LOCAL HIGHLIGHTS

Lake Windsor on Great Inagua is well worth a visit to see the flamingoes. The lake is just a short drive from the airport and Matthew Town; a local guide will take you there. In the Union Creek Reserve, also near Matthew Town, turtles are being studied and the surrounding land is inhabited by Bahama parrots, West Indian tree ducks, hummingbirds, spoonbills, pelicans, egrets, wild donkeys and pigs. The local wardens can take you on a day trip by jeep.

Erickson's Public Library and Museum, Gregory Street, Matthew Town has some interesting Taino Indian artefacts and antiques from early European settlers, as well as some excellent historical maps.

The red night shrimp (Rhynchocinetes rigens) is a creature of the night.

The Marine Environment

When Christopher Columbus first discovered the Bahamas on his way to the East Indies he wrote in his diary, 'Here the fish are so different from ours that it is a wonder . . . blues, yellows, reds . . . painted in a thousand ways. No man would not wonder at them or be anything but delighted to see them.'

The waters around the Bahamas are some of the clearest and least polluted in the world. There are no rivers flowing into the sea other than the fresh water which has percolated through the limestone mantle and flows out through various sinkholes, and little or no sewage is pumped into the sea. Consequently there is no sedimentation in the water and what planktonic sediment there is rapidly sinks into the depths.

When discussing the Bahamas, it is important to think not only of islands, but also of submarine banks and the sea itself. The Bahamas are the island tips of a vast series of subterranean plateaus which were once some 6m (20ft) above the present level of the sea. The changing sea level has created vast blue holes, many with interlocking underground tunnels and caverns; also as the sea level rose the fringing and barrier reefs rose accordingly, creating massive living barriers around all of the islands. The Andros Barrier Reef, 268km (167 miles) long, is regarded by some as the third largest in the world and the second largest in the northern hemisphere, although Anegada in the British Virgin Islands is fairly close in length. Much of the coastline lies within the protection of a fringing reef and this sheltered lagoon environment provides a major breeding area for many species of fish and invertebrates.

The Bahamas National Trust already manage two Land and Sea Parks, in the Exumas and on Abaco. They have earmarked 12 further locations as Protected Marine Parks and five areas for future National Parks. It is within these areas that divers can perhaps best understand the beauty and diversity that the Bahamas have to offer. The entire island archipelago is swept by the nutrient-rich Gulf Stream, which is a primary factor in the construction of the reefs and the richness of the marine environment.

TYPES OF REEF

The sublittoral regions can be divided into a number of different areas or habitats. Although all of the features below are found in the Bahamas, local variations do occur. Directly from the shore you will encounter a fringing reef. In most cases this is fairly flat and connects to the fossilized ironstone shoreline. It is generally uninspiring and sandy on the top due to the constant battering it has received over the centuries by tide, weather and man, with only the occasional knob of hard coral or sea fan. Juvenile fish and hermit crabs are the most common species found here. In further open sand areas, or what becomes a lagoon, you will usually find turtle grass. Such

sandy areas will eventually lead to an outer fringing reef, often referred to as a double reef.

Beyond, you will then encounter a steeply inclined sand stage interspersed with large clumps of hard coral and sea fans, sometimes known as bommies, but generally referred to as a patch reef system. The patch reef is where you will find the highest proportion of marine life during your diving and any night diving you do will probably be in this environment. Derelict ships sunk deliberately as artificial reefs are always located within a patch reef system as it encourages a faster growth of marine life.

Such coral formations gradually take on the characteristics of a spur and groove reef. The spur is a finger of coral growth and the groove is a sand chute. In many cases these then lead over the edge of the wall and are regarded as being part of the drop-off or wall. Alternatively the spur and groove reef may eventually form a much larger barrier reef consisting of elkhorn, boulder, star, brain and staghorn corals. Barrier reefs always grow parallel to the coastline. Spur and groove reefs always run perpendicular to the shore, so it is easy to find your way back up into shallower water.

The wall or drop-off is a vertical reef face which often marks the edge of the continental shelf, and may descend to great depths. The two largest Bahama banks are divided by oceanic troughs ranging from 1500m (5000ft) to 1800m (6000ft) deep, and it is along the edge of these troughs that all the drop-offs of the northeastern Bahamas are located. Here some spectacular diving can be found.

CORALS AND INVERTEBRATES

There are over 120 species of hard corals, soft corals, sea fans and sea plumes, of every conceivable shape and size, in Bahamian waters. They are all incredibly delicate organisms and the majority of the reef is actually a thin crust of living organisms building over the ancient skeletons of their ancestors, changing in shape and structure as the environment changes around it.

The largest of the hard or stony corals (the main reef builders) is the great star coral (*Monastrea cavernosa*). Each individual colony can grow up to 3m (10ft) across. The boulder star coral (*Monastrea annularis*) grows to the same dimension but has a more knobbly effect. Brain corals such as *Colpophyllia natans* can grow up to 2m (7ft), although the species whose form most resembles the convolutions of the human brain is the smaller *Diploria labyrinthiformis*. Sheet coral (*Agaricia grahamae*) can be found on the outer edges of the wall tumbling into the depths. On wrecks and under shaded overhangs can be found one of the smallest yet brightest corals, the golden cup coral (*Tubastrea coccinea*). Gorgonian sea fans come in many different varieties and, given the geographical position of the Bahamas, are an indication that there is a

---

Opposite: *The reefs of the Bahamas frequently feature lush growths of soft and hard corals.*

higher than average concentration of planktonic species cast adrift in the Gulf Stream as it passes directly through the heart of the island chain. Always be careful when approaching these corals because they bend and sway in the current and it is very easy to misjudge your distance underwater and bump into them.

Invertebrates make up a large proportion of all creatures living in the sea and the Bahamas island chain, due to its eastern location across the path of the Gulf Stream, supports most of the species known to occur in the Caribbean. These include sponges, jellyfish, hydroids, anemones, corals, tube worms, flatworms, segmented worms, crustaceans, molluscs, octopus, squid, nudibranchs, echinoderms, bryozoans and tunicates. Invertebrates are perhaps the most rewarding for the inquisitive diver and underwater photographer. Generally, they are a delight to study: their colours are often bright, and many of the creatures have interesting behavioural patterns.

A FRAGILE ECOSYSTEM

Coral reefs everywhere in the world are living communities made up of many thousands of species and tens of thousands of individuals, and the reefs around the Bahamas are no exception. To damage one part damages the whole ecosystem. There are over 1000 species of animals and plants found in the near-shore waters of the Bahamas and many of the animals are interdependent. The major inhabitants are the corals and algae. Algae grows much faster than coral. (In fact, the fastest growing living thing is a marine alga.) If a coral is accidentally

A SUMMARY OF THE FISHERIES (RESOURCES) REGULATIONS

• Use of bleach or other noxious or poisonous substances for fishing, or possession of such substances on board a fishing vessel without the written approval of the Minister is prohibited.
• Use of firearms or explosives for fishing is prohibited.
• Spearfishing within the following areas is prohibited:
  - one mile off the coast of New Providence
  - one mile off the southern coast of Freeport, Grand Bahama
  - 200 metres off the coast of all other Family Islands.
• Nets used for fishing must have a minimum mesh gauge of 6cm (2in).
• Scale fish traps are required to have self-destruct panels and minimum mesh size of 3x6cm (1x2in) for rectangular wire traps.
• The taking of corals is prohibited.
• The close season for collecting crawfish is 1 April–31 July.
• The possession of 'berried' (egg bearing) crawfish is prohibited.
• The removal of eggs from 'berried' female crawfish is prohibited.
• The harvesting of juvenile conch (without a lip) is prohibited.
• The capture or possession of any hawksbill turtle is prohibited.
• The taking or possession of turtle eggs is prohibited.
• The capture of bonefish by nets is prohibited.
• The capture of grouper and rockfish weighing less than 1.36kg (3lbs) is prohibited.
• The harvesting of female stone crabs is prohibited.
• The capture or molesting of marine mammals is prohibited.

damaged, algae take a very fast grip on the damaged area and can soon smother and kill the coral. These two groups are in constant competition with each other.

Some varieties of coral such as staghorn and elkhorn coral are often encountered by divers and snorkellers and are thus particularly exposed. The living tissue found in corals is on and just below the surface and if this is damaged the entire coral may die. It is imperative that divers maintain full control over their buoyancy, as a misplaced fin or equipment console can seriously wound or kill the coral. Even placing your hand on the coral can remove the protective mucus and expose the coral to stress and damage. The average yearly growth of coral is incredibly small. Brain coral grows about 1cm ($^1/_3$in) each year. Elkhorn can grow up to 10cm (4in) each year, and staghorn slightly faster, but even this is not enough to compensate for damage caused by careless actions.

PROTECTING MARINE LIFE

When approaching marine life, you must do so sensitively and with empathy. Try and understand that what you are looking at is just one small link in one of the most complex ecosystems on earth. Divers MUST also master the art of self control and buoyancy technique to keep well clear of the reef and its inhabitants.

Turtles, for example, are fascinating and graceful creatures, but please do not try to hold onto them. If you find one sleeping at night, stay well clear because to grab hold of it could give the creature such a shock that it might blunder into a cave and be drowned or seriously damage itself and the corals around it.

Pufferfish should also be left untouched. They have a natural defence mechanism of sucking in water very rapidly until they are balloon-sized with any defensive spines jutting out. They look comical when inflated and cannot swim properly, but continual handling of these fish will remove the protective mucous membrane over their skin, and in turn let infection set in which can kill the fish.

Long-spined black sea urchins must also be treated with caution. Apart from the very obvious danger of getting spines embedded in soft parts of your flesh due to a lack of control, it is also illegal to cut up these creatures to feed other animals on the reef. The urchins play an important part in controlling algae and they are only just beginning to recover after being almost completely wiped out in the Caribbean due to disease in 1983.

Barrel sponges should be treated with respect. Some of the larger species can grow to over 2m (7 ft), but to climb inside one can kill it.

Generally, most fish are slow in their growth patterns and if the marine habitat of a particular fish or invertebrate, such as coral, is damaged, the spin-off on the rest of the reef's population can be catastrophic. A 2% reduction in the coral community can not only make the reef look less inviting or pretty to a visiting diver, but will also drastically reduce fish stocks and populations of other creatures such as shrimp, lobster and octopus.

COMMON REEF FISH AND INVERTEBRATES

Angelfish (family Pomacanthidae)

There are four species of angelfish in the Bahamas. The rock beauty (*Holacanthus tricolor*), with its yellow face and tail and wide black body, grows up to 30cm (12in) and can be fairly shy. The grey angelfish (*Pomacanthus arcuatus*) is actually brown in colour and one of the largest species. The French angelfish (*Pomacanthus paru*) is dark blue-grey-black with yellow rims on its scales and around the eyes, while the queen angelfish (*Holacanthus ciliaris*), which can grow up to 45cm (18in), has an electric blue body running to gold fins, tail and face.

Grey angelfish (*Pomacanthus arcuatus*)

Basslets (family Grammidae)

The fairy basslet (*Gramma loreto*) is one of the most strikingly coloured fish to be found in the reef environment, with its golden-headed front and violet rear. These fish are usually found in recesses and under shaded areas of the reef.

Fairy basslet (*Gramma loreto*)

Blennies (families Clinidae, Blennidae, Tripterygiidae)

Blennies are similar to gobies in that few have swim bladders and they tend to perch on coral heads and rubble. Most live in cracks or in holes vacated by another marine organism, which they defend vigorously. The arrow blenny (*Lucayablennius zingaro*) is an exception to this rule, preferring to drift along the reef wall with a cocked tail. Spinyhead blennies (*Acanthemblemaria spinosa*) can appear quite comical when they are seen poking their heads out of an old feather worm tube.

Diamond blenny (*Malacoctenus boehlkei*)

Butterflyfish (family Chaetondontidae)

There are six species of butterflyfish in the Bahamas and two of the prettiest are the spotfin butterflyfish (*Chaetodon ocellatus*) and the foureye butterflyfish (*Chaetodon capistratus*). The spotfin has a white body with a yellow trim and a black vertical band through its face and eye, while the foureye has a large eye 'painted' near its tail and numerous dark thin lines and a darker bar through the eye. The longsnout butterflyfish (*Chaetodon aculeatus*) is one of the shyest of the species.

Longsnout butterflyfish (*Chaetodon aculeatus*)

Gobies (family Gobiidae)

Always associated with blennies, gobies spend their lives living on coral heads. They do not have swim bladders and so swim only in short speedy bursts. Among the more common gobies are the peppermint goby (*Coryphopterus lipernes*) and the cleaning goby (*Gobiosoma genie*), which is very similar to the neon goby (*Gobiosoma oceanops*). Found only on sand and coral rubble, the bridled goby (*Coryphopterus glaucofraenum*) is also common.

Sharknose goby (*Gobiosoma evelynae*)

Red grouper (*Epinephelus morio*)

Balloonfish (*Diodon holocanthus*)

Caribbean reef shark (*Carcharhinus perezi*)

Wire coral shrimp (*Periclemines amboinensis*)

Flamingo tongue (*Cyphoma gibbosum*)

Grouper/seabass (family Serranidae)

The grouper, seabass and soapfish family comprises some 42 species. One of the most common species is the tiger grouper (*Mycteroperca tigris*), which can grow up to 1m (3ft). A smaller grouper is the coney (*Cephalopholis fulvus*), which can grow up to 40cm (16in) and always appears to be standing guard on a coral head. These fish come in various colour variations from a dark reddish-brown to bright yellow.

Pufferfish/boxfish (families Tetraodontidae, Ostraciontidae)

Pufferfish and porcupine fish are very common, as are their close relatives, boxfish. The balloonfish (*Diodon holocanthus*) should not be handled (nor, in fact, should any of the species), as their skin can be diseased. The smooth trunkfish (*Lactophrys triqueter*) is seen regularly. Sharpnose puffers (*Canthigaster rostrata*) can always be found during night dives resting in sponges or on sea fans while the bandtail puffer (*Sphoeroides spengleri*) prefers to rest in a shallow depression on the sand.

Sharks (families Rhincodontidae, Requiem, Mackeral and Sphyrnidae)

Unlike other areas of the Caribbean, sharks are fairly common in the Bahamas, though only in the various localized areas where they have become used to humans feeding them. The most frequently sighted is the Caribbean reef shark (*Carcharhinus perezi*), with nurse sharks (*Ginglymostoma cirratum*) a close second.

Shrimps (phylum Crustacea, order Decapoda)

The banded coral shrimp (*Stenopus hispidus*) is found in all of the world's tropical oceans. It is a small, colourful shrimp with long pincers and distinctive waving antennae. The cleaning shrimp (*Periclimenes pedersoni*) is the most commonly found of the shrimps; the red night shrimp (*Rhynchocinetes rigens*) is seen only at night, hiding in the coral recesses, its bright green eyes reflecting the light from divers' torches.

Snails (phylum Mollusca, class Gastropoda, subclass Prosobranchia)

The mollusc family is well represented in the Bahamas and the range and diversity of the animals in it is vast. The queen conch (*Strombus gigas*) is the species most often harvested for food. Perhaps one of the more brightly coloured of the Caribbean shells is the flamingo tongue (*Cyphoma gibbosum*). Its speckled mantle folds up around the body of the shell and it can be found feeding on sea fans.

Snapper (family Lutjanidae)

Closely associated with grunt, snapper such as the schoolmaster (*Lutjanus apodus*) are often seen around the outcroppings of elkhorn coral. The blue-striped grunt (*Haemulon sciurus*) is often found in association with them. Perhaps the most common of the snapper family is the yellowtail snapper (*Ocyurus chrysurus*). This inquisitive fish can congregate in fairly large schools which are forever following the divers, looking for morsels.

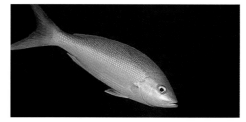

Yellowtail snapper (*Ocyurus chrysurus*)

Sponges (phylum Porifera)

The yellow tube sponge (*Aplysina fistularis*) and the pink vase sponge (*Niphates digitalis*) are two particularly common species of sponge to be found on the deeper reefs off the wall. You will also find stovepipe sponges (*Aplysina archeri*), but perhaps the most dramatic of all is the giant barrel sponge (*Xestospongia muta*).

Tube sponge (*Aplysina archeri*)

Squirrelfish/soldierfish (families Holocentridae, Priacanthidae)

Squirrelfish and soldierfish are found around all the reefs of the Bahamas. The common squirrelfish (*Holocentrus adscensionis*) has white triangular markings on the tips of its dorsal spines and is reddish in colour overall with light silvery stripes running horizontally along the body. The bigeye (*Priacanthus arenatus*) is a close relative and is usually a uniform dark red in colour. They drift in small groups over the edge of the deeper reefs and are more commonly seen at night.

Squirrelfish (*Holocentrus adscensionis*)

Starfish (phylum Echinodermata, classes Crinoidea, Asteroidea, Ophiuroidea)

Crinoids or feather starfish crawl out onto the coral surface as night begins to fall, while brittle starfish prefer to curl around sea fans and whips. Basket starfish (*Astrophyton muricatum*) are the largest of the species and extend their multi-jointed arms over 50cm (1½ft) into the current.

Brittle starfish (*Ophiothrix suensonii*)

Tube Worms (class Polychaeta, families Sabellidae, Serpulidae)

The most colourful of the segmented or tube worms are the social featherduster worm (*Bispira brunnea*), found in small clumps at the base of sea fans or on wrecks, and the magnificent featherduster worm (*Sabellastarte magnifica*), a solitary animal. However, the beauty of them all is without doubt the Christmas tree worm (*Spirobranchus giganteus*), only 3cm (1½in) high. This worm is more often noticed when it disappears rapidly down into its tubes in the coral as you swim close by.

Christmas tree worm (*Spirobranchus giganteus*)

OTHER FISH AND INVERTEBRATES

Anemones (phylum Cnidaria, superclass Anthozoa, order Actinaria)

Anemones come in many different shapes and sizes. The giant anemone (*Condylactis gigantea*) has quite long tentacles tipped with a purple or green knob, all armed with stinging cells with which to paralyse prey. Small shrimps are always found in association with this anemone. The branching anemone (*Lebruna danae*) is usually found amongst corals and often has several Pederson's cleaning shrimps in residence.

Barracuda (family Sphyraenidae)

The largest of the silvery predators on the reef is the great barracuda (*Sphyraena barracuda*). This aggressive-looking fish is usually found on its own and often stays close to mooring buoys, where it will lie in wait under the shadow of a moored dive boat. Barracuda can grow up to 1.8m (6ft).

Chromis/damselfish (family Pomacentridae)

Very common around all of the Caribbean, chromis and other damselfish are generally small and oval in shape. Some cultivate a garden of algae amongst the coral, which they defend with a passion, while others such as the sergeant major (*Abudefduf saxatilis*) feed on plankton. The sergeant major is the largest of the damselfish. On the reeftop, at the edge of the wall, large schools of blue chromis (*Chromis cyanea*) can be found.

Crabs (phylum Crustacea, intraorders Anomura, Brachyura)

The red reef hermit (*Paguristes cadenati*) can be wary of divers and will retreat into its mobile home. The white speckled hermit (*Paguristes punticeps*) is much larger and can grow up to 12cm (5in). The arrow crab (*Stenorhynchus seticornis*) is the one most commonly found in the Caribbean; its huge relative the channel clinging crab (*Mithrax spinosissimus*) is also seen on virtually every night dive.

Drum (family Sciaenidae)

Spotted drums (*Equetus punctatus*) are timid fish living under coral overhangs and in shaded areas. The juveniles attract most attention, due to their active gyrations and beautiful long striped dorsal fins. They only become spotted when they reach maturity.

Filefish/triggerfish (family Balistidae)

There are 12 species of filefish and triggerfish recorded from the Bahamas. Among the commonest is the slender filefish (*Monacanthus tuckeri*), which lives amongst sea fans, rods and plumes. Also common is the most brilliantly coloured of the triggerfish, the queen triggerfish (*Balistes vetula*), which lives amongst the patch corals where it excavates the sand and rubble for small shellfish and crustaceans.

Fireworm (phylum Annelida, family Amphinomidae)

The bearded fireworm (*Hermodice carunculata*) can grow up to 15cm (6in) and is particularly exotic. The fine hairs or bristles along its body can easily penetrate the skin and cause a painful skin irritation.

Flounders (family Bothidae)

Flounders are sand dwellers. In the Bahamas there are peacock flounders (*Bothus lunatus*) and eyed flounders (*Bothus ocellatus*), which are quite skittish when approached and take off over the sand plains at great speed. Both species are regular prey to dolphins.

Frogfish (family Antennariidae)

The longlure frogfish (*Antennarius multiocellatus*) is perhaps the most difficult of all the Caribbean fish to find, due to their fantastic camouflage technique. They can sit still amidst algae or sponges and take on the colours of their background, rather like a chameleon. They have adapted ventral fins which they use more as feet than as fins.

Garden eels (family Congridae)

The garden eel (*Heteroconger halis*) lives in vertical burrows in the softer sand areas and quite often large numbers of them can be seen swaying gently in the current, picking off plankton as it drifts past. They are extremely shy and withdraw into their burrows long before you can get to them for a closer look.

Goatfish (family Mullidae)

Yellow goatfish (*Mulloidichthys martinicus*), when feeding, can be found in small groups foraging in the sand with their adapted pectoral fins. These whisker-like barbels are used like fingers in search of small crustaceans and worms.

Grunt/margate (family Haemulidae)

Found in large shoals alongside snapper, white margate (*Haemulon album*) can be seen stacking up on the outer edges of the reef along with white grunt (*Haemulon plumieri*). White grunt have bluer stripes on their head compared to the higher-backed pearl grey-blue appearance of margate. The species is named after the grunting noise they make underwater.

Gurnards (family Dactylopteridae)

Flying gurnards (*Dactylopterus volitans*) are uncommon reef dwellers, usually found in fairly shallow water of under 10m (33ft). They tend to remain in lifelong mating pairs and are seen skimming over the surface of the sandy seabed with their large extended pectoral fins, or 'walking' over the seabed with modified spines from their ventral fins.

Hamlets (family Serranidae)

Hamlets are members of the seabass family and there are several striking representatives in the Bahamas. The indigo hamlet (*Hypoplectrus indigo*) is the most common and is also found as far away as Bermuda. The golden hamlet (*Hypoplectrus gummingatta*) is perhaps the brightest of all with its golden body and curious blue and black markings on its cheeks.

Hawkfish (family Cirrhitidae)

The redspotted hawkfish (*Amblycirrhites pinos*) is the only Caribbean example of these curious reef dwellers which, though rather timid, make excellent photographic subjects with their red spotted faces and comical stance amidst the corals and anemones.

Hogfish/razorfish (family Labridae)

Very closely related to wrasse and parrotfish, the common hogfish (*Lachnolaimus maximus*) and the Spanish hogfish (*Bodianus rufus*) are both found in this area of the Caribbean. Common hogfish are quite often found near feeding stingrays. The larger adults develop a pronounced snout and the first three spines of the dorsal fin are long. The Spanish hogfish is much more brightly coloured with a purple upper band on its forebody changing to a yellow-gold belly and tail.

Hydroids/jellyfish (phylum Cnidaria, superclasses Hydrozoa, Scyphozoa)

Jellyfish and hydroids are closely related: in essence, the jellyfish is a free-swimming stage of the same type of creature as the hydroid. The moon jellyfish (*Aurelia aurita*) is one of the few animals found in every ocean of the world. A common hydroid is the stinging hydroid (*Aglaophynia latecarinata*), which has feather-like plumes which can inflict a rather nasty sting on the softer areas of your skin if you brush up against it. A close relative to be found on shallow reefs and wrecks is fire coral (*Millepora alcicornis*) which, although it looks like coral, is actually a hydroid.

Jacks (family Carangidae)

Bar jacks (*Caranx ruber*) are very common on the sand flats amongst compact coral heads. They are often seen in mating pairs and, while one stays silvery blue, the mate turns almost completely black and looks and acts like the others' shadow. They are also closely associated with the southern stingray and are seen feeding alongside them. Horse-eye jacks (*Caranx latus*), black jacks (*Caranx lugubris*) and almaco jacks (*Seriola rivoliana*) are always found at the shark-feeding stations, stealing scraps.

Jawfish (family Opistognathidae)

Related to blennies and gobies, the jawfish (*Opistognathus aurifrons*) is a curious fish found amidst the coral rubble. It has a yellowish head and a pale body and can be seen hovering above its burrow. The male incubates eggs in its mouth.

Lizardfish (family Synodontidae)

Named after their lizard-like heads, lizardfish or sand divers (*Synodus* spp.) are bottom dwellers, and are often partially submerged in sand as they sit and wait for their prey to swim by. They will move only when you come too close to them.

Lobsters (phylum Crustacea, intraorder Panilura)

Slipper lobsters (*Parribacus antarcticus*) and spiny lobsters (*Panulirus argus*) inhabit reef ledges, always hiding from direct sunlight and foraging at night. They can retreat rapidly by fast movements of their tail, propelling them backwards.

Moray eels (family Muraenidae)

Moray eels are common around all of the reefs of the Bahamas, with the green moray (*Gymnothorax funebris*) being the largest found in the eastern Caribbean. The spotted moray (*Gymnothorax moringa*), at only 60cm (2ft) long, is perhaps one of the most common around the dive sites. Similar in size is the goldentail moray (*Gymnothorax miliaris*), which has small yellow spots over brown. The much rarer chain moray (*Echidna catenata*) is larger with a dark brown to black body with irregular yellow bars and yellow eyes.

Nudibranchs and other sea slugs (phylum Mollusca, class Gastropoda, subclass Opisthobranchia)

Nudibranchs and other sea slugs feed on a number of different animals and algae and are invariably brightly coloured to advertise to would-be predators that they are harmful. The lettuce leaf sea slug (*Tridachia crispata*) can be camouflaged by the surrounding algae and is difficult to find in the shallows and dead coral rubble areas. The white-speckled nudibranch (*Phyllodesmium* sp.) is commonly found on sea whips and sea rods, which it eats.

Octopus and squid (phylum Mollusca, class Cephalopoda)

Of all the invertebrates, octopus and squid have the most highly developed nervous systems and are often found prowling the reefs at night. Squid in particular appear fascinated by divers' lights and the obvious food which these lights attract.

Parrotfish (family Scaridae)

Some parrotfish begin life as females and grow through various colour changes until a few eventually attain a supermale size. The princess parrotfish (*Scarus taeniopterus*) is quite small, with the supermale growing to 32cm (13in), while the smaller striped family groups and juveniles grow to only 10–18cm (4–7in). One of the larger parrotfish to be found regularly is the stoplight parrotfish (*Sparisoma viride*), which can reach a supermale size of 60cm (2ft). Redband parrotfish (*Sparisoma aurofrenatum*) are perhaps the most difficult to identify due to the assortment of colour changes they go through in their life.

Rays (order Rajiformes)

The spotted eagle ray (*Aetobatus narinari*) is most commonly found along the edges of walls and sand chutes. This large ray has a snout like a pig's, which it uses to forage beneath the sand for crustaceans and molluscs. The electric or torpedo ray (*Torpedo nobiliana*) is smaller in size and grows up to a length of around 1.5m (5ft). It has a rounded body and two electrical organs with which it stuns its prey. The yellow stingray (*Urolophus jamaicensis*) can be found in shallow water; circular in shape, it grows to a maximum of only 50cm (15in), and has a strong tail with a venomous spine near the end, similar to the southern stingray (*Dasyatis americana*).

Sand tilefish (family Malacanthidae)

Sand tilefish (*Malacanthus plumieri*) live on the sand plain amidst coral rubble and are easily spotted as they hover over their large coral rubble nests. They are long and white with a pale yellow crescent-shaped tail.

Scorpionfish (family Scorpaenidae)

Scorpionfish are only rarely found around the Bahamas due to their excellent camouflage techniques. They can be found more readily at night, when divers' torches will pick up the brightly coloured pectoral fins as they move off. The most common species is the spotted scorpionfish (*Scorpaena plumieri*). Scorpionfish have venomous spines.

Silversides (families Atherinidae, Clupeidae, Engraulididae)

These small fish, which grow only as large as 8cm (3in), comprise several species such as anchovies, herring and scad. During their juvenile stage they are at their most vulnerable and tend to group together in huge shoals amongst the gulleys and caves of the patch reef.

Snake eel (family Ophichthidae)

Snake eels, which have a fin which travels the length of the back, live under the sand and in coral crevices during the day. They are active foragers at night and there are a few species recorded in Bahamas waters, including the sharptail eel (*Myrichthys breviceps*) and the gold-spotted eel (*Myrichthys ocellatus*). Both are very rare, but can be approached fairly easily due to their bad eyesight.

Soapfish (subfamily Grammistidae)

The greater soapfish (*Rypticus saponaceus*) is an active predator at night but generally 'sleeps' on the reef during the day, usually lying on its side. They are unafraid of divers.

Trumpetfish (family Aulostomidae)

Trumpetfish (*Aulostomus maculatus*) are a fairly common sight around the Bahamas. They can grow up to 1m (3ft) and show many different colour variations from yellow to a colour which is almost like Scottish tartan. They are distinguished by the trumpet-shaped mouth.

Tunicates (phylum Chordata, class Ascidiacea)

Tunicates or sea squirts are fairly common and, although it is quite small, you can be sure to spot the lightbulb tunicate (*Clavelina picta*). It is found in clumps from a few to several hundred individuals and is generally attached to gorgonian fan corals and black coral.

Wrasse (family Labridae)

The largest wrasse is the pudding wife (*Halichoeres radiatus*), which has greenish blue scrolls on its head and is blue to green overall. It occasionally has a mid-white body bar and grows up to 50cm (18in). The most common of the smaller species are the yellow-head wrasse (*Halichoeres garnoti*) and the bluehead wrasse (*Thalassoma bifasciatum*). Both these species go through a number of colour changes before reaching maturity.

Underwater Photography and Video

For those who want to record their dives more accurately than in a log-book or diary, then underwater photography is the answer. From my earliest days of diving, I struggled to remember every detail of a dive or to be able to describe the intricacies of the colour markings on a species of fish to try and identify it properly. In fact, there were very few identification books available at the time. In the past 30 years, however, all that has changed dramatically. The world's first amphibious camera for the mass market was designed by Jean de Wouters d'Oplinter and developed by Jacques-Yves Cousteau. From there, the industry has evolved to making specialized lenses, flash and waterproof housings to fit the world's most advanced camera systems and technology.

EQUIPMENT

For the beginner, perhaps the best way to start is with an instant disposable camera. These are inexpensive and, of course, give instant results. However, such cameras are usually only good to about 2m (6ft) of depth. An alternative is to rent a waterproof box which will allow you to use your land camera down to 30m (100ft). Submersible waterproof housings can be bulky, but they are strong and reliable and work out cheaper than the last and most sophisticated option, a dedicated underwater camera such as the Nikonos RS-AF. In Nassau and Freeport a number of diving operators sell disposable underwater cameras as well as renting more sophisticated equipment.

To take photographs underwater, you must think not only of the camera. As your ability progresses, your camera needs to form a fully operational system, compatible with as great a variety of equipment as possible. This will include a choice of lenses, a flash and the means to connect it to the camera. Lighting underwater is always with a waterproof flash of some type and needs to be compatible with whichever camera or housing you choose. If you are unsure of which system to buy, then a sensible option is to rent an outfit from one or other of the main photo retailers in New Providence or Grand Bahama and perhaps attend an instruction course to learn about the intricacies and problems of each type of camera system.

No matter what type of system you choose, whether it be the amphibious type such as the Nikonos RS-AF or Sea & Sea system, or an SLR camera housed in a waterproof box, you must always treat it with the greatest respect and care. Before any trip, ensure that all of the connections are clean and that all 'O' rings are free of dust and are given a light coat of silicone grease. Also check for any nicks or cuts in the seals. Ensure that the flash fires correctly with the camera shutter and that you have sufficient power to operate. For those with rechargeable flash, make certain that the recharger works and that it is compatible with the electrical supply on the islands.

The best film for underwater use is generally of the slide or transparency variety with film speeds of between 50 and 100 ISO. This allows for better sharpness and colour reproduction. For instant cameras, print film with a film speed between 200 and 400 ISO is more common.

WIDE-ANGLE PHOTOGRAPHY

Wide angle is by far the most popular form of underwater photography. A wide-angle lens will allow you to take perspective photographs, for example, of the deep canyons and gulleys off The Tongue of the Ocean or any of the wrecks in the Bahamas. To see a diver surrounded by huge sponges with a deep blue background gives a wonderful feel for the scene you are viewing. Wide-angle photographs are also the most published by magazines, and this type of lens is the preferred choice of many professional underwater photographers.

WIDE-ANGLE APPLICATIONS

- Cliff and reef drop-off panoramas
- Exteriors of shipwrecks
- Interiors of shipwrecks and caves
- Divers in action
- Divers and fish/animal interaction
- Large fish
- Available light and silhouettes
- Wide-angle flash and flash-fill techniques

BENEFITS OF MACRO PHOTOGRAPHY

- A different perspective
- High magnification
- Maximum colour saturation
- Sharp focus
- Ease of learning and execution
- Can be done anywhere, under almost any conditions
- Easiest to use on night dives
- Greatest return for the least investment

MACRO PHOTOGRAPHY

Macro photography is a form of underwater photography where the camera lens is positioned very close to a subject to record a relatively large image on film and produce an image of high magnification of the subject. I recommend that you start underwater photography with a macro system, as it is undoubtedly the easiest form of underwater photography. The frustrations common to many other types of photography are minimized and very soon you will be amazed by the sharp images and vibrant colours that only macro photography can produce.

The different perspective that macro photography gives opens up a whole new world of tiny animals and plants not normally seen during average diving conditions. Your eyes quickly learn to find creatures small enough to fit the format and, as a result, what were once boring dives on gravel beds or sandy bottoms or under jetties suddenly start to yield a wealth of life.

A BEGINNERS' GUIDE TO TAKING SUCCESSSFUL UNDERWATER PHOTOGRAPHS

With macro photography it seems as if you can almost become an expert overnight, but the pursuit of underwater images is a life-long experience. Allow time to learn more about composition, and little by little you will find your technique steadily improve.

Prior to taking up underwater photography, it is also recommended that you attend an underwater photography workshop. There are a number of centres specifically organized for this type of instruction, and classes are scheduled throughout the year. Even non-photographer 'buddies' will benefit from the classes, since modelling, composition and buoyancy are all important factors in the successful photograph.

- Approach one photographic technique or problem at a time. Do not try to do everything at once.
- Record the technical details of each photograph (aperture, speed, distance etc.) as you take them, to find out which settings get the best results.

- Keep your flash or strobe well away from the camera (unless working in a macro situation). Position it to the top left of the camera so that the light beam makes an angle of 45° along the camera-to-subject axis.
- Pre-aim your flash out of the water at first to obtain the correct camera-to-subject position. If you need to change the setting underwater, aim the flash one-third behind the apparent position to counter the effects of light refraction.
- Find the aperture that produces the most consistent results for you. Next time you take photographs at that setting take an extra photograph, one either side of that aperture (one stop lower and one stop higher). Called 'bracketing', this will take care of subjects with different degrees of brightness.
- Get as close as you can to your subject. Close-ups have the most impact and better colour saturation.
- Note the position of the sun when you enter the water. Use the sun to create back-lit shots to add depth and interest.
- Never take pictures below you; always shoot horizontally or upwards.
- Pre-set your focus and allow the subject and yourself to approach each other slowly and carefully.
- Take your photographs in clear water and bright sunlight if you can.
- Never use the flash when the camera-to-subject distance is greater than one-fifth of the underwater visibility. If the visibility is 5m (16½ft), focus and use the flash at only 1m (3ft), which will cut down the reflection or 'back scatter' of particles in suspension in the water.
- Set your camera to the fastest aperture that the flash will synchronize to (unless using an automatic housed system).
- Be ruthless. The only way you can learn is by self criticism, so put as much film through the camera as possible and learn by your mistakes.

FILM AND CAMERA TIPS

- If you have to buy film locally, do so from a top photography outlet or a major hotel, where the turnover of stock will be reasonably swift and where the film will have spent most of its storage life in cool conditions.
- If you keep film refrigerated, give it at least two hours to defrost before putting it in a camera.
- Do not assemble underwater cameras in cool, air-conditioned rooms or cabins. Condensation is likely to form inside them when you take them into the water.
- Normal cameras that have been in an air-conditioned environment will mist up when you take them out into the warm atmosphere. You need to wait at least ten minutes for the condensation to dissipate before you can take clear photographs.

Underwater Video

Stills photography is all very well for recording that tiny moment in time of a marine subject. But when you are faced with the prospect of swimming through a hole in the wall surrounded by millions of silversides, then video is what you need. People are transfixed by the moving image and nothing tells the story of the dancing wonders of the reef better. Several dive stores in the Bahamas have underwater video equipment for rent and by renting you can soon find out for yourself which of the many systems on offer you prefer. The format is changing constantly and it is difficult to keep up with the latest technological developments in underwater video.

EQUIPMENT

Virtually all video cameras available are primarily designed for the terrestrial holiday market, and the sophistication of the waterproof housings which have been developed for them sometimes seems nonsensical. Housings come in a variety of styles and sizes: all have waterproof controls to allow you to use the camera's functions, though some are more awkward to handle than others, especially with lights attached. It is important to choose a system with a good-quality housing, such as those made by Sony, Panasonic and other well known manufacturers. These are readily available by mail order from most diving-related magazines.

The quality of the video image has improved by leaps and bounds in recent years, while in the meantime cameras have become smaller and lighter. One problem with systems now being so light is that with hand-held shots you may get camera shake. Whenever possible, with close-up work or a marine life study, make use of a tripod.

Lighting systems have also undergone a revolution these last few years. Many of the lights fixed on the video housing are very light, and the bulky and heavy battery pack may be extended to a clamp which attaches onto your diving air tank. On a number of other housings, the battery pack is held in a sling under the housing, which helps with the stability of the system.

A basic advantage of video over photography is that there is no waste of film. You can re-use the tape at any time. The only major problem you are likely to come up against with underwater video is rechargeable power packs. You need always to remember to change each pack before you dive and to make sure that you have enough power in store to catch that magic moment that may arise during a dive.

BUOYANCY CONTROL

As an underwater photographer, I am acutely conscious of very occasional moments of accidental contact that I have with the coral reef. All divers MUST master the art of buoyancy control. Apart from the primary need to avoid damaging corals, buoyancy control is an important aspect of taking good underwater photographs and videography.

The basic need is to be able to hover both horizontally and vertically close to the reef or the bottom without a need to actually make contact. Buoyancy is principally controlled by inflating or deflating your buoyancy compensator at various depths. Once expert buoyancy has been achieved, you will notice a drastic reduction in your air consumption, see more marine life on each dive and find your pleasure increase accordingly, as well as, of course, dramatically cutting down on accidental environmental damage.

SHOOTING SEQUENCES

Try and plan your shooting sequences before entering the water and stick to that plan as best you can. Of course, there is always the chance that something totally unexpected will happen and you should be ready for all eventualities. It is best to avoid diving with inexperienced divers or trainees, as they will inevitably get in the way. Train your buddy to help you.

Try not to prolong the sequence that you are filming. Too long a sequence is boring and more difficult to edit. Keep the direction of movement of divers constant and whenever possible have the divers and fish swimming towards the camera. The best situation is for your diving buddy/model to swim to the other side of the reef and then swim towards you. As they approach, the fish in front of the person will automatically swim towards you, making for a more interesting shot. Take occasional cut-away shots – small vignettes of diver portaits, fish behaviour, close-ups of anemone tentacles and so on.

EDITING

Editing your video is fun, but can also be frustrating, as you have to be ruthless with your choice of clips. The difficulty is not what to leave in, but rather what to take out. Your audience will soon get bored if the video is too long and of the same subject matter. Study any of the wildlife films on television and try to emulate them: this is as good a way as any for learning editing technique. Your video will also be greatly enhanced by the addition of sound and commentary – again, try not to get too technical and perhaps use someone else's voice to add a touch of professionalism.

Health and Safety for Divers

The information on first aid and safety in this part of the book is intended as a guide only. It is based on currently accepted health and safety guidelines, but it is merely a summary and is no substitute for a comprehensive manual on the subject – or, even better, for first aid training. We strongly advise you to buy a recognized manual on diving safety and medicine before setting off on a diving trip, to read it through during the journey, and to carry it with you to refer to during the trip. It would also be sensible to take a short course in first aid.

We urge anyone in need of advice on emergency treatment to see a doctor as soon as possible.

WHAT TO DO IN AN EMERGENCY
- Divers who have suffered any injury or symptom of an injury, no matter how minor, related to diving, should consult a doctor, preferably a specialist in diving medicine, as soon as possible after the symptom or injury occurs.
- No matter how confident you are in making a diagnosis, remember that you are an amateur diver and an unqualified medical practitioner.
- If you are the victim of a diving injury do not let fear of ridicule prevent you from revealing your symptoms. Apparently minor symptoms can mask or even develop into a life-threatening illness. It is better to be honest with yourself and live to dive another day.
- Always err on the conservative side when treating an illness or an injury. If you find that the condition is only minor you – and the doctor – will both be relieved.

FIRST AID
The basic principles of first aid are to:
- do no harm
- sustain life
- prevent deterioration
- promote recovery.

If you have to treat an ill or injured person:
- First try to secure the safety of yourself and the ill or injured person by getting the two of you out of the threatening environment: the water.
- Think before you act: do not do anything that will further endanger either of you.
- Then follow a simple sequence of patient assessment and management:
  1 Assess whether you are dealing with a life-threatening condition.
  2 If so, try to define which one.
  3 Then try to manage the condition.

Assessing the ABCs:
Learn the basic checks – the ABCs:
A: for AIRWAY (with care of the neck)
B : for BREATHING
C: for CIRCULATION
D: for DECREASED level of consciousness
E: for EXPOSURE (a patient must be exposed enough for a proper examination to be made).

- **Airway (with attention to the neck):** check whether the patient has a neck injury. Are the mouth and nose free from obstruction? Noisy breathing is a sign of airway obstruction.

- **Breathing:** look at the chest to see if it is rising and falling. Listen for air movement at the nose and mouth. Feel for the movement of air against your cheek.

- **Circulation:** feel for a pulse (the carotid artery) next to the windpipe.

- **Decreased level of consciousness:** does the patient respond in any of the following ways?
  A - Awake, aware, spontaneous speech.
  V - Verbal Stimuli: does he or she answer to 'Wake up'?
  P - Painful Stimuli: does he or she respond to a pinch?
  U - Unresponsive.

- **Exposure:** preserve the dignity of the patient as much as you can, but remove clothes as necessary to carry out your treatment.

Now, send for help
If, after your assessment, you think the condition of the patient is serious, you must send or call for help from the nearest emergency services (ambulance, paramedics). Tell whoever you send for help to come back and let you know whether help is on the way.

Recovery position
If the patient is unconscious but breathing normally there is a risk that he or she may vomit and choke on the vomit. It is therefore critical that the patient be turned on one side with arms outstretched in front of the body. This is called the recovery position and is illustrated in all first aid manuals.

If you suspect injury to the spine or neck, immobilize the patient in a straight line before you turn him or her on one side.

If the patient is unconscious, does not seem to be breathing, and you cannot feel a pulse, do not try to turn him or her into the recovery position.

Do **NOT** give fluids to unconscious or semi-conscious divers.

If you cannot feel a pulse

If your patient has no pulse you will have to carry out CPR (Cardiopulmonary Resuscitation). This consists of techniques to:
- ventilate the patient's lungs (expired air resuscitation)
- pump the patient's heart (external cardiac compression).

CPR (Cardiopulmonary Resuscitation)

Airway

Open the patient's airway by gently extending the head (head tilt) and lifting the chin with two fingers (chin lift). This lifts the patient's tongue away from the back of the throat and opens the airway. If the patient is unconscious and you think something may be blocking the airway, sweep your finger across the back of the tongue from one side to the other. If you find anything, remove it. Do not try this if the patient is conscious or semi-conscious because he or she may bite your finger or vomit.

Breathing: EAR (Expired Air Resuscitation)

If the patient is not breathing you need to give the 'kiss of life', or expired air resuscitation (EAR) – you breathe into his or her lungs. The 16% oxygen in the air you expire is enough to keep your patient alive.
1 Pinch the patient's nose to close the nostrils.
2 Place your open mouth fully over the patient's mouth, making as good a seal as possible.
3 Exhale into the patient's mouth hard enough to make the chest rise and fall. Give two long slow breaths.
4 If the patient's chest fails to rise, try adjusting the position of the airway.
5 Check the patient's pulse. If you cannot feel one, follow the instructions under 'Circulation' below. If you can, continue breathing for the patient once every five seconds, checking the pulse after every ten breaths.
- If the patient begins breathing, turn him or her into the recovery position (see page 166).

Circulation

If, after giving expired air resuscitation, you cannot feel a pulse, you should try external cardiac compression:
1 Kneel next to the patient's chest.
2 Measure two finger breadths above the notch where the ribs meet the lower end of the breastbone.
3 Place the heel of your left hand just above your two fingers in the centre of the breastbone.
4 Place the heel of your right hand on your left hand.
5 Straighten your elbows.
6 Place your shoulders perpendicularly above the patient's breast bone.
7 Compress the breast bone 4–5cm (1½–2in) to a rhythm of 'one, two, three . . .'
8 Carry out 15 compressions.

Continue giving cycles of two breaths and 15 compressions, checking for a pulse after every five cycles. The aim of CPR is to keep the patient alive until paramedics or a doctor arrive with the necessary equipment.

Check before you dive that you and your buddy are both trained in CPR. If not, get some training – it could mean the difference between life and death for either of you or for someone else.

DIVING DISEASES AND ILLNESSES

Acute decompression illness

Acute decompression illness is any illness arising from the decompression of a diver – in other words, by the diver moving from an area of high ambient pressure to an area of low pressure. There are two types of acute decompression illness:
- decompression sickness ('the bends')
- barotrauma with arterial gas embolism.

It is not important for the diver or first aider to be able to differentiate between the two conditions because both are serious, life-threatening illnesses, and both require the same emergency treatment. The important thing is to be able to recognize acute decompression illness and to initiate emergency treatment. The box on page 168 outlines signs and symptoms to look out for.

The bends (decompression sickness)

Decompression sickness or 'the bends' occurs when a diver has not been adequately decompressed. Exposure to higher ambient pressure underwater causes nitrogen to dissolve in increasing amounts in the body tissues. If this pressure is released gradually during correct and adequate decompression procedures, the nitrogen escapes naturally into the blood and is exhaled through the lungs. If the release of pressure is too rapid, the nitrogen cannot escape quickly enough and bubbles of nitrogen gas form in the tissues. The symptoms and signs of the disease are

---

AMBULANCE/AIR AMBULANCE SERVICES

Able Aviation & Air Ambulance, Inc.
  tel: 1 880 ABLE JET (225 3538); collect (407) 465 0893
Advanced Air Ambulance (AAA)
  tel: 1 800 633 3590; collect (305) 232 7700
Aero Ambulance Intl.
  tel: 1 800 443 8042; collect (945) 776 6800
Air Ambulance Network Inc. (AANI)
  tel: 1 800 522 3467; collect (813) 934 3999
Air Ambulance Professionals Inc. (AAPI)
  tel: 1 800 752 4195; collect (305) 491 0555
Air-Evac Intl.
  tel: (954) 772 0003
Amelia Airways - Air Ambulance
  tel: 1 800 546 4648
Associates Air Ambulance Inc. (AAA)
  tel: 1 800 546 4648; collect (954) 771 3151
Commercial Airline Escort Services
  tel: 1 800 752 4195; collect (305) 491 0555
Global Med-Tec (ground ambulance services)
  tel: (242) 394 3388/2582
Med-Evac Air Ambulance Service (ground ambulance services)
  tel: (242) 322 2881/323 8919
All except the last two of these numbers are in the USA. Charges for use of the services are made against your medical insurance.

related to the tissues in which the bubbles form and it is described by the tissues affected – joint bend, for example.

Symptoms and signs include:
- nausea and vomiting
- dizziness and weakness
- malaise
- pains in the joints
- paralysis
- numbness
- itching of skin
- incontinence.

Barotrauma with arterial gas embolism
Barotrauma is the damage that occurs when the tissue surrounding a gaseous space is injured following a change in the volume of air in that space. An arterial gas embolism is a gas bubble that moves in a blood vessel; this usually leads to the obstruction of that blood vessel or a vessel further downstream.

ROUGH AND READY TESTS FOR THE BENDS

If you suspect a diver may be suffering from the bends, carry out these tests. If the results of your checks do not seem normal, the diver may be suffering from the bends and you must take emergency action. Take the action outlined on this page even if you are not sure of your assessment – the bends is a life-threatening illness.

1 Does the diver know:
who he/she is?
where he/she is?
what the time is?

2 Can the diver see and count the number of fingers you hold up? Hold your hand 50cm (20in) in front of the diver's face and ask him/her to follow your hand with his/her eyes as you move it from side to side and up and down. Be sure that both eyes follow in each direction, and look out for any rapid oscillation or jerky movements of the eyeballs.

3 Ask the diver to smile, and check that both sides of the face have the same expression. Run the back of a finger across each side of the diver's forehead, cheeks and chin, and ask whether he/she can feel it.

4 Check that the diver can hear you whisper when his/her eyes are closed.

5 Ask the diver to shrug his/her shoulders. Both should move equally.

6 Ask the diver to swallow. Check that the adam's apple moves up and down.

7 Ask the diver to stick out his/her tongue at the centre of the mouth – deviation to either side indicates a problem.

8 Check the diver has equal muscle strength on both sides of the body. You do o this by pulling/pushing each of the diver's arms and legs away from and back toward the body, asking him/her to resist you.

9 Run your finger lightly across the diver's shoulders, down the back, across the chest and abdomen, and along the arms and legs, feeling upper and underside surfaces. Check that the diver can feel your finger moving along each surface.

10 On firm ground (not on a boat) check that the diver can walk in a straight line and, with eyes closed, stand upright with feet together and arms outstretched.

Barotrauma can occur in any tissue surrounding a gas-filled space. Common sites and types of barotrauma are:
- ears (middle ear squeeze) → burst ear drum
- sinuses (sinus squeeze) → sinus pain/nose bleeds
- lungs (lung squeeze) → burst lung
- face (mask squeeze) → swollen, bloodshot eyes
- teeth (tooth squeeze) → toothache.

Burst lung is the most serious of these since it can result in arterial gas embolism. It occurs following a rapid ascent during which the diver does not exhale adequately. The rising pressure of expanding air in the lungs bursts the delicate alveoli – air sacs in the lungs – and forces air into the blood vessels that carry blood back to the heart and, ultimately, the brain. In the brain these air bubbles block blood vessels and obstruct the supply of blood and oxygen to the brain. This causes brain damage.

The symptoms and signs of lung barotrauma and arterial gas embolism include:
- shortness of breath
- chest pain
- unconsciousness.

Treatment of acute decompression Illness:
- ABCs and CPR (see pages 166–7) as necessary
- position the patient in the recovery position (see page 166) with no tilt or raising of the legs
- give 100% oxygen by mask or demand valve
- keep the patient warm
- remove to the nearest hospital as soon as possible. The hospital or emergency services will arrange for recompression treatment.

Carbon dioxide or carbon monoxide poisoning
Carbon dioxide poisoning can occur as a result of skip breathing (diver holds breath on SCUBA), heavy exercise on SCUBA or malfunctioning rebreather systems. Carbon monoxide poisoning occurs as a result of: exhaust gases being pumped into cylinders; hookah systems; air intake too close to exhaust fumes.

Symptoms and signs of carbon monoxide poisoning:
- blue colour of the skin
- shortness of breath
- loss of consciousness.

Treatment of carbon monoxide poisoning:
- get the patient to a safe environment
- ABCs and CPR (see pages 166-7) as necessary
- 100% oxygen through a mask or demand valve
- get the patient to hospital.

Head injury
Any head injury should be treated as serious.

Treatment of a head injury:
- the diver must surface and do no more diving until a doctor has been consulted
- disinfect the wound

- if the diver is unconscious, contact the emergency services
- if breathing and/or pulse have stopped, administer CPR (see page 167)
- if the diver is breathing and has a pulse, check for bleeding and other injuries, and treat for shock
- if the wounds permit, put the injured person into recovery position and, if possible, give 100% oxygen
- keep the patient warm and comfortable and monitor pulse and respiration constantly.

Hyperthermia (raised body temperature)
A rise in body temperature results from a combination of overheating, normally due to exercise, and inadequate fluid intake. A person with hyperthermia will progress through heat exhaustion to heat stroke, with eventual collapse. Heat stroke is an emergency: if the diver is not cooled and rehydrated he or she will die.

Treatment of hyperthermia:
- move the diver as quickly as possible into a cooler place and remove all clothes
- call the emergency services
- sponge the diver's body with a damp cloth and fan him or her manually or with an electric fan
- if the patient is unconscious, put him or her into the recovery position (see page 166) and monitor the ABCs as necessary
- if the patient is conscious you can give him or her a cold drink.

Hypothermia (low body temperature)
Normal internal body temperature is just under 37°C (98.4°F). If for any reason it falls much below this – usually, in diving, because of inadequate protective clothing – progressively more serious symptoms may follow, and the person will eventually die if the condition is not treated rapidly. A drop of 1C° (2F°) causes shivering and discomfort. A 2C° (3F°) drop induces the body's self-heating mechanisms to react: blood flow to the hands and feet is reduced and shivering becomes extreme. A 3C° (5F°) drop results in memory loss, confusion, disorientation, irregular heartbeat and breathing and eventually death.

Treatment of hypothermia:
- move the diver as quickly as possible into a sheltered and warm place; *or:*
- prevent further heat loss: use an exposure bag; surround the diver with buddies' bodies; cover his or her head and neck with a woolly hat, warm towels or anything else suitable
- if you have managed to get the diver into sheltered warmth, remove wet clothing, dress your patient in warm, dry clothing and wrap him or her in an exposure bag or heat blanket; however, if you are still in the open, the diver is best left in existing garments
- if the diver is conscious and coherent administer a warm shower or bath and a warm, sweet drink

- if the diver is unconscious, check the ABCs (see page 166), call the emergency services, make the patient as warm as possible, and treat for shock (see page 170).

Near-drowning
Near-drowning is a medical condition in which a diver has inhaled some water – water in the lungs interferes with the normal transport of oxygen from the lungs into the bloodstream. A person in a near-drowning condition may be conscious or unconscious.

Near-drowning victims sometimes develop secondary drowning, a condition in which fluid oozing into the lungs causes the diver to drown in internal secretions, so all near-drowning patients must be monitored in a hospital.

Treatment of near-drowning:
- get the diver out of the water and check the ABCs (see page 166); depending on your findings, begin EAR or CPR (see page 167) as appropriate
- if possible, administer oxygen by mask or demand valve
- call the emergency services and get the diver to a hospital for observation, even if he/she appears to have recovered from the experience.

Nitrogen narcosis
Air contains about 80% nitrogen. Breathing the standard diving mixture under compression can lead to symptoms very much like those of drunkenness (nitrogen narcosis is popularly known as 'rapture of the deep'). Some divers experience nitrogen narcosis at depths of 30–40m (100–130ft). Down to a depth of about 60m (200ft) – which is beyond the legal maximum depth for sport-diving in the UK and the USA – the symptoms are not always serious; but below about 80m (260ft) a diver is likely to lose consciousness. Symptoms can occur very suddenly. Nitrogen narcosis is not a serious condition, but a diver suffering from it may do something dangerous.

Treatment of nitrogen narcosis: the only treatment for this condition is to get the diver to ascend immediately to shallower waters.

TRAVELLING MEDICINE

Many doctors decline to issue drugs, particularly antibiotics, to people who want them 'just in case'; but a diving holiday can be ruined by an ear or sinus infection, especially in a remote area or on a live-aboard boat, where the nearest doctor or pharmacy is a long and difficult journey away.

Many travelling divers therefore carry with them medical kits that could lead the uninitiated to think they were hypochondriacs. Nasal sprays, ear drops, antihistamine creams, anti-diarrhoea medicines, antibiotics, sea-sickness remedies . . . Forearmed, such divers can take immediate action as soon as they realize something is wrong. At the very least, this may minimize their loss of diving time.

Always bear in mind that most decongestants and remedies for sea-sickness can make you drowsy and therefore should NEVER be taken before diving.

Shock

Shock is a medical condition and not just the emotional trauma of a frightening experience. Medical shock results from poor blood and oxygen delivery to the tissues. As a result of oxygen and blood deprivation the tissues cannot carry out their functions. There are many causes; the most common is loss of blood.

Treatment for medical shock:
This is directed at restoring blood and oxygen delivery to the tissues:
- check the ABCs (see page 166)
- give 100% oxygen
- control any external bleeding by pressing hard on the wound and/or pressure points (the location of the pressure points is illustrated in first-aid manuals); raise the injured limb or other part of the body
- use a tourniquet only as a last resort and only on the arms and legs
- if the diver is conscious, lay him/her on the back with the legs raised and the head to one side; if unconscious, turn him or her on the left side in the recovery position (see page 166).

MARINE-RELATED AILMENTS

Sunburn, coral cuts, fire-coral stings, swimmers' ear, sea-sickness and bites from various insects are perhaps the most common divers' complaints – but there are more serious marine-related illnesses you should know about.

Cuts and abrasions

Divers should wear appropriate abrasive protection for the undersea environment. Hands, knees, elbows and feet are the areas most commonly affected. The danger with abrasions is that they become infected, so all wounds must be thoroughly washed and rinsed with water and an antiseptic as soon as possible after the injury. Infection may progress to a stage where antibiotics are necessary. If the site of an apparently minor injury becomes inflamed, and the inflammation spreads, consult a doctor immediately – you may need antibiotics to prevent the infection spreading to the bloodstream.

Swimmers' ear

Swimmers' ear is an infection of the external ear canal caused by constantly wet ears. The condition is often a combined fungal and bacterial infection. To prevent it, always dry your ears thoroughly after diving. If you know you are susceptible to the condition, insert alcohol drops after diving. If an infection occurs, the best treatment is to stop diving or swimming for a few days and apply ear drops such as:
- 5% acetic acid in isopropyl alcohol; *or*
- aluminium acetate/acetic acid solution.

FIRST-AID KIT

Your first-aid kit should be waterproof, compartmentalized and sealable, and, as a minimum, should contain the following items:
- a full first-aid manual – the information in this appendix is for general guidance only
- contact numbers for the emergency services
- coins for telephone
- pencil and notebook
- tweezers
- scissors
- 6 large standard sterile dressings
- 1 large Elastoplast/Band-Aid fabric dressing strip
- 2 triangular bandages
- 3 medium-size safety pins
- 1 pack sterile cotton wool
- 2 50mm (2in) crepe bandages
- eyedrops
- antiseptic fluid/cream
- bottle of vinegar
- sachets of rehydration salts
- sea-sickness tablets
- decongestants
- painkillers
- anti-AIDS pack (syringes/needles/drip needle)

Sea or motion sickness

Motion sickness can be an annoying complication on a diving holiday involving boat dives. If you suffer from motion sickness, discuss the problem with a doctor before your holiday – or at least before boarding the boat. But bear in mind that many medicines formulated to prevent travel sickness contain antihistamines, which make you drowsy and will impair your ability to think quickly while you are diving.

Biting insects

Some regions are notorious for biting insects. Take a good insect repellent and some antihistamine cream to relieve the effects.

Sunburn

Be sure to take plenty of precautions against sunburn, which can cause skin cancer. Many people get sunburned on the first day of a holiday and spend a very uncomfortable time afterwards recovering. Pay particular attention to the head, the nose and the backs of the legs. Always use high-protection factor creams, and wear clothes that keep off the sun.

Tropical diseases

Visit the doctor before your trip and make sure you have the appropriate vaccinations for the regions you intend to visit on your trip.

Fish that bite

- **Barracuda** These very rarely bite divers, although they have been known to bite in turbid or murky, shallow water, where sunlight flashing on a knife blade, a camera lens or jewellery has confused the fish into thinking they are attacking their normal prey.

  Treatment: clean the wounds thoroughly and use antiseptic or antibiotic cream. Bad bites will also need antibiotic and anti-tetanus treatment.

- **Moray eels** Probably more divers are bitten by morays than by all other sea creatures added together – usually through putting their hands into holes to collect shells or lobsters, remove anchors, or hide baitfish. Once it bites, a moray often refuses to let go, so you may have to persuade it to by gripping it behind the head and exerting pressure with your finger and thumb until it opens its jaw. You can make the wound worse by tearing your flesh if you pull the fish off.

  Treatment: thorough cleaning and usually stitching. The bites always go septic, so have antibiotics and anti-tetanus available.

- **Sharks** Sharks rarely attack divers, but should always be treated with great respect. Their attacks are usually connected with speared or hooked fish, fish or meat set up as bait, lobsters rattling when picked up, or certain types of vibration, such as that produced by helicopters. The decomposition products of dead fish (even several days old) seem much more attractive to most sharks than fresh blood. Grey reef sharks can be territorial. They often warn of an attack by arching their backs and pointing their pectoral fins downward. Other sharks often give warning by bumping into you first. If you are frightened, a shark will detect this from the vibrations given off by your body. Calmly back up to the reef or boat and get out of the water.

  Treatment: a person who has been bitten by a shark usually has severe injuries and is suffering from shock (see page 170). If possible, stop any bleeding by applying pressure. The patient will need to be stabilized with blood or plasma transfusions, so get the diver to hospital. Even minor wounds are likely to become infected, so the diver will need antibiotic and anti-tetanus treatment.

- **Triggerfish** Large triggerfish – usually males guarding eggs in 'nests' – are particularly aggressive and will attack divers who get too close. Their teeth are very strong, and can go through rubber fins and draw blood through a 4mm (⅙in) wet suit.

  Treatment: clean the wound and treat it with antiseptic cream.

Venomous sea creatures

Many venomous sea creatures are bottom dwellers – they hide among coral or rest on or burrow into sand. If you need to move along the sea bottom, shuffle along, so that you push such creatures out of the way and minimize the risk of stepping directly onto sharp venomous spines, many of which can pierce rubber fins. Antivenins require specialist medical supervision, do not work for all species, and need refrigerated storage, so they are rarely available when they are needed. Most of the venoms are proteins of high molecular weight that break down under heat.

General treatment: tie a broad bandage at a point between the limb and the body and tighten it. Remember to release it every 15 minutes. Immerse the limb in hot water (perhaps the cooling water from an outboard motor if no other supply is available) at 50°C (120°F) for two hours, until the pain stops. Several injections around the wound of local anaesthetic (such as procaine hydrochloride), if available, will ease the pain. Young or weak people may need CPR (see page 167). Remember that venoms may still be active in fish that have been dead for 48 hours.

- **Cone shells** Live cone shells should never be handled without gloves: the animal has a mobile, tubelike organ that shoots a poison dart. This causes numbness at first, followed by local muscular paralysis, which may extend to respiratory paralysis and heart failure.

  Treatment: tie a bandage between the wound and the body, tighten it, and release it every 15 minutes. CPR (see page 167) may be necessary.

- **Fire worms** These worms with white hairs along their sides display bristles when touched. They easily break off in the skin causing a burning feeling and intense irritation.

  Treatment: bathe the affected part in methylated spirit, vinegar (acetic acid) or hot water.

- **Fire coral** Corals of the genus *Millepora* are not true corals but members of the class Hydrozoa – i.e., they are more closely related to the stinging hydroids. Many people react violently from the slightest brush with them – producing blisters sometimes as large as 15cm (6in) across, which can last for as long as several weeks.

  Treatment: bathe the affected part in methylated spirit or vinegar (acetic acid). Local anaesthetic may be required to ease the pain, though antihistamine cream is usually enough.

- **Jellyfish** Most jellyfish sting, but few are dangerous. When seasonal changes are favourable you can encounter the Portuguese Man-of-War (*Physalia physalis*). These are highly toxic and continued exposure to the stinging cells may require hospital treatment. Sea wasps (*Carybdea alata*) can be found in shallow warm water at night and are attracted to light. These creatures often swarm and stings can be severe, causing muscle cramps, nausea and breathing difficulties. Whenever the conditions are favourable for thimble jellyfish (*Linuche unguiculata*), there is always the chance of much smaller and almost invisible micro-organisms in the water column. Wear protection such as a wet suit or the new style of Lycra skin suit.

Treatment: in the event of a sting, the recommended treatment is to pour acetic acid (vinegar) over both animal and wounds and then to remove the animal with forceps or gloves. CPR (see page 167) may be required.

- **Scorpionfish** These are not considered dangerous in Caribbean waters, but care should always be taken against the spines on top of their dorsal fin.

Treatment: inadvertent stinging can be treated by bathing the affected part of the body in very hot water.

- **Sea urchins** The spines of some sea urchins are poisonous and all sea urchin spines can puncture the skin, even through gloves, and break off, leaving painful wounds that often go septic.

Treatment: for bad cases bathe the affected part of the body in very hot water. This softens the spines, making it easier for the body to reject them. Soothing creams or a magnesium sulphate compress will help reduce the pain, as will the application of the flesh of papaya fruit. Septic wounds need to be treated with antibiotics.

- **Stinging hydroids** Stinging hydroids often go unnoticed on wrecks, old anchor ropes and chains until you put your hand on them, when their nematocysts are fired into your skin. The wounds are not serious but they are very painful, and large blisters can be raised on sensitive skin, which can last for some time.

Treatment: bathe the affected part in methylated spirit or vinegar (acetic acid). Local anaesthetic may be required to ease the pain, though antihistamine cream is usually enough.

- **Stinging plankton** You cannot see stinging plankton, and so cannot take evasive measures. If there are reports of any in the area, keep as much of your body covered as you can.

Treatment: bathe the affected part in methylated spirit or vinegar (acetic acid). Local anaesthetic may be required to ease the pain, though antihistamine cream is usually enough.

- **Stingrays** Stingrays vary considerably in size from a few centimetres to several metres across. The sting consists of one or more spines on top of the tail; although these point backward they can sting in any direction. The rays thrash out and sting when they are trodden on or caught. The wounds may be large and severely lacerated.

Treatment: clean the wound and remove any spines. Bathe or immerse in very hot water and apply a local anaesthetic if one is available; follow up with antibiotics and anti-tetanus.

- **Other stinging creatures**
Venoms can also occur in soft corals, the anemones associated with clownfish and the nudibranchs that feed on stinging hydroids. If you have sensitive skin, do not touch any of them.

Cuts

Underwater cuts and scrapes, especially those caused by coral, barnacles and sharp metal, will usually, if they are not cleaned out and treated quickly, go septic; absorption of the resulting poisons into the body can cause more serious medical conditions.

After every dive, clean and disinfect any wounds, no matter how small. Larger wounds will often refuse to heal unless you stay out of seawater for a couple of days. Surgeonfish have sharp fins on each side of the caudal peduncle; they use these when lashing out at other fish with a sweep of the tail, and they occasionally use them to defend their territory against a trespassing diver. Their 'scalpels' may be covered in toxic mucus, so wounds must be cleaned and treated with antibiotic cream.

As a preventive measure against cuts in general, the golden rule on the reef is: do not touch. Be sure to learn good buoyancy control so that you can avoid touching anything unnecessarily – never forget for an instant that every area of the coral you touch will inevitably be killed.

Bibliography

Berg, Daniel and Berg, Denise: *Tropical Shipwrecks* (1989), Aqua Explorers Inc., New York

Blount, Steve and Walker, Lisa: *Diving and Snorkelling Guide to the Bahamas: Nassau and New Providence Island* (1991), Gulf Publishing Co., Texas

Buettner, Dan: *Inside Grand Bahama* (1990), Fair Prospect Press, Atlanta, Georgia

Cohen, Shlomo: *Bahamas Divers Guide* (1977), Seapen Books, Israel

Colin, Dr Patrick I.: *Caribbean Reef Invertebrates and Plants* (1978), TFH Publications Ltd.

Humann, Paul: *Reef Coral Identification* (1993), New World Publications, Florida

Humann, Paul: *Reef Creature Identification* (1993), New World Publications, Florida

Humann, Paul: *Reef Fish Identification* (1993), New World Publications, Florida

Keller, Bob and Charlotte: *Diving and Snorkelling Guide to the Bahamas: Family Islands and Grand Bahama* (1995), Gulf Publishing Co., Texas

Palmer, Rob: *Bahamar* (1995), Immel Publishing, London

Palmer, Rob: *Deep into Blue Holes* (1997), Media Publishing, Nassau

Saunders, Gail: *The Bahamas: A Family of Islands* (1993), Macmillan Press, London

Sefton, Nancy and Webster, Steven K.: *Caribbean Reef Invertebrates* (1986), Sea Challengers, California

Index